# 90 DAYS

# 90 DAYS

## THE TRUE STORY OF THE HUNT FOR RAJIV GANDHI'S ASSASSINS

Anirudhya Mitra

HarperCollins *Publishers* India

First published in India by HarperCollins Publishers 2022
4th Floor, Tower A, Building No. 10, Phase II, DLF Cyber City,
Gurugram, Haryana –122002
www.harpercollins.co.in

2 4 6 8 10 9 7 5 3 1



P-ISBN: 978-93-9440-756-5
E-ISBN: 978-93-9440-761-9



Typeset in 11.5/15.2 Bembo Std at
Manipal Technologies Limited, Manipal

Printed and bound at
Thomson Press (India) Ltd

*To my wife Ruma Mitra, and sons Arjun and Prithvi Mitra.*
*Pets Bruno, Sasha, Sugar and Whitu.*

# PROLOGUE

Rajiv Gandhi, a former Prime Minister of India, was assassinated on 21 May 1991 at a place called Sriperumbudur in Tamil Nadu. The assassin was an adolescent girl named Dhanu who was made into a human bomb. She got herself exploded at 10.19 p.m. at close proximity with the visiting former Prime Minister. In a trice the life of Rajiv Gandhi was snuffed out and his body smashed into smithereens. As for the assassin, nothing except a few pieces of charred limbs and her sundered head were found. In the explosion, the lives of eighteen others were also extinguished. Investigation pointed to a minutely orchestrated cabal, masterminded by conspirators to extirpate the former Prime Minister from this terrestrial terrain. In the final charge sheet made by the Central Bureau of Investigation (CBI), all the twenty-six appellants now before us were arraigned as members of the conspiracy, which targeted, inter alia, Rajiv Gandhi. The Special Judge who tried the case found all the twenty-six appellants guilty of various offences charged, the gravamen of them being Section 302 read with Section 120-B of the IPC. All of them were hence convicted of those offences and sentenced to death.[1]

Justice K.T. Thomas J.
Supreme Court of India

# PREFACE

It's been thirty years that I have been asking myself whether to write a book on the assassination of India's former Prime Minister Rajiv Gandhi. It is during these three decades that friends, seniors and government officials have asked me why I have never thought of writing a book even after extensively covering one of the biggest crimes in modern Indian history for the *India Today* magazine. And when I finally did, the very first question my publisher asked me was why I wrote the book after all these years.

The story 'Rajiv Assassination: The Inside Story' on the 15 July 1991 issue of the *India Today* magazine had got people talking. While the general response was euphoric, a section of the media felt I was sensationalizing it. The truth is, I had suppressed much more information than I could and had revealed. By the time the Central Bureau of Investigation (CBI) filed the charge sheet, which was eleven months after the assassination, I had a surfeit of concealed facts: the former Prime Minister's assassination was the product of a conspiracy; the plotters and key operators came not just from the Tamil guerrilla separatist organization LTTE (the Liberation Tigers of Tamil Eelam) but had links across the globe. And as the probe gained traction, followed by the seizure of incriminating documents and arrests made, Sivarasan emerged as the mastermind of the complex web that eventually took Rajiv Gandhi's life. It became evident that he was regularly in touch with contacts in Singapore, Saudi Arabia, the UAE, Sweden, France and the UK before and after carrying out the assassination.

There have been many theories and conclusions, including the Supreme Court of India's verdict based on the findings of the CBI's special investigation team (SIT), upholding the death sentence awarded to the assassins. The number of death sentences awarded to the twenty-three accused in the Madras TADA (Terrorist and Disruptive Activities [Prevention] Act) court came down to seven in the Supreme Court but the fate of the key conspirators such as Santhan, Murugan, Nalini and gang remained unaltered. The Jain Inquiry Commission, headed by Justice Milap Chand Jain, set up to look into the 'larger conspiracy' behind the assassination, was flooded with allegations against the P.V. Narasimha Rao government, slowing down the pace of inquiry and ignoring, hiding and suppressing vital evidence that could have led the investigators to the doorstep of some influential people in Delhi. But what nobody could throw light on was Rao's motive.[1]

One of the finest officers in the SIT, Amit Verma was later inducted into the commission to assist Justice Jain. Incidentally, Verma had huge differences of opinion with his chief, D.R. Kaarthikeyan, over the possibility of a 'foreign hand' in the assassination. The commission was looking into one Amos Radia and Giorce Betchar as agents operating for the Israelis in India.

And in the days that followed, startling depositions and intelligence intercepts made before the commission indicated that Subramanian Swamy may have had prior knowledge of a threat to Rajiv and had communicated the same to the former Prime Minister's party, but no one, whether in his party or the government, had reacted in a timely manner. In fact, Swamy had had an argument with the then Research and Analysis Wing (R&AW) chief in a Cabinet committee meeting that was held within hours of the killing. Justice Jain devoted separate chapters to three key Indian players who were suspected, one way or the other, to have had prior knowledge of the assassination. The evidence looked more circumstantial, though, but a political will to examine them further was shamelessly ignored by New Delhi.

In my journalism career spanning over ten years, there was no place better than *India Today* for investigating the Rajiv Gandhi assassination case. It was my greatest experience, the most rewarding and, yes, the most controversial. While *India Today* backed me to the hilt, there was no dearth of opposition. After the breaking story of how the conspiracy was hatched, a celebrated journalist from a southern daily accused me of yellow journalism, a fellow crime reporter suggested I was writing fiction, a leading politician from Tamil Nadu labelled me anti-Tamil and the LTTE supremo called me an agent of the CBI in his interview to the Western media. A former Prime Minister called my editor and asked if the story of the dry run conducted in his political rally in Tamil Nadu was true. An official from 10 Janpath asked if I could share my stories with Rajiv's family before they were published. Even the SIT boss called parts of my story figments of my imagination. But he had no explanation to offer when three well-known people, who were named in the story, were arrested by the same SIT. The celebrated journalist from the southern daily, too, kept quiet, failing to substantiate his charges. Understandably, my editor-in-chief was concerned. He tapped his own sources in the government and was told that every story published by the magazine was factually correct, thus adding to my motivation to keep chasing the bigger story.

But then the threats started coming in from other quarters. Suspicious characters would follow my car in Madras, call my hotel room and not speak or leave a note under my door telling me not to visit Jaffna in Sri Lanka. It's another matter that I was not granted a visa to visit Jaffna, but an incident that soon followed shocked me.

The chief metropolitan magistrate (CMM) was hearing the application of the police remand of the accused, including key conspirators Nalini, Murugan, Peraribalan and Robert Payas. The investigating officer (IO) of the case, K. Ragothaman, was standing between Murugan in handcuffs and me. The CMM had asked something and Ragothaman had stepped forward to answer. Murugan turned, gave me a cold stare and said something in Tamil, a language not unfamiliar to me. But his accent was heavily Sinhalese. I figured he was trying to find out if I was a 'reporter'. He repeated his query to Ragothaman, who, of course, didn't pay him any attention. At the end of the hearing, someone stopped me outside the courtroom and conveyed Murugan's message to me: 'Stay away from maligning freedom fighters.' It was a cold-blooded threat, but I was told not to worry as my stories were 'getting noticed'.

Meanwhile, I was getting involved in the investigation deeper and deeper, even as the legend of 'One-Eyed Jack', as Sivarasan was sometimes called, grew larger by the day. He managed to stay ahead of the CBI, R&AW, the Intelligence Bureau (IB), Military Intelligence (MI) and state police across the country, in a clear indication that India's biggest manhunt so far was not good enough to catch him. But one thing was clear to the CBI—Sivarasan was holed up somewhere in India. While the agencies left no stone unturned to find him, the mastermind played his own tricks. He hand-picked his lookalikes from the cadres of his organization and sent them across the country in disguise just to keep the security agencies engaged in chasing 'him' to every corner of the country and then return disappointed.

Unlike the SIT, mine was a one-man army, and I was lucky to have the right contacts in the CBI. The SIT boss Kaarthikeyan was not too happy with my 'overenthusiastic' approach to staying ahead of rival publications but would rarely refuse to grant me an appointment. However, covering the developments on the trail of the assassin had become equally challenging for me. I didn't know which lead to follow and which to ignore. However, the relentless chase brought hope when the Indian Navy intercepted a coded communication between Madras and Jaffna, indicating that Sivarasan was asking his boss, Pottu Amman, in Jaffna for a boat. But the breakthrough was short-lived. Sivarasan discovered his communication with Jaffna was being intercepted by the Indian security agencies. As I wrote in one of my stories in the *India Today* magazine,

> Instead of ceasing transmission, he used the knowledge to run rings around the SIT. On one occasion, the SIT rushed a 60-man force to Pulicat lake on the Tamil Nadu-Andhra Pradesh border. They combed every inch of the 600 sq km lake only to find they had been handed another red herring.[2]

The Robert Ludlum-like plot continued to thicken, and the tasks and targets kept multiplying. Raids by the SIT's tracking team kept failing. Fingers were pointed at the SIT and their inability to catch the mastermind, who, showing a clean pair of heels, sneaked out of Tamil Nadu hiding in an oil tanker and landed in neighbouring Karnataka. Sivarasan had, by then, grown bigger than everyone. I visited the residence of retired director general (intelligence) of

Tamil Nadu police, Kondath Mohandas. The ace sleuth questioned the 'intriguing circumstances' in which Sriperumbudur had been added to Rajiv Gandhi's itinerary despite objections from several quarters. He pointed out an earlier report where Yasser Arafat, chairman of the Palestine Liberation Organization, had warned India about a possible threat from the Mossad, Israel's national intelligence agency. Mohandas emphatically claimed that the LTTE was being used as a front by vested interests operating not just from Jaffna.

Meanwhile, I could see a clear divide within the SIT. While one section felt the investigation did not need to not look beyond the LTTE, a few others felt overlooking the foreign links of Sivarasan would not only be a disservice to their profession but also an injustice to Rajiv Gandhi. They dared to do what no other CBI official attempted—bring Rajiv's true assassins to justice. Ridiculed by the press, denounced by their seniors and harassed by New Delhi, these officers were tormented by those who clung fast to the idea of the LTTE as the only villain in the conspiracy. With their career on the line, at least two officers persisted in the belief that the footprints of the assassins would lead them beyond Jaffna.

This, therefore, is the story of the officers who successfully brought the conspirators to trial but were prevented every step of the way from unearthing the larger conspiracy. This is also the story of the pervasive subterfuge, outright lies and deceptions of the intelligence agencies, the sympathetic stance of some very senior policemen from Tamil Nadu who owed their allegiance to the LTTE, and the mysterious deaths of key witnesses just before their testimonies were due. It was a complex web, where not only was the truth forbidden but also where the necessity to catch the mastermind alive was systematically jeopardized.

Over the years it was my inability to decide what information to keep and what to leave out, if any at all, that stopped me from writing on a subject as sensitive as the assassination of a world leader. When I reconnected with some of the officials who had cracked the case, I realized that the assassination had continued to haunt some of them even after thirty years. I have chosen to write this book as a mark of respect for their stellar work and for the generation of today—to tell them about this intriguing piece of investigative journalism and to help them gain a deeper understanding of the events—and the attempted cover-up that followed—of what was surely a turning point in our nation's history.

Anirudhya Mitra
11 April 2022

# A BRIEF NOTE ON THE INDIAN PEACE KEEPING FORCE (IPKF)

THE VIOLENT SRI LANKAN CIVIL WAR SAW A SUDDEN INFLUX OF refugees into India. The Indian government, first under Indira Gandhi and then under Rajiv Gandhi, sympathized with the Tamil insurrection, owing to the strong support for the cause in Tamil Nadu. The state soon became a sanctuary for separatists and a channel for the LTTE to smuggle weapons to Sri Lanka. Sri Lanka chose to limit its intervention even when LTTE supremo Prabhakaran was arrested and then released in Tamil Nadu in 1982.

The first round of civil violence flared in 1983 when the killing of thirteen soldiers of the Sri Lanka Army sparked anti-Tamil pogroms—the Black July riots—in which approximately 3000 Tamils were killed.[1] With militant attacks on the rise, as well as political and ethnic turmoil, Rajiv Gandhi's government attempted to maintain cordial diplomatic relations and restrict all aid to Tamil militants.

In June 1987, the Sri Lankan army laid siege to Jaffna, leading to mass civilian casualties. Fearing the prospect of a backlash from its own Tamil population, India sent unarmed ships for humanitarian assistance, but the convoy was intercepted and sent back by the Sri Lankan navy. In July 1987, India airdropped food parcels into Jaffna. This triggered a round of negotiations, and the Indo-Sri Lanka Accord was signed by Prime Minister Rajiv Gandhi and Sri Lankan President J.R. Jayawardene in 1987. The primary task of the IPKF was to disarm the LTTE and all other rebel groups that took to arms to champion its cause. The LTTE was resistant to the terms of the agreement,[2] which stated (a) the devolution of power to provinces (b) the withdrawal of Sri Lankan troops to their northern barracks and (c) the disarmament of the Tamil rebels.

Starting 30 July 1987, Indian army troops started getting stationed in Sri Lanka to watch over the regional council. At its peak, the IPKF deployment included a large Indian paramilitary force, the Indian special forces, the Indian air force and the Indian navy. Though no Tamil militant groups were part of the peace negotiations, most accepted it. The LTTE, on the other hand, declared war on the IPKF on 7 October 1987.[3] Following an assault on the IPKF, which led to the death of five Indian para-commandos, the Indian army launched a month-long ruthless anti-LTTE campaign to regain control of the Jaffna peninsula. The intervention of the IPKF was opposed by the Sri-Lankan Tamils and the Sinhalese alike. The IPKF launched a number of combat operations aimed at destroying the LTTE-led insurgency. It soon escalated into repeated skirmishes between the IPKF and LTTE.[4]

Following his election as President, Ranasinghe Premadasa started negotiations with the LTTE and ordered the Sri Lankan army to discreetly hand over a consignment of arms to the LTTE to fight the IPKF. Following tactical success but several intelligence failures, the IPKF started leaving the country. In its wake were left a string of controversies and accusations that gained traction even after the last members left Sri Lanka by March 1990.

# A BRIEF NOTE ON THE LIBERATION TIGERS OF TAMIL EELAM (LTTE)

THE LIBERATION TIGERS OF TAMIL EELAM (LTTE) WAS A MILITANT separatist organization fighting to attain a proposed independent state (the Tamil Eelam) spread across the north and east of Sri Lanka. The group was founded by Sri Lankan Tamil guerrilla Velupillai Prabhakaran on 5 May 1976 and was active until Prabhakaran's death at the hands of the Sri Lankan armed forces on 18 May 009.

The genesis of the LTTE can be attributed to discriminatory state policies and oppression of the minority Sri Lankan Tamils at the hands of the majority Sinhalese, which often included island-wide ethnic riots. The 1956 anti-Tamil pogrom in Gal Oya Valley and the 1958 riots in Ceylon led to inter-community polarization. The conflict escalated when, in 1971, the policy of standardization was introduced by the government to curtail the enrolment of Tamil students in certain universities across the nation. The Tamil diaspora, united under Prabhakaran's leadership, and the LTTE rose to prominence after defeating many insurgent Tamil militant groups. Prabhakaran reportedly believed that the LTTE was the only Tamil militant group truly dedicated to armed struggle while perceiving the others as likely to give in to political rhetoric.[1] The LTTE had its own military wing, which included an intelligence wing, a navy, an airborne unit and a specialized attack unit. Apart from following a strict code of moral conduct and undertaking gruelling military training, it was mandatory for LTTE cadres to read specialized literature and view LTTE films.[2]

The LTTE gained global notoriety for training women and children as insurgents and were recognized as a terrorist organization by thirty-three countries. Major attacks were launched by the LTTE on civilians as well as the Sri Lankan army, which included gunfire attacks, planting bombs in planes and cars, massacres of police officers, attacks on Buddhist holy sites as well as mosques, and army ambushes.[3] They perfected the use of the suicide vest, which comprised of several bombs, worn by a lone assassin.[4] The perpetrators were the LTTE's elite suicide-bombing unit called the Black Tigers.

In hopes of resolving the Sri Lankan Civil War, the Indo-Sri Lanka Peace Accord was signed by Sri Lankan President J.R. Jayawardene and Indian Prime Minister Rajiv Gandhi in July 1987. The Indian Peace Keeping Force was deployed in Sri Lanka to enforce disarmament. The accord was denounced by the LTTE, and after several months of tension, it declared war on the IPKF on 7 October 1987.[5] The last members of the IPKF left the country in March 1990 and the LTTE regained territorial control.

This was followed by the high-profile assassinations of former Indian Prime Minister Rajiv Gandhi in 1991 and Sri Lankan

President Ranasinghe Premadasa in 1993; both were carried out by suicide bombers. In the final months of conflict, the defence lines of the LTTE began to crumble. As the Sri Lankan army annexed the LTTE territory, the top leadership retreated and more than 100 fighters were killed. Following the death of Prabhakaran, the sole first-generation leader left alive, Selvarasa Pathmanathan, assumed the position of the new leader but was captured in Malaysia by the Sri Lankan military intelligence unit a mere fifteen days from the announcement.

# CAST OF CHARACTERS

## THE INVESTIGATORS

**D.R. KAARTHIKEYAN (52):** Head of the SIT

D.R. Kaarthikeyan is a lawyer-turned-police officer from the 1964 batch of the IPS. He was appointed to head the SIT by then Prime Minister Chandra Shekhar in consultation with the director of the Central Bureau of Investigation (CBI), Vijay Karan. Though not very high-profile at the time, Kaarthikeyan was chosen for the job for his managerial skills, varied experiences in non-police assignments attached to diplomatic missions and his wide network of influential people. He was known to be shrewd and intelligent, and knew how to deal with politicians. Rajiv Gandhi's assassination was a very sensitive case with political overtones.

In the SIT, his journey could not have been very smooth, given the nature of the task. But he stuck to it and succeeded in proving the guilty in the court of law and secured justice for the victims. Kaarthikeyan handled his team with care, supervised the progress of the investigation despite non-stop obstacles, visited Sonia Gandhi, Rajiv Gandhi's wife, in Delhi and briefed her on the progress of the investigation, faced the media onslaught with diplomatic replies and retained his uniform spotless with the same elan.

As time passed and the mastermind of the assassination, Sivarasan, remained elusive, Kaarthikeyan's reputation took a hit. In the final strike on Sivarasan at the Konanakunte hideout in Bangalore (now Bengaluru), Kaarthikeyan earned the wrath of the media and some fellow members for 'delaying the operation' and not allowing the National Security Guard (NSG) commandos to try and 'catch Sivarasan alive'. But Kaarthikeyan alone was definitely not empowered to take calls. CBI boss Vijay Karan was himself present and taking calls, at times bypassing Kaarthikeyan. Whatever might have been the outcome in Bangalore, Kaarthikeyan succeeded in nailing the LTTE and securing the conviction of the assassins right up till the Supreme Court.

**AMIT VERMA (37):** SP, CBI-Delhi

Amit Verma was a 1978-batch IPS officer from the Tamil Nadu cadre and was handpicked by the director of the CBI, Vijay Karan, for his notable experience in Tamil Nadu before joining the CBI and cracking cases such as that of the forged letter by Devi Lal, the HDW (Howaldtswerke-Deutsche Werft) submarine deal, the army chief General Vaidya's assassination and then eventually catching the most dreaded Khalistani terrorist Harjinder Singh 'Jinda'. While many officers refused to join the SIT fearing political interference, Verma instantly thanked Vijay Karan for giving him the opportunity. He was known for his courage and perseverance, and for owning a sharp detective's mind. Somehow, he had an inkling that the LTTE was involved in Rajiv Gandhi's assassination from the moment he heard about it. I was present with him at that moment. Verma, along with DSP K. Ragothaman from the Madras (now Chennai) branch of the CBI, became the face of the field investigation. He would be present at every raid, interrogation of the key accused, examination of important clues and liaising with the Tamil Nadu forensics lab, which didn't see eye to eye with the SIT. But his SIT journey was a bumpy one when it came to picking up various leads. At times, he was at loggerheads with some of his seniors on the direction of the investigation. He wanted to pursue the larger conspiracy theory about what was beyond the LTTE, but the SIT management never allowed him to do that. His proposed trip to France to investigate LTTE man Pushpraj, the alleged foreign link of the mastermind Sivarasan, was rejected. He eventually took up the matter with his additional director, S.K. Datta, who promised Verma an 'opportunity at an appropriate time'. And Datta kept his word. He sent him to the Jain Commission, which later inquired into the larger conspiracy angle.

Verma passed away in June 2010 in Tamil Nadu.

**K. RAGOTHAMAN (44):** DSP, CBI-Madras

A post-graduate in economics, Ragothaman joined the CBI in 1968 and was appointed as the chief investigation officer of the Rajiv Gandhi assassination case. He was chosen for his good record in solving murder cases. He was known for his composure while interrogating hardened, strong-headed criminals and extracting confessions. Soft-spoken by nature, Ragothaman, however, did not succumb to pressure or threats, which is why he ran into conflicts with his seniors at times. His intentions were above board.

He formed a formidable force with Amit Verma and went deep into the investigation in spite of having no clue where to begin. It was Ragothaman who suggested that Vijay Karan visit the spot of crime—the blast site at Sriperumbudur—and adopt the procedural way from ground zero at a time when there was no clue but speculations galore. He kept the SIT apprised of the attempts and persons behind any disinformation campaign trying to malign the investigation and derail it. That way he had to face the maximum strain and stress in the SIT. Unlike other investigators, Ragothaman, being the IO of the case, had to stand in the witness box and deal with cross-examinations. In fact, the task took a toll on him and he suffered a stroke soon after the TADA court gave its verdict sentencing all the twenty-six accused to death.

**AMOD KANTH (45):** DIG, CBI-Delhi

A 1974-batch UT-cadre IPS officer, Amod Kanth's rise to fame was his fearless handling of the 1984 anti-Sikh riots. Thereafter, he cracked many sensitive cases, including the assassination of Indira Gandhi and Congress leader Lalit Maken. Kanth solved the mystery of the transistor bomb blasts that killed 105 people in Delhi in 1985. He spent the next six years in the crime branch—the longest tenure for any officer—during which many more cases were solved, including the arrest of several Punjab terrorists. He was serving as a DIG in the CBI when Rajiv Gandhi was assassinated. Kanth, given his experience, was a natural induction into the SIT.

Kanth had a charming personality. He was both ruthless and witty during his interrogation of the Tamil Tigers. He could call their bluff despite his total unfamiliarity with their language. There were times when Murugan and Santhan would just not speak, but Kanth's crafty psychological manipulation induced them to open their mouths. He couldn't care much about being told to be more patient with the accused, who were from the southern side of the Indian subcontinent while he was from the north.

He would see the 'criminal' in a suspect and not his 'colour' or 'creed'. He cracked the diabolical backup plan of Sivarasan killing Rajiv Gandhi in New Delhi in case his Tamil Nadu plan failed. With the help of his wide network of informers from the crime world of northern India, Kanth detected and scuttled Sivarasan's efforts to escape through the India–Nepal route. He then alerted the Mumbai underworld and warned them against any possible attempt to help him.

In the SIT, he formed an excellent duo with fellow DIG Radhavinod Raju and cracked the sensational assassination case of Eelam People's Revolutionary Liberation Front (EPRLF) leader K. Padmanabha, which had remained unsolved until the assassination of Rajiv Gandhi. As a result, the SIT was able to draw a parallel between the two assassinations and discovered that both had been conceived by the same person. This was a big breakthrough for the SIT. During the course of the investigation, Kanth took a stand in support of looking into the scope of the larger conspiracy—to see if anyone was involved beyond the LTTE. But he was not encouraged. While fulfilling his obligations at the SIT, Kanth, however, did probe the larger conspiracy theory and made substantial progress, which later became useful for the separate inquiry commissions set up to look into the 'security lapse' and the 'the larger conspiracy' during Rajiv's assassination.

**RADHAVINOD RAJU (42):** DIG, CBI

An IPS officer of the 1975-batch Jammu and Kashmir cadre, Raju had rich experience in tackling insurgency problems, and hence had a fine understanding of militancy and a militant's mind. Also, as SP, CBI, he had solved many cases of murder and corruption in the mid-1980s in Kerala. But his speciality was dealing with counter-insurgency, hence chosen for the job in the SIT. As number two to

Kaarthikeyan, he played a key role in cracking the LTTE angle and proving it in the trial until the case was decided.

As earlier mentioned, he formed a strong duo with fellow DIG Amod Kanth and made the first big breakthrough in the case by solving the assassination case of EPRLF leader K. Padmanabha, which eventually led the SIT to suspect Sivarasan behind Rajiv Gandhi's assassination too. While Kaarthikeyan would be busy running around between Madras, Hyderabad and Delhi, Raju would lead the investigation.

Raju passed away in Kochi in June 2012.

**CAPTAIN A.K. RAVINDRAN (33):** National Security Guard

National Security Guard commando unit head Captain A.K. Ravindran was asked to be on standby with a thirty-member team of the Black Cat commandos by the Cabinet Secretariat hours after Rajiv Gandhi's assassination. They waited at the Palam airport in Delhi for two days before returning to their base in Manesar, Haryana. Captain Ravi felt devastated at the death of Rajiv Gandhi and was determined to punish the killers. He had a rich experience in tackling militants and in close-combat war with terrorists in Jammu and Kashmir and Punjab.

He reached Madras with his team in the third week of June and formed the tracking team to nab Sivarasan and gang along with the SIT. He had to face many setbacks in the course of tracking the mastermind due to the indecision of the senior members of the SIT and bureaucratic tangles. While he was trained to take swift action on suspects, his co-members from the local police were comparatively slow and operated only by the rulebook. This led to no results at all, often raising his frustrations. In the final countdown to catching Sivarasan in Konanakunte, Bangalore, Captain Ravi repeatedly pleaded for timely action on the hideout where Sivarasan and gang were holed up. But it took the agencies thirty-six hours to act and allow him to storm the hideout.

**P. CHANDRASEKHARAN (44):** Director, Tamil Nadu Forensics Lab

He was considered the czar of Indian forensic science. He made the first breakthrough in the Rajiv Gandhi assassination case while the CBI was groping in the dark. His deconstruction of the bomb and analysis of the evidence collected from the scene of crime revealed that the former Prime Minister was killed by a 'human bomb' and deduced that she was wearing a denim vest jacket underneath her salwar kameez. The bomb had been packed in the vest jacket. Within forty-eight hours, from the evidence collected from the blast site, he reconstructed the vest bomb, and its mechanical and electrical circuit. From the photographs published in newspapers, Chandrasekharan spotted a camera stuck in the heaps of bodies. Suspecting the final moments of the assassination had been captured on a camera, he launched a hunt for it and eventually got it from the CID, Madras Police. The camera belonged to the photographer Haribabu, who died in the blast. Chandrasekharan developed the film roll from the camera and extracted ten photographs, of which the first showed the human bomb Dhanu and the mastermind behind the assassination, Sivarasan. His achievement gave a major boost to CBI's investigation.

## THE ASSASSINS

**SIVARASAN (33):** The mastermind

He has been one of the most elusive fugitives in history. He had a reward of Rs 15 lakh on his head but made sure he wasn't caught alive. He managed to flee from a hideout a day—just hours, really—before the tracking team arrived. He found eleven LTTE boys who resembled him and got them to hang around in different parts of Tamil Nadu wearing different make-up. So 'Sivarasan' would be seen as a Muslim cleric, a Catholic priest, a bald Hindu priest and a turbaned Sikh to send the sleuths off in the wrong direction.

And when he ran out of hideouts in Tamil Nadu, Sivarasan escaped sitting inside a water tanker and travelled 350 km to Bangalore, crossing a dozen police checks without being caught. When he found that the police had surrounded his hideout in Konanakunte, he didn't immediately die by suicide. He knew the agencies would like to catch him alive, and yet he waited thirty-six hours for them to finally break into his hideout. It's only then that he shot himself through his temple. He was cunning, ruthless, brutal and devoted to his Tamil cause.

He was the one to crack the assassination plan and direct its execution. He used several aliases, of which Sivarasan and Raghuvaran were the most widely known. As per a report by D.B.S. Jeyaraj, first published in *The Hindu* and later in several other publications, Sivarasan's comrades called him 'Ottraikkannan', a one-eyed person, since he had lost an eye. Later, the Indian media referred to him as 'One-Eyed Jack' from a Marlon Brando film.

According to Jeyaraj's report, Sivarasan's real name was Chandrasekharampillai Packiachandran. He hailed from Udupiddy, a town about 32 km from Jaffna city and not far from the hometown of Prabhakaran and the cradle of Tamil armed militancy. He was the LTTE's prime hitman thanks mainly to his ability to fluently speak Tamil, Telugu, Malayalam and Hindi. Contrary to reports, his Tamil was sans a Lankan accent. He was also familiar with the Indian topography, which stood him in good stead in eluding the super sleuths tailing him. One of his major advantages was the stark contrast between his side and front profiles. There was hardly any similarity between Haribabu's photograph of him, which showed him in profile, and the front view that appears on his driving licence.

According to Indian intelligence agencies, Sivarasan was assigned the task of killing the EPRLF leader K. Padmanabha. The slain leader was opposed to the LTTE's violent practices. Sivarasan, along with a deputy, Santhan, devised a plan and carried out Padmanabha's assassination in broad daylight in Madras in June 1990. Impressed by his work, the LTTE's intelligence chief, Pottu Amman, chose him for the task of killing Rajiv Gandhi.

**MURUGAN (30):** Explosive expert

Murugan Sriharan was just twenty-one years old at the time of Rajiv Gandhi's assassination. A member of the LTTE's intelligence wing, he was trained in close-combat warfare and the making of bombs. He became an important member of the hit squad and was recognized for his expertise in explosives. He, too, was handpicked by Pottu Amman and sent to India to assist Sivarasan. The investigators called him 'a terrorist who turned Romeo'. He came to Madras to assist Sivarasan, provide logistics to the human bombs and hideouts where the assassins could be sheltered. While carrying out his task meticulously, Murugan fell in love with a local girl named Nalini, used her in his scheme of things and later married her. She became a key conspirator who facilitated the crime. He had reportedly surprised his own boss by procuring locally sourced RDX to be used later in the making of the bomb.

He also aided in a dry run carried out at the political rally of former Prime Minister V.P. Singh at Nandanam near Madras. The idea was to check if the 'plan' was foolproof. After Rajiv Gandhi's assassination, Murugan took Nalini and her mother Padma to the Tirupati temple, and the couple got married. He was a man of few words. Along with his wife Nalini, he refused to give in to the interrogators for almost three days. When Amit Verma slapped him during an interrogation, Murugan told him in front of everybody that he would kill him after his release. He was the only accused who made an attempt to escape from the SIT office in Malligai, Madras.

His death sentence was upheld by the Supreme Court in May 1999. However, on appeal, it was commuted to life term by the apex court in February 2014, citing the eleven-year delay on the part of the Centre in deciding his mercy plea.

**BHAGYANATHAN (31):** Key conspirator

A young LTTE activist from Madras, Bhagyanathan was the first recruit of the assassination plot and was involved at every stage of the killing. He wanted to bring out a political journal attacking New Delhi's Sri Lanka policy but lacked the financial resources. He fell into the LTTE's lap. LTTE activist Baby Subramaniam sold his printing press to him for just Rs 5,000 then. And the printing press became the new hub of LTTE activists and publication of LTTE literature. Bhagyanathan brainwashed his sister Nalini and mother Padma against the former Indian Prime Minister and brought them into the LTTE fold. And thereafter, he extended support to everything Sivarasan wanted to accomplish. While there were different people assigned to different tasks, anyone could go to Bhagyanathan and seek help. He was the most popular member of the gang.

He is currently serving life term in jail.

**NALINI (27):** Gave refuge to the human bombs

She gave refuge to the human bomb Dhanu who killed Rajiv Gandhi. A key conspirator and facilitator of the assassination, Nalini was a tough nut to crack. It took the SIT almost three days to make her talk about the crime. During the interrogation, she openly abused Rajiv and compared the SIT investigators with the IPKF, calling them 'butchers of innocent Tamils'. She became an easy recruit in the assassination team; she even started working on a book titled *Satanic Forces* and subtitled 'Heinous Crimes of the Indian Peace Keeping Force' at her brother Bhagyanathan's printing press.

Brainwashed by both Murugan and her brother Bhagyanathan, Nalini did not join the LTTE but provided all possible support to the assassins. A graduate in English from Madras University, Nalini shifted from hideout to hideout to keep the two human bombs—Dhanu and the backup Shubha—safe. She took them around on weekends and attended sessions held by Sivarasan discussing the plan. She studied LTTE literature spewing venom against the IPKF, and Rajiv Gandhi in particular, holding him responsible for the 'massacre of innocent Tamils in Jaffna'. She took Dhanu and Shubha to a garment store to purchase the salwar kameez that they would wear on the night of the assassination.

Nalini showed no sign of nervousness after the assassination and attended office work normally until two cops landed at her workplace and inquired about why a member of the LTTE would have her telephone number on his person. Feigning ignorance, she dealt with the cops smartly and never returned to office after that. She is the lone survivor of the assassins who had visited Sriperumbudur on that fateful night. But she did not talk for sixty hours after her dramatic arrest from the Saidapet bus terminus in Madras.

Her death sentence was upheld by the Supreme Court in May 1999. However, on appeal, it was commuted to life term by the apex court later.

**SANTHAN ALIAS SUTHENTHIRARAJA ALIAS RAJA (30):** Logistics, support base

Santhan was like a shadow to Sivarasan. He, besides his boss, was the only LTTE member to be involved in two assassinations carried out by the LTTE on Indian soil. He had assisted Sivarasan at every step while planning and executing the assassination of EPRLF leader K. Padmanabha exactly a year before Rajiv Gandhi's killing.

Santhan's main task was to provide a support base for the assassins. He was part of the first batch of three operatives who reached India in September 1990. A close friend of the human bomb, Dhanu, he was seen off at Jaffna by the LTTE's intelligence chief Pottu Amman. That showed his importance in the organization. Nalini, in her confession, said that Santhan, along with Sivarasan, did not spare anyone who did not cooperate with them. A Sri Lankan national in his twenties at the time of the assassination, Santhan was a member of the intelligence wing of the LTTE and was close to Sivarasan. He was sent to Madras to continue his studies, and after coming to India, studied at the Indian Institute of Engineering & Technology in Kodabakkam, where his fees were paid by the LTTE. He was a crucial cog in the planning of Rajiv Gandhi's assassination and was one of the few conspirators who were informed early on about their target. He met Sivarasan on the day of the assassination and saw him off.[1]

The Supreme Court upheld his death sentence in May 1999. Later it was commuted to life term by the same court in February 2014 following an appeal where Santhan cited the eleven-year delay on the part of the Centre in deciding his mercy plea.

**ARIVU PERARIBALAN (20):** The bombmaker

He arranged the equipment for the bomb that was used to kill Rajiv Gandhi and carried out a location scout of former Prime Minister V.P. Singh's rally in Madras to assess security arrangements. He was just twenty years old at the time. Peraribalan was the son of a Tamil poet and had been part of the LTTE since 1989. He was involved in the sale of LTTE literature and even met LTTE chief Prabhakaran and other leaders when he went to Jaffna in 1990. He aided in the movement of LTTE cadres into India and prepared a sketch of the Vellore fort to free LTTE prisoners.[2] He had completed a diploma in electronics and communication engineering at the time of his arrest in 1991.

The Supreme Court first upheld his death sentence and then reduced it to life term after he cited in an appeal the eleven-year delay by the government in deciding his mercy petition. As per media reports, the apex court forwarded his case to the governor of Tamil Nadu to decide his remission petition.

**ROBERT PAYAS (27):** Gave refuge to the mastermind

With help from Murugan, he gave shelter to Sivarasan in his house in Madras before and after the assassination. A Sri Lankan Tamil, Payas had come from Jaffna in September 1990 and sought political asylum in Tamil Nadu. He was accompanied by his wife.

His plea before the authorities was that he had lost his child in the atrocities committed by the IPKF. Later, he took a vow to avenge his loss. Payas confessed his role in hatching the conspiracy to kill Rajiv Gandhi and was convicted.

Payas is currently serving life term in jail.

# 1

It was 22 May 1991. Seven o'clock, Wednesday morning. Too early to wake up. Especially after a late night. Anirudhya tried to figure out what she was saying by waving around the morning paper. He fumbled with the bunch of newspapers his wife had dropped right on top of him and said, 'Rajiv Gandhi is dead.' Headlines across the newspapers said the very same thing—the former Prime Minister of India had been assassinated the previous night at an election rally in Sriperumbudur, Tamil Nadu.

Anirudhya's wife, Rupa, had gone back to the kitchen. The telephone rang. Anirudhya picked up the receiver. The coordinator of the news desk of *India Today* magazine was on the line. Anirudhya had been called to office early. He had been working for *India Today* for just over a month and was always looking for a good story. But this appeared much more than that. The assassination of a former head of state who was tipped to be returning to power was much more than what he had been doing—investigative pieces on kickbacks paid in defence deals, political appointments of bureaucrats and narco-terrorism. He had left his previous job at another newspaper to chase bigger investigative stories. It seemed he had got that served on a platter.

Anirudhya parked his Kinetic Honda scooter in Connaught Place F-block and climbed the narrow, steep stairs that led to one of India's most respected news fortnightlies. The magazine's large newsroom encircled by editors' cabins was usually quiet until about eleven, even if a sub-editor or two were at work. As Anirudhya peeped into the coordinator Harpal Singh's cubicle to check if there was any message from Editor-in-Chief Aroon Purie, he called from behind him, standing at the door of Managing Editor Inderjit Badhwar. Badhwar had been instrumental in getting Anirudhya over to *India Today*.

Badhwar told him that Senior Editor Shekhar Gupta was on his way to Madras (Chennai), so Anirudhya should hang around the 'North Block' and pick up whatever information he could about the ghastly incident from the previous night.

For a moment Anirudhya was disappointed. It was clear that he was not going to Madras to investigate. Shekhar Gupta was *India Today*'s senior editor. Naturally he would be the one sent to the scene of crime before anyone else. As Anirudhya stepped out of Badhwar's cabin, Copy Editor Dilip Bobb caught him. 'Get me your copy latest by six in the evening,' he said.

The office was full at eleven. Anirudhya sat at his desk and asked the pantry for a soft drink with extra ice. People usually drank tea in newsrooms, but the culture in *India Today* seemed different. Here people spoke with an accent, were more stylishly dressed and had a chip or two on the shoulder.

Anirudhya tried to recollect what he had been doing the previous night. He was playing badminton with his friend in the CBI, Amit Verma, outside the latter's Pandara Road official residence. Verma's wife, Shobhana, had interrupted the game, telling Verma that he had an urgent call. The next thing Anirudhya knew, his friend had changed into jeans and a T-shirt and asked Anirudhya if he could be dropped at the Delhi residence of the chief secretary to the state of Tamil Nadu, T.S. Sundaram. He, a Tamil Nadu-cadre IPS officer, had been called for a meeting.

Anirudhya made three calls while waiting for his iced soft drink. First to a source in Delhi Police, second to another in the Intelligence Bureau (IB) and third to Verma and tried to piece together the events of the previous night. He thought he had better type a story straightway. Around 10.25 p.m. Sonia Gandhi received a call from someone asking if everything was fine. The Gandhis had been preparing to call it a night, and Rajiv Gandhi's personal secretary, Vincent George, had left for the day. Sensing trouble, Sonia Gandhi immediately summoned George, who had just reached home and found every phone in his residence ringing—the callers were from Madras. When Sonia Gandhi got through to one of George's lines, he was on another phone call with Madras. She waited for George to finish his call, but Rajiv Gandhi's personal secretary could not muster up the courage to tell her what had happened on the phone. He chose to rush back to 10, Janpath, where he tried to narrate in fragmented sentences what had happened in Sriperumbudur.

By that time, Congress leaders had started gathering at 10, Janpath. According to some of them, Sonia Gandhi had an attack of asthma as she cried inconsolably. She was not in a position to take control of the events unfolding; no one knew what needed to be done. However, Priyanka Gandhi, her daughter, gathered herself and asked George to arrange for their travel to Madras, where the body of Rajiv Gandhi had been taken.

Reportedly, President R. Venkataraman, upon learning that the Gandhis were planning to go to Madras, advised them against it as the situation was bad. But Priyanka insisted, and some three hours later, past midnight, they reached Madras in a special Indian Air Force plane, only to be told that they could not see the face of Rajiv Gandhi—he was lying in a coffin.

It was clear to Anirudhya why Verma was in such a hurry last night. Sundaram's residence in Pandara Park, which mostly housed senior bureaucrats, was at a kilometre's distance from Verma's residence. Anirudhya didn't get a chance to ask what had happened—why would a CBI officer be called at 10.55 at night unless a raid was taking place? The number of cars parked outside Sundaram's residence was unusual at that hour. Anirudhya had asked his friend what the matter was, but the latter had left without giving him any answers.

Anirudhya went back to typing.

Reports filed by other correspondents on the situation at Lutyens' Delhi were pouring in—so were the agency copies from PTI, UNI, AP and AFP. Prime Minister Chandra Shekhar was on his way back from Bhubaneswar, leaving his political rally halfway. White ambassador cars filled the parking space outside the North and South Block. The PM's secretary, C.B. Gautam, had already called the Cabinet Secretary Naresh Chandra to call a Cabinet Committee meeting. Minister of State for Home Subodh Kant Sahay was in Ranchi when Gautam called. Finding a flight at that hour was not easy. An otherwise quiet night in the capital was taking a serious turn with every senior bureaucrat appearing to be baffled. The news of the assassination was that unexpected.

Anirudhya had a quick coffee at Triveni in Mandi House with the head of IB's Delhi unit and got a basic story in place to start with: The Director of CBI, Vijay Karan, would be leaving for Madras the next morning in a special aircraft, the interim Prime Minister of the country, Chandra Shekhar, had rushed back from Bhubaneswar and held a series of closed-door meetings with Cabinet Secretary

Naresh Chandra, Home Secretary R.K. Bhargava, Research & Analysis Wing (R&AW) chief G.S. Bajpai, Director of IB M.K. Narayanan, Director of CBI Raja Vijay Karan, the defence secretary and the three service chiefs (of the navy, army and air force) and the director of the Military Intelligence (MI). He also learnt that thirty Black Cat commandos of the National Security Guard (NSG) were on standby at the airport, ready to leave for Madras at any time.

The Prime Minister, in consultation with CBI Director Vijay Karan and Additional Director S.K. Datta, had set up a Special Investigation Team (SIT). The inspector general (IG) of the Central Reserve Police Force (CRPF) D.R. Kaarthikeyan was chosen to head the team. He said he had received a call from Datta, who said intelligence agencies such as the R&AW, MI, the Joint Intelligence Committee (JIC) and IB had no clue about the identity of the assassin. Unlike the assassinations of Mahatma Gandhi and Indira Gandhi, where the assassins were witnessed committing the crime and caught immediately, the assassins of Rajiv Gandhi had vanished into thin air. Not a single name had come up. It reminded them of US President John F. Kennedy's assassination. Datta reportedly told Kaarthikeyan that he was the best for the job. Kaarthikeyan, a 1964-batch IPS officer, had done law before clearing the UPSC. He was well connected, had strong managerial skills and had varied experiences, including on diplomatic missions and non-police organizations. And, more importantly, he could handle political pressure. But why would someone from the CRPF be brought in when the CBI had more than a dozen sleuths with enviable track records in investigating big cases? The idea, Anirudhya inferred, was to induct officers who knew the Tamil language, at a time when Tamil Nadu Police was seen divided between various political camps. New Delhi did not feel comfortable picking one of them to head the SIT.

The structure of this SIT was going to be different from those in the past. The SIT headed by Anand Ram, which had probed the assassination of Indira Gandhi, reported to the cabinet secretary and the home minister. But the SIT under Kaarthikeyan would be functioning as an independent unit within the CBI and Kaarthikeyan would report to Director Vijay Karan and his deputy S.K. Datta.

Kaarthikeyan took up the challenging task, laying down a few conditions that were all accepted by the bosses. But within hours he understood it was going to be a much bigger challenge than he had initially thought. Many fellow officers told him there was still time to get out of this one as it was a 'blind case' and that he would never succeed. His batchmates from the IPS told him that the political pressure on this case would be humongous. Kaarthikeyan told Anirudhya later that, after all this, he felt even more motivated to crack the case.

The formation of the SIT's core group was already being discussed at the CBI's Lodi Road headquarters. Bobb wanted a quick profile of them to go in the next *India Today* cover story. Getting the details, therefore, was crucial for Anirudhya. Names started pouring in, starting with Radhavinod Raju and Amod Kanth. Anirudhya dialled Verma's Delhi residence and asked Shobhana for a number where he could reach him. She laughed and said she didn't know any other than his direct line. Next Anirudhya dialled Kanth's home number and got an almost identical reply from his wife, Rekha Kanth. He got the message. He need not call them again.

Raju was a 1975-batch Jammu and Kashmir cadre. He had handled sensitive terrorist cases and knew how to read a militant's mind. He had cracked cases of financial scams in Kerala and a few murder cases too. His speciality was counter-insurgency, which is why he had spent so much time in J&K. Kanth, too, was high-profile because of his sensitive handling of the anti-Sikh riots in 1984 Delhi. He had handled investigations into two assassination cases—Indira Gandhi's and Lalit Maken's. He had been instrumental in nabbing India's most dreaded terrorist, Harjinder Singh Jinda.

As Anirudhya stopped typing and dialled the pantry for tea, he noticed that the only question doing the rounds was who killed Rajiv Gandhi in the middle of the country's general elections. Was it an insider job to create sympathy in favour of his party and pull up its dwindling popularity? It was too soon to respond to any such speculation.

Anirudhya telephoned Verma on his direct line. Unexpectedly, his secretary responded. Verma had asked Anirudhya to see him later. There was no clarity on when and where, though. But it didn't take long for them to catch up over a quick coffee at Khan Market. Verma took him through what had happened in the wee hours of 22 May.

Verma, Vijay Karan's executive assistant and a Tamil Nadu-cadre 1986-batch IPS officer, was waiting to throw his hand into the ring. But he knew that being Karan's chief assistant, he couldn't just opt for another assignment. Also, the names had been cleared by the PMO. Seeing Karan look tired on their way back to office in the same car, Verma asked how the Cabinet committee meeting in the wee hours had gone. Karan told him the R&AW didn't think that the LTTE had a hand in the assassination. Verma instantly countered, 'They know nothing, sir. It's the LTTE.' The chief, slightly miffed, wanted to know what made him so sure. Verma started his batting. He said he was not 'sure' but backed it with a counter-question. Who else would dare to choose the soil of Tamil Nadu for such an action? Most likely the neighbour. The LTTE had turned Tamil Nadu into a hideout, courtesy of a friendly government, political allies and sympathizers. The strategy of the LTTE, Verma thought, was to 'kill someone in Sri Lanka and then escape to India' or 'kill someone in India and then escape to Sri Lanka'. It would take not more than a few hours.

Karan saw his argument but felt it was too early to jump to any such conclusion. He stressed the argument based on the track record of the LTTE. They were far more brutal than even the Colombian mercenaries who worked for the drug lord Escobar. The LTTE guerrillas took no less than fifty lives in every attack, sometimes over 100. Many Tamil rebels fought for 'liberation', but it was Prabhakaran who had split from them and formed the LTTE, declaring war against the Sri Lankan government. He had inducted teenagers and given them guns and grenades. And he hated Rajiv Gandhi for signing the Indo-Sri Lanka Accord with President Jayawardene. Karan, however, suggested that Verma not get carried away. Verma had asked his boss point-blank, 'Sir, I want to join the SIT.' Karan had turned him down, saying he could not let the staff run his office, but Verma had reminded him there was no dearth of officers wanting to join the office of the CBI director. He had asked Karan to consider his credentials—that he was a Tamil Nadu-cadre IPS, that he spoke fluent Tamil, knew the state like the back of his hand and that he had deep knowledge of the LTTE's functioning. Also that he definitely wanted to thrash those who had killed the former Prime Minister. After giving it thought, Karan had called his deputy, Datta, from the car phone and asked his opinion of Verma even as the latter sat beside him. It didn't take more than a minute for Verma to be inducted into the SIT.

Sub-editor Binoo John came rushing in with the fax copy of Shekhar's story from Madras. Oh god, he had already started filing. Anirudhya tried to sneak a look at the copy. But John said, 'A reporter could not peep into a senior editor's copy, sorry.' All Anirudhya could manage to see were two more bylines next to Shekhar's—Anand Viswanathan and Kavitha Shetty. He knew they were both from *India Today*'s Madras bureau.

Anirudhya looked across the newsroom. Bobb's cabin was diagonally across from him. He had set the deadline at six. And no one messed with Bobb's deadlines. He asked Bobb if he had to file his copy that evening since the story was not meant for publication the next morning, *India Today* being a fortnightly and not a daily. If Anirudhya had come to the magazine with the reputation of being a Page One reporter, Bobb was a prima donna who had been there since its inception and was credited with setting up the magazine's style of writing.

Bobb was sunk in piles of computer printouts. He looked up and asked with a poker face if Anirudhya could file by six. The editors in office knew that Anirudhya's skill lay in news gathering and not writing perfect copies. His copy would have to go through Bobb.

Bobb looked at Anirudhya's copy later in the day and said that Shekhar had already filed most of that information. 'He did that from Madras?' 'Yes, a journalist of Shekhar Gupta's repute can access information from anywhere,' came the response. 'See what else you can give me. By tonight.' Bobb went back to his printouts.

That night, Verma called and said something that could have far-reaching implications. Anirudhya telephoned Bobb and asked if he could come now to meet him.

'Tell me over the phone. You need not come to the office.'

'Law Minister Subramanian Swamy claimed at the Cabinet Committee on Political Affairs meeting that he suspected the Tamil guerrilla outfit LTTE behind the assassination. But the R&AW chief G.S. Bajpai ruled out any involvement of the Tamil Tigers in the assassination.'

Bobb asked Anirudhya to come to the office and hung up. Swamy was a close confidant of the Prime Minister. The information was sensitive. The story was better discussed threadbare in person.

—✦—

The first details of the *India Today* cover story were falling into place, with reporters sending their inputs from Madras, Colombo, London, New York, Singapore and New Delhi. Anirudhya was desperately trying to catch hold of Subramaniam Swamy, a politician known for making sensational—and often revealing—claims. Anirudhya had the luck to catch up with him in his car from his South Avenue residence to his party's parliamentary office.

Apparently, Swamy, on multiple occasions, had cautioned the Congress party about its inept handling of the Indo-Sri Lanka Accord. He claimed to have told a senior Congress leader from the south, known for her proximity to Rajiv Gandhi and Internal Security Minister P. Chidambaram, that the LTTE supremo Velupillai Prabhakaran would strike directly at the former Prime Minister. According to Swamy, Prabhakaran was upset with Rajiv Gandhi and felt like a wounded tiger after Rajiv's refusal to review the Indo-Sri Lanka Accord that he, as Prime Minister, had signed with the Sri Lankan President. Swamy said no one in the Congress party had cared to follow up on his information.[1]

Swamy went on to claim that Chief Election Commissioner T.N. Seshan had come to his residence on the morning of 22 May and said that Israel's intelligence outfit Mossad was the real mastermind behind the LTTE's assassination of Rajiv Gandhi. When Swamy had asked Seshan the basis of such a charge, the latter had told him that he would do so only if made the home minister in the government. But that was not going to be possible because the government was functioning only as a caretaker. Even then, chief of the AIADMK, J. Jayalalithaa, knowing of the LTTE's hostility towards the Congress leader, declined to address any public meeting jointly with Rajiv Gandhi, despite both their parties contesting the election in an alliance.[2]

The Ministry of Information and Broadcasting's Press Information Bureau (PIB) issued a release that inter alia said that the Central government, while announcing the formation of the SIT to investigate the assassination, had simultaneously announced a separate one-man Judicial Commission of Inquiry, headed by a sitting judge of the Supreme Court, Justice J.S. Verma, to look into the security lapses that led to the tragic incident.

If anything was certain about the assassination, it was the aspect of the 'security lapse'. A contact from the CBI told Anirudhya that the Madras unit of the agency had registered a fresh case—9/91-SCB (Special Crime Branch) with a DSP-rank officer K. Ragothaman as the investigation officer (IO). Anirudhya did a quick check on the IO's background from his contacts in Madras and learnt that Ragothaman was an officer with a fine track record. A colleague of his from the CBI Madras told him that Ragothaman didn't feel very upbeat about his new high-profile assignment. 'Maybe because he is becoming the IO of a case that will be very difficult to solve as there is absolutely no clue. In such a situation, collection of evidence is next to impossible. Also, the local politics can act as a deterrent,' said the contact. Actually, that was the feeling across the board. The top brass of the police didn't see any hope of cracking the case.

Even as the security agencies were struggling to find a clue, *The Hindu*, then Tamil Nadu's premier English daily, published a photograph that seemed likely to be a breakthrough. It showed a salwar-kameez-wearing bespectacled woman carrying a sandalwood garland, flanked by another woman and a teenage girl. The newspaper suspected the girl carrying the sandalwood garland was the assassin. But publication of the photograph, which was potentially a great piece of evidence and a lead, upset the SIT. Any lead at that stage was meant for investigation and not for public consumption. In no time, a section of the IPS lobby blamed the forensics boss P. Chandrasekharan for trying to hog publicity.

Those in the press who didn't get the picture and were outsmarted by *The Hindu* sought an explanation from the SIT chief Kaarthikeyan. How could such vital information be leaked to the press even before the investigators had got wind of it? *The Hindu*'s executive editor N. Ram's clarification of 'the freedom of press' did not make the sleuths happy. Kaarthikeyan tried to douse the fire by telling his team, 'You have to learn to live with it.'

If the SIT was becoming desperate for a clue, time was running out for Anirudhya as well. After working for a month in *India Today*, he had realized that working for a fortnightly was very different from working for a daily. A periodical, whether a weekly or a fortnightly, got to look beyond what the dailies published. The most preferred word in a newsmagazine was 'exclusive'. If your story did not carry exclusive information, the only place your copy would land up in was the trash bin.

Anirudhya arrived in the office of the head of IB's Delhi unit. It had taken him years to cultivate 'sources'—contacts such as this one. But nobody seemed to know anything except the mundane. The head of IB Delhi was a harried man. His team in Madras had intercepted a message but could not decode it. The communication was between a rogue station somewhere in the south of Madras and Jaffna across the Palk Strait, the den of the Tamil Tigers. He had rushed to the airport to catch up with his boss M.K. Narayanan, who was about to board an eight-seater BSF plane with Joint Director Ajit Doval, in charge of operations, and LTTE expert E.S.L. Narasimhan. He thought Narayanan could get it deciphered with the help of his friends in Military Intelligence (MI). But the plane had taken off and Narayanan had returned to office in a foul mood. There he had found Anirudhya waiting to see him.

Seeing his IB contact unwilling to cough up any information, Anirudhya did most of the talking. With everyone so tightlipped, the SIT indeed had a daunting task at hand, with no clue in sight. It was the perfect murder. The sleuths were groping in the dark, leading to multiple theories and multiple suspects. It could be anybody and not just the LTTE, though it had emerged as the main suspect courtesy of the media. The Punjab militants had seen Indira Gandhi dead. How could one rule out even the Kashmiri extremists or the insurgents from the North-Eastern states? Or even the Naxalites from Andhra Pradesh or Bihar, for that matter? Or any other foreign hand?

But the all-important intelligence specialist was not answering any of Anirudhya's questions. An assistant brought in an urgent telex report. Narayanan went through it twice, and, in a sudden change of mind, tossed it to Anirudhya. It was an eye-opener. It was a logical extension of the photograph of the suspected assassin published by *The Hindu* the day before.

The Tamil Nadu forensics boss Chandrasekharan claimed to have made a breakthrough in the investigation. The telex report suggested that on the morning of 22 May in Sriperumbudur, while Chandrasekharan was collecting evidence from the blast site, a young policeman had whispered something to his ear and slipped an envelope containing a strip of exposed negatives into his hand. Those came from a camera that the young cop had recovered from the blast site on the fateful night. The young policeman did recall hearing IG R.K. Raghavan, in charge of security arrangements at the venue, saying that 'someone must pick up the camera' from the scene of devastation moments after the blast. Anyone with basic investigative knowledge would know that the camera could provide vital clues.

Anirudhya thanked his IB friend and left for office. Around eight in the evening, Bina from *India Today*'s reception called Anirudhya at his desk, saying Chandrasekharan was on the line, and connected the two.

Chandrasekharan told *India Today* that while going through the photographs of the blast site published across newspapers, the forensics team had noticed a camera among the heaps of bodies. His instant reaction was that the pictures taken by the camera could be of immense value. He had asked his team why the camera had not been acquired. Chandrasekharan had further checked with his photographer to bring in the video footage of the morning when he and his team were collecting evidence at the blast site. A replay of the video did not show any camera at the spot. Someone must have picked it up at the time of clearing the bodies, Chandrasekharan told his team, adding it be retrieved at the earliest.

Chandrasekharan did not waste even a minute. He headed for Kanchipuram Hospital. But nobody could give him any information on the camera at the morgue. There he saw two unidentified, dismembered bodies—one male and one female—brought in from the blast site. He suspected something very serious. While examining the corpses at the morgue, he learnt that one of them was a freelance photographer. He tried to join the dots—camera seen in the heaps of bodies and a dead photographer. It was highly likely that he had captured the last moments of Rajiv Gandhi's assassination. Further inquiry by his team revealed the name of the photographer as Haribabu; he had been seen clicking photographs of Rajiv Gandhi upon his arrival in Sriperumbudur.

Chandrasekharan was determined to get hold of Haribabu's camera. He went back to the blast site the following morning. But nobody knew anything about the camera. He went back to his laboratory and found a young policeman from the CID waiting for him. The young policeman was a police photographer who had collected the camera at the instruction of the IG (CID) R.K. Raghavan. The senior cop had thought on the same lines as the senior forensics man. The police photographer told

Chandrasekharan that he could not develop the film roll inside the 'Chinon' camera retrieved from the crime scene due to a bandh observed in the city following the assassination. He, therefore, sought the help of the laboratory to develop the film roll and print copies for the crime branch. Chandrasekharan's deputy, Watson, made copies and printed them—a set of ten photographs.

One of the photographs showed a bespectacled woman wearing a green-and-orange salwar kameez, carrying a sandalwood garland. Another woman and a teenage girl could also be seen, and a white kurta-pyjama-clad man standing a little away from them. Chandrasekharan took the chance of a lifetime. He gave a copy of the photograph to Special Correspondent Prakash Swamy of *The Hindu,* who had tagged along with Chandrasekharan since morning and was present in his office even at that point of time. The forensics expert thought its publication would inspire people to volunteer information about the people in the photograph.

The forensics laboratory started working at full steam. It pieced together what appeared to be the explosive device that was used to assassinate Rajiv Gandhi. They found pieces of tattered blue denim cloth with electrical wires attached to them and bits and pieces of the green-and-orange salwar kameez that the bespectacled woman was wearing in the photograph. They matched what was still found attached to the dismembered female body at the morgue earlier. This was followed by DNA tests, and it appeared that the female was a human bomb that killed Rajiv. This was a first in Indian history.

While Chandrasekharan was congratulated by all and sundry for his breakthrough, the SIT was desperately trying to find out the identity of those in the photograph and their antecedents. During the interrogation of those who had attended Rajiv's rally at Sriperumbudur, one woman identified the two females in one of the pictures taken by Haribabu and claimed she had seen them mingling with the 'human bomb' and the white-kurta-pyjama-clad man seen in Haribabu's first picture. The two girls were later found to be Nalini and the second human bomb, Shubha.

But why had Chandrasekharan given the photograph to a newspaper before sharing it with the investigators? His reply was through a counter-question to Anirudhya. 'Did it hamper the investigation or help the investigation at a time when the CBI was clueless about which direction to head in?' His intentions could have been above board but no one in the SIT approved of his leaking a crucial piece of evidence to the media while keeping the SIT in the dark.

Anirudhya felt he had got something that, in the cardinal language of journalism, was truly 'exclusive', something that would make his editors happy. He finished writing his interview of the person who was considered the forensic czar of India and sent it to his editors.

—∞—

Bobb's printer churned out the final copy of Shekhar Gupta's story, part of which read:

> The short, stout, dark and bespectacled, woman, somewhere in her mid-30s, would have mingled indistinguishably in any Tamil election crowd but for one incongruity: she wore a salwar-kameez. But so many Tamil women have discarded the sari for the more practical northern dress, particularly in Madras. So, a mere 50 km away, the police were not about to get unduly perturbed by the sight of a nondescript woman just because she was clad in salwar-kameez. Twelve hours later, with no more than two dismembered legs, a severed head, bits of a denim-and-velcro belt, fragments of a detonating switch

> and battery as clues, some of the country's top investigators, forensic scientists and explosives experts from the NSG were struggling to piece together the rest of the jigsaw, the key to which lay in the identity of the dead assassin.[3]

Shekhar, with inputs from the Madras bureau and Anirudhya in Delhi, went on to write that Rajiv's personal security officer, ACP Pradip Dutta, had recently told him that he was aware of Rajiv's careless attitude towards security restrictions while mingling with the crowd at public meetings. But the ACP had assured him that if anything were to happen to Rajiv, it would be over his own dead body. Ironically, that's exactly what happened. ACP Dutta's body was recovered next to Rajiv's, along with that of sixteen others, including the local superintendent of police Mohammed Iqbal and Congress workers who had come to catch a glimpse of their leader. The rest were lucky to have escaped the outcome of the blast. The Congress candidate from Sriperumbudur, Maragatham Chandrasekar, for whom Rajiv had gone to campaign, Tamil Nadu Congress Committee (TNCC) chief Vazhappady Ramamurthy, Congress general secretary G.K. Moopanar, prominent Congress politician Jayanthi Natarajan, Ramamurthy's PA and Arasu Nachiappan, a TNCC office-bearer, were in close proximity but managed to run away soon after the blast, fearing more explosions. Ramamurthy, Natarajan and Moopanar rushed back only to find Rajiv's mangled body at the site. Ramamurthy spotted Rajiv's Lotto shoe and screamed. Moopanar tried to lift Rajiv's body; his hands were smeared with blood and flesh and Rajiv lay motionless, with one-quarter of his skull missing.

*India Today*'s Madras bureau kept sending a blow-by-blow account of the post-assassination scene over the next twenty-four hours. For the first half an hour or so, total confusion reigned on the spot. By the time the police recovered their composure, the accomplices, if any, had ample time to hide either in metropolitan Madras or flee to the coast and then across the Palk Strait to the safety of Jaffna. Even the driver of the car in which Rajiv had arrived at the venue from the airport had fled the scene.

A former journalist who was then working in the Ministry of Home Affairs (MHA) informed Anirudhya that all states were being told to put their security forces on alert to pre-empt any backlash. The black memory of the time that followed Indira Gandhi's assassination was still vivid in the minds of many. Delhi was given special attention by the MHA and the army headquarters with the deployment of army columns. Security was beefed up in areas such as Karol Bagh, which had a sizeable Tamil population.

While the Madras bureau was sending ground reports, Anirudhya called a friend in Madras, Dr K. Chokalingam, a trauma surgeon and also the chairperson of the Congress party's medical cell. He was at the Madras General Hospital, where the post mortem had been conducted. Dr Chokalingam said the doctors faced a lot of difficulty trying to suture the fragmented body. The skull had broken open, exposing the brain cavity, through which grey matter had been lost. The face had received too many hits, with the lips, nose and the eyes destroyed. Despite being a veteran in his field, Dr Chokalingam could not look at the mangled body of his leader for more than a minute. Earlier, he said, Dr Cecilia Cyril had found twenty-two injuries on Rajiv's body at the Madras General Hospital when asked to conduct the post mortem. She had observed that Rajiv's face was severely damaged. Deep wounds were observed on the left portion of the trunk and the face. Anirudhya hung up.

---

Anirudhya had been waiting outside the office of S.K. Datta for more than two hours only to find out who else had been picked to join the SIT. Finally, when he walked into Datta's office, the Number 2 of the CBI was pondering over the matter of the 'human bomb'. He was looking at various reports, including the forensic analysis from the Tamil Nadu Forensics Lab, Central Forensic Science Laboratory of New Delhi and explosive experts from the NSG. These reports, put together, indicated that the body of a woman from the corpses collected after the blast threw significant leads. The torso and the right limb of the woman were blown into bits. The dismembered body showed pellet marks and burns. If the forensics maestro Chandrasekharan had pointed the finger of suspicion at the girl carrying the sandalwood garland standing inches away from Rajiv Gandhi moments before the blast, it was the SIT's responsibility to prove that the girl was indeed the human bomb that had killed Rajiv.

The CBI was still upset with Chandrasekharan leaking crucial evidence to the media before sharing it with the SIT. Even before the investigation started in full swing, lack of cooperation and blame games had ensued between the agencies. The R&AW was in disagreement with the IB on the role of the LTTE in the assassination. Tamil Nadu Police felt there was no point going after the LTTE in a state where the terrorist organization from Jaffna enjoyed support from certain political parties. The Tamil Nadu Forensics Lab asked why an agency (read the CBI) from New Delhi was coming to take all the credit. Even the CBI did not take the findings of the lab—that the assassination was the work of a human bomb—at face value and sent the results to the Centre for Cellular and Molecular Biology in Hyderabad for verification. So tissues collected from the dismembered female body with remains of the green-and-orange salwar kameez, the vest bomb and the blast site were sent again to Hyderabad. The scientists upheld the findings and conclusions arrived at by Chandrasekharan. However, Datta did not agree with that observation. According to him, the CBI always got evidence collected by other agencies verified.

Meanwhile, Shekhar Gupta learnt that, based on a video film shot minutes before the blast, the two women who were seen in the first picture taken by Haribabu had been identified as S. Kokila and Latha Kannan, standing with the suspected human bomb. Latha Kannan was a Congress worker and must have had secured permission to greet Rajiv in the red carpet area through party seniors. The million-dollar question was how the suspected assassin knew Kannan. Did she gain access to the red carpet area, which was meant only for VVIP security, with Kannan's help? Obviously, it was too early to get that answer, even for the investigators. Therefore, speculations could not be stopped. Security across Tamil Nadu was beefed up with the deployment of paramilitary units and army columns in areas that had Sri Lankan refugee camps.

—∞—

Inderjit Badhwar, wearing a tracksuit, walked into the newsroom. 'That's a hell of a story from Shekhar and team,' he told everyone and then turned to Anirudhya. 'Sonny, it's your turn now. Go to Suri and give him your travel plans for Madras.'

Two things struck Anirudhya. First, that he was finally going to the scene of crime for his story, and, second, that the managing editor had come into office wearing a tracksuit. Was he coming straight from a jog? Well, no one jogged at noon in Delhi's summer. Anirudhya asked a colleague where he could find Suri.

*India Today*'s legendary cartoonist Ajit Ninan sat in a cubicle adjacent to the reception. An hour of his life wouldn't pass without him cracking a joke or bringing a smile to your face. Anirudhya stopped by and Ninan said, 'You still haven't moved your ass to Madras?' Anirudhya asked who Suri was and where he sat. Ninan gave him a serious look and said, 'Be careful with him. His name is

Arun Suri, very similar to that of the boss Aroon Purie.' Anirudhya didn't react. He was too new in the set-up.

Ninan called out, 'Suri?' The guy sat right opposite the cartoonist's cubicle. Ninan introduced Anirudhya to him. Suri took a look at the newcomer and said he would check with Badhwar and get back on whether Anirudhya needed to travel to Madras. Ninan, in his inimitable style, poked Suri, '*Footage baad mein khana*, do his work now. Poor chap has to leave for Madras ASAP.'

# 2

THE DELHI–MADRAS INDIAN AIRLINES FLIGHT VIA HYDERABAD was on time. It took four hours and ten minutes to land at the Meenambakkam airport. Arun Suri had arranged everything perfectly. He got the Madras office of *India Today* to send a car to pick up Anirudhya from the airport and take him to the hotel where Suri had booked him.

Anirudhya was coming back to the capital of Dravidian culture exactly a decade after he finished college in the city. Nothing much had changed, he felt, while passing Gemini Studios. Next was the Sapphire cinema complex. It appeared unaltered. The Anand restaurant, Spencer's ice cream soda joint and the Thousand Lights mosque. So many memories! All looked the same. The car entered pulled up at the hotel around 1.30 p.m. Anirudhya had heard that *India Today*'s reporters always stayed in five-star hotels. This was his first.

'Welcome to the Taj, Mr Mitra,' a woman's voice came from behind him. She was dressed in a meticulously draped brick-colour Kanjivaram silk sari. How did she know his name, Anirudhya asked, when he hadn't even checked in? 'It's not difficult, sir,' she replied, guiding him to his room on the ground floor. 'Room No. 40, a corner one. Hope you have an enjoyable stay here, sir.' She left. Soon the telephone rang. The receptionist was requesting his presence for his signature. He was impressed by *India Today*'s clout and the hotel's hospitality.

After doing the relevant paperwork, the first thing Anirudhya did was dial Amit Verma at the SIT's office. He came on the line through the operator.

'Hi! You reached?'

'Yes, I did.'

'So?'

'You tell me, you've got all the news.'

'Let's catch up after a couple of days. Meanwhile, check out the local police?'

'Why the local police when the CBI has taken over?'

'You never know what comes up,' Verma said and hung up. Anirudhya understood the forensics lab leaking vital evidence to a newspaper was still fresh in the SIT's mind.

But what did he mean by 'catch up after a couple of days'? What would he do in the next 'couple of days' if he could not meet his source and get an idea of how the investigation was progressing? That, too, at the cost of five-star luxury! He sensed trouble. Dilip Bobb would be expecting his copies on a daily basis. So would Inderjit Badhwar. He checked the room, the wardrobe and the minibar; he took a look at the price list and headed for a shower.

Now he would have to look for food outside the hotel. *India Today* kept its reporters in five-star hotels but paid a daily allowance, or DA, of 200 bucks, which would no way take care of food and laundry in a five-star facility.

It was about 3 p.m., and Madras was pretty hot and sultry. *India Today*'s Madras office was within walking distance from the hotel. Anirudhya dropped at an Udupi café and ordered a non-veg thali. Having spent five years in college in the city, he was familiar with the local cuisine. But today it was not to his taste. Something was wrong. He cleared the bill and got up. Nothing had been going right since he had landed.

Finding the Madras office on Binny Road was, however, easy. He pushed the swing door inwards, introduced himself and asked for Anand Viswanathan and Kavitha Shetty. Those were the only two names from the Madras bureau he knew. Both had gone out on assignments. Madras was under the lens of the world since the assassination. The action was outside and not inside a journalist's office. He was about to leave and get back to the hotel when someone called out to him.

'Anirudhya?' a stocky, handsome guy with a thick moustache asked.

'Yes?'

'Hi, I am Shyam Tekwani. Photographer.' He extended his hand for a shake.

Anirudhya was happy to meet Tekwani. He was famous for his coverage of the mutilation of IPKF soldiers at the hands of LTTE members in 1987. He shook Tekwani's hand with pleasure. 'Come inside,' the photographer took him to his cabin. It didn't take Anirudhya long to figure out the top brass of Tamil Nadu Police with Tekwani's help. He suggested that Anirudhya meet IG R.K. Raghavan. He was overall in charge of the security arrangements at Sriperumbudur.

The IG's office took Anirudhya's contact details in Madras and said it would get back to him.

Next day, Anirudhya visited his alma mater and met some of the staff from his time. Next was a trip to Marina beach to have coconut water; then to one of the Velu Military food joints for 'mutton fry' with 'lachha paratha' before getting back to the hotel. The receptionist handed him the room key with four messages—three from Harpal Singh, the editorial coordinator at the Delhi office. He was checking about the progress in work. The fourth message was from Bobb, which just said, 'Call back.'

Anirudhya felt he had had it. What would he tell Singh or Bobb? The last thing he would like to say was that his 'sources' were unavailable to talk to him, giving the impression that he was on a paid vacation. He called Singh first, who told Anirudhya that he need not worry if he had nothing to file that night—it happened often to reporters—and hung up. Anirudhya didn't tell Singh that Bobb had asked him to call back. Then he called on Bobb's direct line. Bobb picked up but did not speak. Anirudhya could hear Bobb's baritone voice yelling at someone. Gosh, he was in a bad mood. Anirudhya thought of hanging up, but suddenly Bobb came on the line.

'Yeah?'

'A-anirudhya here. Can we t-talk?'

'Oh, hi ... Yeah, go right ahead.'

'I don't have much to file today ... Actually, still catching up with my sources. They are extremely busy.'

'That was expected. You stick around. Let me know if you get something worthwhile.'

Bobb hung up.

He had sounded very polite, just the opposite of how he had been seconds ago to whoever he was shouting at in office. What a relief! Anirudhya picked up the TV remote and paused at CNN. He thought of having a drink. He had saved a hundred from his first day's allowance. The room service menu suggested not even a pint of beer would come in that amount. He took a shower and hit the bed.

The phone rang. It was from the office of IG R.K. Raghavan of Tamil Nadu Police. Anirudhya was inside a taxi headed to meet Raghavan in the next five minutes.

Raghavan was waiting for Anirudhya. Even though the SIT had taken over the investigation, Raghavan was as busy as ever. The SIT was new and needed backup and ground support. More than that, Raghavan, in charge of the security arrangements at Rajiv Gandhi's rally, took it as his moral responsibility to crack the assassination case.

'We came to know of Rajiv Gandhi's itinerary in the state on 17 May. Immediately we got down to making the required security arrangements in collaboration with the state and central security agencies,' Raghavan told Anirudhya.

The latter switched on his tape recorder, hoping Raghavan would not object. But he did. 'Look, I have nothing to hide. But since the CBI has taken over the investigation, it won't be fair on my part to comment on the case officially,' he said. The tape recorder was put back in its place.

Raghavan resumed talking. His office had issued instructions on 20 May to ensure there would be crowd and access control at the venue. Senior officers were deputed to coordinate with the organizers of the meeting, mostly from the Congress party, to prepare a list of VVIP guests to be allowed for a 'meet and greet' with Rajiv Gandhi. Metal detectors were sanctioned to screen them. More than 300 police personnel were stationed there that night to guard the red carpet area and keep an eye on guests. But, most unfortunately, the female police who were assigned the task of frisking the female VVIP guests could not do so for lack of cooperation from the organizers. They probably thought it might bruise the ego of the VVIPs.

'Organizers meaning ... ?' Anirudhya asked.

'The Congress party.'

An orderly brought in steaming filter coffee, with an accompaniment of local sweets.

'I was certainly unhappy to see the way some party functionaries conducted themselves at the venue. I asked them why the wooden barricades were not made to the specifications provided by the police department. I didn't get a satisfactory answer. My juniors complained of lack of support from the event organizers whenever any security concern was raised. Security issues were least on their list of their priorities,' said Raghavan. Anirudhya was making notes fast. But, inside, he wasn't happy with the outcome. A mere line or two criticizing the Congress party's attitude didn't make for a good story. The dailies were full of such reports. Raghavan was talking about security lapses, whereas Anirudhya was looking for material on the killers. The senior IG promised to meet him again.

Next morning Anirudhya visited the Madras bureau again and got a warm welcome from Viswanathan. Tekwani and Shetty were out on an assignment. Viswanathan was following AIADMK (All India Anna Dravida Munnetra Kazhagam) supremo J. Jayalalithaa's campaign for the assembly election. After a cup of hot filter coffee, Viswanathan invited Anirudhya along, unless he had prior engagements.

Hanging around with Viswanathan paid dividends at the end of the day when the Madras bureau chief thought of dropping in at the DMK (Dravida Munnetra Kazhagam) party office to get their reaction to media speculations about the party's sympathetic attitude towards the LTTE. Rajiv Gandhi had earned the wrath of the party ever since he had forced Chandra Shekhar's minority government in New Delhi to dissolve the DMK's government in Tamil Nadu and impose President's Rule in the state.

So Viswanathan had thought a visit to the party office could get Anirudhya something.

As luck would have it, Anirudhya ran into an old intelligence contact from Delhi who was then stationed in Madras for the past year, monitoring the affairs of the DMK. He was not a very senior officer in the country's domestic intelligence-gathering agency. He was a 'field man'. And such officials, or 'moles', always proved to be effective as they went by facts and not mere conjecture or analysis.

Anirudhya caught up with him early next morning at the Marina beach. He was done with his morning jog. The beach was not crowded. They spoke over some fresh idli followed by filter coffee. Anirudhya's first query was if there was any mystery behind Rajiv Gandhi's coming to Tamil Nadu to address just one rally. His 'field man' tried to give him some perspective. One was not sure of a mystery behind the leader's trip to the state but destiny calling him there could not be ruled out. Intelligence officials are not known for using words such as 'destiny' and 'fate'. Anirudhya was even more curious as the 'field man' went into the events that had led Rajiv to visit Sriperumbudur.[1]

Congress General Secretary Margaret Alva had finalized Rajiv's tour programme on 13 May for Orissa (now Odisha) and Tamil Nadu, where Maragatham Chandrasekar's constituency, Sriperumbudur, had not been included. When going through the draft itinerary of his tour, Rajiv, in his own handwriting, had included 'Aunty's' constituency and only a day for Tamil Nadu. Was he writing his fate? But there was much more to it than that.

Rajiv's tour programme was published across all newspapers on 17 May. Something very interesting happened. TNCC President Vazhappady Ramamurthy sent a fax to Rajiv asking if his tour of Tamil Nadu was necessary, considering that the Congress party was in alliance with the AIADMK, whose leader, Jayalalithaa, had a very strong hold on the state. The state Congress chief was not endorsing Rajiv's visit to the state, let alone to Sriperumbudur. Rajiv had simply noted 'So what' on the fax sent by Ramamurthy. Was it destiny pulling him to Sriperumbudur?

In fact, the DMK supremo M. Karunanidhi was to address a rally on the same Sriperumbudur temple ground on the same date. But the party's event management team had not asked for the temple ground on time. They had sought police permission on 19 May. The police could not allow two big meetings addressed by such big leaders on the same day in the same town. Eventually, the DMK dropped out and Chandrasekar had her way. And she had insisted on the temple ground, as some of her real estate developer relatives owned it. Rajiv's meeting would have brought it into the limelight.

Rajiv's tryst with destiny didn't end there. After touring Orissa in a helicopter, Rajiv took a chartered plane hired by his party to Vizag in Andhra Pradesh on 21 May. He was to take off for Tamil Nadu by 4.30 p.m. Captain Subhash Chandok was flying him. He found that the 'King Air' plane had developed a communication error. Rajiv, an experienced Boeing pilot himself, looked into the problem and said he felt sorry for 'Aunty Chandrasekar' as he wouldn't be able to attend the political rally in her constituency. The aircraft was not fit for flying—Rajiv would have to spend the night there and return to Delhi the next morning due to no landing or take-off facility at the Vizag airport after 6 p.m.

Shortly, however, the pilot managed to find the required spare part from the ground staff, fixed the communication error and declared that the aircraft was ready to take off. A happy Rajiv himself piloted the aircraft and landed in Madras around 8 p.m—keeping his date with destiny.

The sun got stronger as Anirudhya and his contact sat on the beach, talking. It was rare to see a 'spy' getting emotional about someone's death. Anirudhya returned to the hotel and filed the next instalment of his story under the title 'Tryst with Destiny'.

The call came early in the evening. Copies filed by reporters went to all the editors. Badhwar read Anirudhya's copy and called his hotel. Anirudhya answered in the middle of shaving. Badhwar's message was loud and clear.

'Hey, we sent you to Madras to collect some hard facts that you are known for in your stories. This "tryst with destiny" could have been done by any of the subs here, Anirudhya! Any problem that you are facing in Madras?'

'No, not at all,' said Anirudhya.

'Good. Just go for the kill. Good luck.'

'Thanks, Inder ... thanks for the ...' Badhwar had disconnected.

—∾—

Kaarthikeyan was submerged in files, books, stacks of printouts and videocassettes.

Unlike the Mahatma Gandhi and Indira Gandhi assassinations, where some of the assailants were caught red-handed on the spot, in the case of Rajiv Gandhi there was no clue about the possible identity of the killers. *The Hindu* photograph was doing the rounds, but the SIT was still trying to figure out the characters in it. That they were Sri Lankan Tamils did not necessarily make them LTTE operatives. Kaarthikeyan feared it might end up like the Kennedy assassination case. He was studying cases of violent attacks and ambushes where extremist groups were involved in Tamil Nadu. There was a knock on the door. He didn't hear. Someone pushed open the door slightly.

It was Radhavinod Raju, second in command in the SIT. Kaarthikeyan still hadn't noticed. Raju cleared his throat.

'Come in.'

'I was leaving, so thought of saying good night.'

'Sure. Good night.'

Raju was about to leave when Kaarthikeyan spoke again.

'The CBI director has a meeting with the PM tomorrow morning. I was making some notes for him. While doing that, I came across some previous cases of crime where extremist groups were involved in Tamil Nadu. Very revealing, I must say.'

'Can I take a look at them?'

'Yes, yes. Let me finish reading them. After that I wanted to pass them on to you anyway.'

'By all means.'

'Thanks. Good night.'

—∞—

The next day, Anirudhya visited *The Hindu* office and looked for Prakash Swamy, who had got the controversial photograph from the forensics giant Chandrasekharan. He wasn't expecting a guest. However, a courteous man, Swamy invited Anirudhya to the canteen for coffee. The latter inquired about the photographs from Haribabu's camera. The senior reporter was all smiles but wouldn't open his mouth to someone he was seeing for the first time—who was also a competitor. However, he did drop one hint for the reporter who had come all the way from Delhi. He said the photo had been edited. There was a white-kurta-pyjama-clad man in it too, who was cropped out of the image on the advice of the forensics boss Chandrasekharan.

About Chandrasekharan 'leaking the photo' to his paper, Swamy told Anirudhya that it was probably that the forensic lab wanted to prove what it was capable of—and, of course, it wanted to help the investigation too. Nobody among the locals was too happy about the way New Delhi had been imposing the SIT on Tamil Nadu officers and stealing all the credit. Chandrasekharan's leaking the photo to the press had been criticized, but it had also helped the SIT get a 'start' on the case. Nobody knew at that point that these photos would prove to be the biggest clue in times to come.

—ꟺ—

At South Block, New Delhi, two crucial meetings took place back to back. In the first, Prime Minister Chandra Shekhar spoke to the chief of R&AW G.S. Bajpai and asked him what the R&AW was doing when speculations about the LTTE's involvement were rife across the media. People would see it as a failure in assessing the threat perceptibility on the former PM's life by a premier intelligence agency such as R&AW. But Bajpai was unwilling to see reason in the speculations. He reportedly told the Prime Minister that a day after the assassination, the chief of the LTTE's International Secretariat in London, Sathasivam Krishnakumar, alias Kittu, had denied the group's involvement in the assassination. The head of R&AW's argument was that the LTTE's official spokesperson, Anton Rajah, had offered the group's condolences saying the LTTE was 'shocked' by the tragedy. Chandra Shekhar could not understand why the spokesperson of a terrorist organization had to be believed. Bajpai cited that terrorist organizations owning responsibility for attacks was nothing new. The PM didn't interrupt him. The R&AW chief also said that the Jammu and Kashmir Liberation Front (JKLF) chairman Amanullah Khan had issued a statement from Rawalpindi, Pakistan, denying its involvement; so had the Sikh militant leader Jagjit Singh Chohan from London.

The R&AW, therefore, didn't believe there was a 'foreign hand' in the assassination. Bajpai also expressed his disapproval of the CBI's arrival on foreign soil—Colombo—without the knowledge of the Ministry of External Affairs (MEA) and R&AW. Bajpai advised the

PM that the serious matter of lapse in internal security that had led to the tragedy had to be investigated. The Verma Commission had already been formed for that very purpose. But Bajpai reportedly tried to push his theory of 'internal sabotage'. Seeing the PM not paying much attention to his claims, Bajpai claimed that a top leader of the LTTE was a R&AW mole. Instantly the PM wanted to know who it was. The reply came after a pause. The 'mole' was Kittu. The PM was surprised. Because the assassination had taken place despite a key member of the terrorist organization being a R&AW mole. There was silence in the room.

Prime Minister Chandra Shekhar was a shrewd politician with more than five decades in the political game, including seven terms in the Parliament. He had earned the top job with the support of just fifty-four Members of Parliament (MPs) against the requirement of 273. Rajiv's party was lending him support from the outside. He had already called the director of the IB (DIB), M.K. Narayanan, and CBI Director Vijay Karan for a meeting and pitted them against Bajpai's claim of 'internal sabotage'. While Bajpai was responsible for gathering 'foreign' intelligence, Narayanan did the same for 'domestic' intelligence. Chandra Shekhar wanted to assess the level of the blame game among the security agencies.

In the second crucial meeting, Narayanan and Karan were seated across from the Prime Minister. The PM deliberately asked a twisted question—whether the LTTE had claimed responsibility for the assassination. Narayanan politely denied it, adding that a caller from Sacramento in California had called the office of *India West*, an Indian ethnic weekly published from California, and 'claimed responsibility on behalf of the LTTE'. That meant nothing to suggest that the LTTE had claimed responsibility.

Both Karan and Narayanan knew where it was coming from. Karan added another incident that had raised eyebrows. The Indian High Commission in Colombo had received a call around

4 p.m. on 21 May, about six hours before the assassination. The anonymous caller had asked whether Rajiv Gandhi was still alive. The junior High Commission staff member who had received the call had asked the caller to repeat his question, and the caller had complied. Then the staff member had asked the caller to identify himself, and the caller had quickly hung up. The PM was shocked to hear this, though he didn't miss the meaningful smile on Narayanan's face. Had it been brought to notice on time, perhaps Rajiv Gandhi's life could have been saved—at the least, security around him could have been tightened. The PM then told the two how Bajpai had been ruling out the LTTE or any Sri Lanka angle in the assassination.

The PM angrily pressed a phone button and asked to get Bajpai back to the PM's office. Sensing the situation might become aggravated, both Narayanan and Karan tried to placate the PM—they requested him to speak to Bajpai after their meeting was over. The PM understood. But there was more to the LTTE connections that both the senior officers wanted to discuss with the PM. They were armed with newspaper clippings, wire messages and phone-tapping reports, and started presenting their case.

Karan tabled a news clip of an article by Sri Lankan Tamil journalist D.B. Jayaraj, which had been carried in *The Hindu*. The writer had given the various aliases and other details of that kurta-pyjama man masquerading as a journalist at the site before the blast. This was after the paper's publication of the photograph of the suspected assassin. The PM laughed seeing how a newspaper was ahead of the security agencies in investigating the case. He appreciated the paper's editor for doing his job well.

Top cops such as Narayanan and Karan had to digest the PM's taunt. Narayanan went on to say that, interestingly, the newspaper's editor, celebrated journalist N. Ram's sister Malini Parthasarathy, had arranged an appointment between Rajiv Gandhi and Kasi Anandan, a known LTTE think tank, on 5 March that year—which was later found to be a red herring in the case. The LTTE wanted to get a sense of Rajiv Gandhi's attitude towards itself at a time when the Congress leader's return to power seemed imminent.

The PM observed, on a lighter note, how the IB was so sure of his defeat in the ensuing elections. Narayanan apologized and said it was nothing like that.

Getting back to the LTTE, probably on the feedback of Kasi Anandan, Kittu, who was in London, had sent another emissary, Arjun Sitrambalam, a Sri Lankan Tamil and a banker in London, to meet Rajiv to judge his attitude towards the LTTE and its leader. The emissary had landed in Delhi with the help of P.V. Narasimha Rao and Romesh Bhandari, India's foreign secretary at the time Rajiv signed the Indo-Sri Lankan Peace Accord in 1987, had got him an appointment for a meeting with Rajiv Gandhi. The emissary had met Rajiv on 15 March. Such incidents could not be ruled out as coincidences. There was a pause. It was critical for the veteran sleuths to know the PM's thoughts about their revelations.

Rajiv had reportedly told the emissary that the issue of Sri Lankan Tamils would be 'resolved' if he returned to power. However, he had said that with a rider—that it would be solved through the implementation of the Indo-Sri Lanka Accord that he had signed in 1987. The same was mentioned in the party's election manifesto. Apparently, Rajiv had sent a message to the LTTE boss Prabhakaran through this emissary, asking the guerrilla outfit to drop arms and come to the negotiation table.

Maybe Chandra Shekhar wanted a break. He asked if they would like some more coffee. But neither Karan nor Narayanan was interested. They didn't want the rhythm of the meeting to be broken. They answered him with a polite 'No sir, thank you'.

The IB chief continued to inform the PM that Rajiv's message was conveyed to Kittu—arms had to be dropped before any peace talk could take place through the foreign office and R&AW. But a clear message like that from Rajiv had upset the LTTE. They understood that the former Indian PM would come down heavy on the Tamil Tigers if he came back to power. There was a wireless message sometime in the latter part of March from the LTTE's intelligence chief Pottu Amman to one 'Jack' to get ready for Delhi and send 'black tigress Gowri' along with 'Uncle' to the Indian capital as backup.

The PM felt it all sounded like a John le Carré thriller. He could not believe that the agencies had sat over so much 'intel' and still done nothing.

There was silence in the room until Karan spoke again. The CBI suspected the LTTE had been at it for quite some time. The question was whether they had finally succeeded in Sriperumbudur. He assured the PM that the SIT would not spare any angle or any clue from investigation; any information that was received, even if it appeared inconsequential on the surface, would be probed. The meeting ended on an encouraging note as the PM showed complete confidence in both. Narayanan was personally very close to Rajiv Gandhi, so he looked somewhat emotional towards the end of the meeting. It didn't go unnoticed by the PM. He turned to Narayanan and said that death came to everyone—whether it came with inner dignity and honour, or was just a pitiful incident depended on how people lived their lives at that particular moment. The PM saw both of them off to the door.

—∾—

Anirudhya's next stop was Malligai, where the SIT office was located. He was not looking into barging into an office where some of his best contacts and friends had been busy trying to crack the most controversial crime in Indian history. He had taken an appointment with Kaarthikeyan, who, over the phone, had promised only five minutes as he was 'not yet authorized to talk to the press directly'. Anirudhya hoped to stretch the brief meeting to a not-so-brief one.

Kaarthikeyan received Anirudhya with warmth, and did not expect a point-blank question to start with.

'Can you please show me the rest of the nine photographs from Haribabu's camera, Mr Kaarthikeyan?'

'What makes you so sure that they are in my custody?' Kaarthikeyan asked with a somewhat sarcastic smile.

'It's all over the press, sir.'

'The press is doing its job—it writes whatever it considers right. I cannot comment on that.'

'All right, sir. Have you got them or not?' Anirudhya was all smiles.

'I have got them. But it's too early for me to talk about them.'

While Anirudhya was looking for his next question, the SIT chief looked like the meeting was over. But Anirudhya was not calling it quits so soon.

'You can talk about the photograph that's already published in *The Hindu*. After all, sir, the SIT has not denied anything about it.'

Kaarthikeyan looked at his watch and said it was 'tiffin time'—would Anirudhya like to join him? Anirudhya jumped at the invitation. Such things always granted a reporter more time with sources.

Kaarthikeyan and Anirudhya went to the dining hall. There was a buffet system—coffee, tea, masala vadai, steaming idli, medu vada, mini-sized imarti and sweet rava. Seeing the boss walk in, the staff already present made way for him and exchanged greetings. Kaarthikeyan filled a plate with 'tiffin' and gave it to Anirudhya and then served himself just two idlis. Was he on a diet? 'No, no. I keep eating throughout the day.'

Meanwhile, other senior officers had joined. Kaarthikeyan introduced Anirudhya to all of them, not even missing one. Anirudhya understood that the seasoned cop was treating Anirudhya with all the respect and attention but creating a situation where Anirudhya would not be comfortable asking questions.

Among the officers who had joined Anirudhya knew a few. Amit Verma grinned from ear to ear when he saw Anirudhya. Kaarthikeyan noticed, quickly handed him over to Verma and moved on.

'Don't tell me you are stalking me,' Verma said, chuckling.

'You were not even there. That's why I took an appointment with your boss.'

'And he gave you all this instead of what you came for.' Verma pointed at Anirudhya's plateful of 'tiffin'.

'Like you gave me?'

'Listen, I will talk to you soon. Till then, just chill in Madras. You studied in this city. Just hang around. What's your problem?'

Kaarthikeyan walked up to them—he must have heard the last line Verma had said. The top cop said, 'Anirudhya's problem is he wants information that we don't have.' He then backed it up with a 'sorry' and left. Verma followed him. Anirudhya was now stranded in the middle of sleuths who were uncomfortable discussing work with each other in the presence of a journalist.

There was no sign of Delhi's famous cop Amod Kanth. Anirudhya had known him ever since he was assigned the crime beat in the *Times of India* some eight years ago. A staffer helped him find Kanth. A plate with some 'tiffin' was on his desk, indicating he was too busy to eat. He didn't offer Anirudhya a seat.

'First, congratulations on your new job. *India Today* is prime.'

'That's true. But the *Times* is the *Times*.'

'Of course, of course.'

'I can see you are busy … Should I wait outside?'

'Listen, we must catch up another time. How long would you be in Madras?'

'I will be around. See you later?'

'Sure thing.'

Two officers walked in. Anirudhya walked out.

—∞—

Back in the hotel room, Anirudhya thought how his position and that of the SIT's were not much different. Both were struggling for a lead that would launch them. He dialled the number of his IB contact in Madras who spied on the DMK's affairs and left a message. Someone knocked on the door. An overweight man in his thirties in a white safari suit stood there with a smile on his face. The golden watch on his wrist was prominent.

'Yes?' Anirudhya asked.

'I am Venu, sir. Superintendent of Police "Amith Berma" has sent me to give you this VHS tape, sir.'

His accent was thick. He handed Anirudhya the tape and left. It contained a film—*The Delta Force*. Intriguing. The doorbell rang again. Suddenly a slew of visitors, Anirudhya thought wrily. It was Verma.

'Hi! Busy?'

'So the VIP cop sent a pilot before landing up himself?' Anirudhya teased as he made way for his friend to come in.

'Say whatever you want to, but, man, I tell you the scene is crazy,' Verma said, throwing himself back on the hotel's king-size bed.

Anirudhya looked at his watch. It was 10.15 p.m.

'Drink?'

'No, man. I got to go back in twenty minutes. Let's have a quick bite instead?'

Anirudhya was slightly disappointed hearing that Verma had come for such a short time.

'So the film is to help me kill time?'

'Watch it.' Saying that, he got up and went to the bathroom.

*India Today*'s reporters were entitled to spend if they had to entertain their sources. He took Verma to the Rain Tree restaurant in the hotel. The place was almost empty. Verma picked a corner table. Anirudhya asked for the drinks menu. In the conversation that followed, Verma agreed with the view that both the SIT and Anirudhya were in a similar situation—waiting for that one clue that would launch them in their mission. And Haribabu's ten photos seemed to be just that. The SIT had taken possession of the Chinon camera that had been found at the site and eventually secured the ten developed negatives from the local forensics office—and at the time it did seem to be the most important piece of evidence. The first photo showed the human bomb in a green-and-orange salwar kameez, flanked by two other women; it also showed a kurta-pyjama-clad man standing at a distance. He was not among the dead, nor among the injured. Who was he, then? Was he connected to the woman? The SIT was looking for that answer first.

Anirudhya hoped Verma wouldn't remember his plan to leave in twenty minutes. But Verma had gone into talking mode. The second photo, he said, gave a view of the gathering in the women's enclosure. The third showed a musician, Shankar Ganesh, speaking to a Congress functionary. The fourth through the ninth photos showed the arrival of Rajiv Gandhi, the crowd gathering around him, party workers greeting him with shawls and garlands, and a teenage girl reading something to him from a piece of paper. In that photograph, the bespectacled woman in the green-and-orange salwar kameez was seen approaching Rajiv. The tenth photograph captured the explosion and showed huge flames—nothing else.

In forensic science, Locard's principle holds that the perpetrator of a crime will bring something into the crime scene and leave with something from it, and that both can be used as evidence. And Haribabu's camera did the same. After joining the dots indicated in Haribabu's ten pictures, the SIT had gone on a drive to secure pictures and videos captured by the media and any freelancers who had attended the Sriperumbudur rally. But strangely, the investigators could not find anything that was taken before the assassination, beyond Haribabu's ten pictures and six from another photographer accompanying Ganesh's music band. Obviously, the crowd of lensmen representing the media could not have imagined what was coming or that assassins were roaming around in disguise.

A sub-inspector of the Tamil Nadu police, Anusuya, seen near Rajiv Gandhi in the photograph before the blast, was not identified among the bodies recovered from the blast site. She had to be traced. Verma and the IO Ragothaman had found her admitted in Madras General Hospital in a critical state. She had lost three fingers on her right hand and her face had been severely burnt. She had narrated the events to them when Ragothaman showed her the first photograph. She had immediately recalled the kurta-pyjama-clad man and the woman in the green-and-orange salwar kameez in the red carpet area, and added that there was a young photographer who had been taking their photographs just before the arrival of Rajiv Gandhi.

Soon after *The Hindu* had published the first photograph taken by Haribabu, another photojournalist, Bhagwan Singh, had got in touch with the SIT and expressed doubts about the man in the kurta pyjama. Singh knew Haribabu and had seen him in Sriperumbudur that night; he said the latter had introduced the kurta-pyjama-clad man as the 'partner' of another photographer,

Ravi Shankar. Next day, when Singh called Shankar and inquired about his so-called 'partner', Shankar admitted to having lent his Chinon camera to Haribabu but declined any knowledge of the man in the kurta pyjama.

Shankar's denial had bothered Singh, especially after hearing about the possible involvement of the LTTE in the assassination. Singh knew Haribabu was well known to senior photojournalist Subha Sundaram, whose close links with the LTTE were no secret. He also knew that Sundaram had contacted Haribabu's father, Sundermani, and advised him to dispose of his photographer son's cache of letters and pro-LTTE propaganda material. Although news of his sympathies for the LTTE had appeared in the local press, Haribabu's home was yet to be raided. Luckily for the SIT, Haribabu's family had not acted upon Sundaram's repeated advice of destroying all LTTE-related material their deceased son had stored at home. Nor had they approached the police to inform them about their son's LTTE connections.

Verma and Ragothaman's interaction with Anusuya and Shankar had helped the SIT establish a connection between the suspected dead assassin, the dead photographer Haribabu and the man holding a pen and notebook in the same photograph, clad in a white kurta pyjama. Anusuya had asked the suspected assassin if she had permission to enter the VVIP area. Before she could give a satisfying answer, the photographer (Haribabu) had come in. His reply to Anusuya was that the girl was supposed to garland Rajiv Gandhi and that he was there to click a picture. In reference to the kurta-pyjama-clad man, his explanation was that he was a 'journalist', thus clearly establishing all three were connected.[2]

It was closing time for the Rain Tree's kitchen. A staff gently inquired if Anirudhya and his guest would like to order anything more. The two were down four bottles of beer. Anirudhya had had his dinner before Verma had showed up. He got a club sandwich packed for his friend. The problem started when it came to settling the bill. Verma insisted that he pay for it. Eventually Anirudhya convinced him to go for it the next time. Verma took a taxi and left. Anirudhya called his IB contact and left a message.

Next morning, the IB contact dropped a sealed envelope at his hotel. It contained information on Madras-based media personnel known to be sympathetic to the LTTE. Subha Sundaram was among them. He had lent his studio to LTTE propagandist Baby Subramaniam for the brainwashing of young Tamil minds. Subramaniam was close to the LTTE supremo Prabhakaran too. Sundaram was politically well connected in India and Sri Lanka both. He had visited Jaffna in March 1990 along with a Tamil Nadu-based journalist and had met Prabhakaran. He had also been in touch with other LTTE leaders, such as Anton Balasingham, Kasi Anandan and Kittu, the head of LTTE's international affairs. In January 1991, Sundaram had written to Kittu and offered his services to the 'protector of Tamils Thalapathi Prabhakaran'. The sealed envelope dropped at my hotel had also highlighted the fact that photojournalist Ravi Shankar and Haribabu both knew one Bhagyanathan, who had been gifted a printing press by Subramaniam. Anirudhya made it a point to dig up more on Subramaniam. He could be linked to the assassins if the LTTE indeed turned out to be responsible for Rajiv Gandhi's assassination.

# 3

THE SMALL CLUSTER OF HUTS IN SAIDAPET, TO THE WEST OF MADRAS, was waking up to the cacophony of ducks, some rushing to the pond for a morning bath and some already in the water. Ragothaman had parked his Jeep about 100 yards away. He didn't remind one of the conventional cop, but the arrival of his police Jeep alerted onlookers. And then faces started peeping out from inside the huts.

He stood in front of a hut and looked around, trying to ascertain if he was at the right address. He didn't want to raise an alarm. Nobody came out of the hut. After a while, he pushed open the door and entered. Inside, he saw two photo frames adorned with garlands—that of Haribabu and Rajiv Gandhi. Haribabu's elderly father figured the man must have come for something in connection with his dead son. He didn't dare ask Ragothaman who he was until the latter introduced himself. Haribabu's father asked him to sit and said he would be back soon with coffee. Ragothaman waved at him to sit and not bother about it.

Pointing to Haribabu's picture next to Rajiv's, Ragothaman asked if the young man was a Congress party worker.

'No, he was my son. A photographer by profession … died at the blast site.'

'I am so sorry to hear that. What was his name?'

'Haribabu.'

'Has his last rites been performed?'

Ragothaman noticed a young girl gaping at him from one side of the hut. The father introduced her as his daughter.

'We cremated the body after getting it back from the hospital.'

Haribabu's mother, Meenakshi, returned from some work outside. Haribabu's father used just one word to describe the guest to his wife: 'Government.'

Ragothaman showed them a photograph of the dismembered body of a man from the morgue. The mother could not check her tears. Both parents confirmed it was their son Haribabu. They had seen their son in that condition earlier at the hospital.

Ragothaman stepped out of the hut and waved at his assistant, Inspector Chelladurai. Ragothaman wanted to help Haribabu's family. He asked Chelladurai to get some bread, biscuits, coffee and milk for the family.

To his surprise, Haribabu's mother instantly objected. 'No, no, no, sir. You are my guest, sir. Guests are like God. Let me do the honours, sir.'

She fished out a bundle of hundred-rupee notes from inside her white blouse, pulled one out and gave it to her daughter. 'Get some biscuits and coffee.'

It was a revelation for the seasoned CBI investigator. Where did she get that much money from? The IO of the world's most sensational case at that moment looked straight at the mother as he spoke. 'Your son is gone. That's very unfortunate. But if you can come up with any information about your son's associates, you will be heavily rewarded. That's my promise.'

The father was about to say something but the mother stopped him. Ragothaman took their leave without waiting for the coffee to arrive. After taking his seat in the Jeep, he told Chelladurai, 'Appearances are always deceptive in our field of work, and things are rarely as they seem to be.'

After a breakfast of poori-kurma at Anand's on Mount Road, Anirudhya called Verma. He said he was busy looking into Bhagwan Singh and that he might raid a place in connection with that. 'Would you like to join me?' he asked.

'Yeah, when?'

'Call me around eight at night?'

Both spoke for a while longer and then disconnected.

—~—

Haribabu's father had made up his mind. He was not going to keep quiet despite a note of caution from his wife. He had gone to meet Ragothaman at the SIT's office in Malligai. He handed Ragothaman a camera tripod and said it belonged to his son. Maybe the cop could find some fingerprints on it? It was thoughtful of the father. Ragothaman had not expected it. He, however, noticed a certain reluctance about the man—maybe he wanted to say something.

'Is there anything else you want to tell me? Please feel free.'

'No, no, sir. That's it, that's it. Give me permission to leave, sir.'

Ragothaman asked Chelladurai to drop Haribabu's father home. 'Please wait outside,' he said. 'My assistant will soon join you.'

The father stepped out. He still looked hesitant about something.

'I believe he wanted to say something to me when I went to his house the other day, but his wife was stopping him. Survey his house when you go to drop him—clandestinely, of course,' Ragothaman told his assistant before they left.

Verma and Ragothaman raided Haribabu's hut the next day. After dropping the father the previous night, Chelladurai had telephoned Ragothaman and claimed that there were bundles of plain paper in the three adjoining huts next to Haribabu's father's for printing books and journals. The family owned these huts as well—two had been recently acquired. Locals, too, had noticed their sudden financial rise, Chelladurai had said. Ragothaman advised Chelladurai to call for additional forces and maintain a watch on the huts that night—nobody should be allowed into the huts until the next morning.

In the raid, the SIT found, among other suspicious things, the original bill of the Tamil Nadu state emporium, Poompuhar, on Anna Salai Road, dated 21 May 1991, for the purchase of a sandalwood garland for sixty-nine rupees. This could be the same garland the assassin had been seen carrying in her hand in Haribabu's photograph. It was undoubtedly a breakthrough in the investigation. Anirudhya could not cover the raid due to a change in its timing but he got the dope he needed.

After the raid, Ragothaman asked Haribabu's mother if there was something she was hiding; if she was, its consequences could land them in jail. The mother started howling and then, recovering herself, said, 'Two photographers, Shubha Sundaram and Ravi Shankar, came to our house early on the morning of 22 May. They were looking for Haribabu's camera. I said Haribabu had not come home since the previous day. But they never told me about my son's death.' Unable to carry on, she started rolling around on the floor and crying loudly.

Ragothaman knew this was the moment he had to press the parents for the truth. Eventually, Haribabu's mother led the SIT to a friend of Haribabu's—Kannan—who confirmed her story to Ragothaman. The SIT started tapping the phones of photojournalist Ravi Shankar and Shubha Sundaram and put both under surveillance.

Verma passed on a box to Ragothaman after he returned to office. 'Ragothaman, it has come from the Q Branch, the special wing of the CID that looked into the LTTE's activities in Tamil Nadu. They received it from an anonymous source. Apparently, Haribabu had kept it hidden at a relative's place. The relative probably thought the contents would help the investigation after reading about Haribabu in the newspapers.'

'Have you gone through it, sir?' Ragothaman asked.

'Nope. You can go ahead.'

Ragothaman took it to his desk for examination. There was a small note addressed to Haribabu from Bhagyanathan, asking him to pay Muthuraja's electricity bill and hand over the receipt to Murugan. It gave the SIT three new names—Bhagyanathan, Muthuraja and Murugan. However, Ragothaman's assistant, who Ragothaman passed on the contents to for making a list, came across a picture of LTTE supremo Prabhakaran, copies of LTTE calendars, a list of a large number of medicines to treat wounds, sketches of the Vellore fort, where a large number of LTTE cadres were detained, and some personal letters from Haribabu's girlfriend Sundari. The love letters immediately caught the assistant's attention, one of which indicated that Haribabu was going on a 'dangerous mission' and Sundari was trying to discourage him.[1]

Haribabu's links with the LTTE were becoming clearer. A colleague of his had already corroborated that he had seen Haribabu with Subha Sundaram at 'Subha Studio', carrying a large envelope inside which he caught a glimpse of the sandalwood garland. It was a vital piece of evidence, which linked Haribabu with the kurta-pyjama-clad man and the woman who had carried the sandalwood garland. And then the bill of purchase of the garland had also been found at the deceased photographer's house.

Haribabu had turned out to be more than a mere photographer, having close ties with the assassin gang as was evident in his girlfriend Sundari's letters to him. She lived in Villupuram, Madurai, and worked as a nurse. After consulting Kaarthikeyan and Raju, Verma had asked the Tamil Nadu Police to pick up Sundari from Villupuram and bring her to Malligai.

Whatever Haribabu's 'dangerous mission' was, there seemed to be one more 'mission' the assassins could have been involved in. Raju and Kanth had been studying the forensic test results of the clue materials gathered from the blast site and similar reports from the NSG explosives experts. They found similarities between explosives used in Rajiv Gandhi's assassination and some other cases of militant action in the state that largely remained unsolved. Kaarthikeyan had given them a file that contained the earlier cases. Similarities in the modus operandi and groups involved also came to light. The killing of a Tamil leader, K. Padmanabha, and his associates had particularly caught their attention. Raju and Kanth wanted to present their findings to Kaarthikeyan.

Padmanabha was the leader of Tamil rebel group EPRLF, whose objectives were openly criticized by the LTTE, although both were fighting for the liberation of Sri Lankan Tamils. And that case still remained unsolved. Recalling the files acquired from the Tamil Nadu police department, Kanth observed that Padmanabha and other EPRLF leaders were killed in a terrorist attack on 19 June 1990 at the Zachariah Colony apartments in Madras. The killers had used grenades and fired from AK-47 rifles, resulting in a massive bloodbath. The killers had come in a white Ambassador car around 6.30 p.m. After killing Padmanabha and his men, the assassins had targeted some of the onlookers to pre-empt eyewitness accounts. And then they had fled.

Investigations had revealed that the killers had hijacked a Maruti van, in which an officer of a private company and his mother were travelling near Villupuram a day later. The attackers then dropped the occupants on the side of the road and took off in the van. The local police traced the owner of the Maruti van, Thomas Charles, and brought him to Malligai. When Raju and Kanth spoke to Charles, he said there were six hijackers. Four of them, in the age group of twenty to twenty-five years, got out of the white Ambassador and forcibly stopped his van. In addition to sophisticated arms, they were carrying walkie-talkies. They threatened him with consequences if he or his family members talked to anyone about the incident. Charles gave Kanth and Raju a general description of the attackers. But there was nothing more he could help with. He said he could not understand the dialect the men used while communicating with each other. It sounded like Sinhala-Tamil.

A breakthrough happened amid the confusion, purely by chance. A routine police check near the Vedaranyam beach, also known for smuggling activities, involved a young man speeding on a motorcycle. The state was already on alert. When the police asked the rider to get off, he said he was in a hurry. From his accent, the police felt he sounded like a Sri Lankan Tamil. That was enough reason for the police to take him in. His interrogation threw up dramatic results. The young man turned out to be Shankar Koneswaran from Jaffna, who had been living there as a 'Sri Lankan refugee'. In the aftermath of Rajiv Gandhi's assassination, any link with Jaffna was treated as 'extra-sensitive'. The Vedaranyam police immediately informed the SIT in Madras about the suspect through a fax message:

> The Tamil Nadu Police has picked up an LTTE militant Shankar Koneswaran alias Ruso in Thanjavur and found telephone numbers that may be of vital use to the investigation. The first telephone number is against two names—Nalini and Das. The second telephone number belongs to a provision store in Porur, Madras, as per inquiry. Further investigation by the 'Q' Branch of Tamil Nadu Police and inquiries made into the said person, Miss Nalini, revealed that she was working with M/s Anabond Silicon Pvt Ltd in Adyar, Madras. However, the 'Q' Branch could not proceed further in the absence of any other incriminating evidence.[2]

Koneswaran was handed over to the CBI. During interrogation, he told the SIT that he was one of the nine-member assassination squad that had reached Kodiakkarai on the Tamil Nadu coast from Jaffna on 1 May 1991 under the command of Sivarasan. It was the first time an LTTE cadre was confessing to the presence of a 'hit squad' in Tamil Nadu—or India, for that matter. The 'Q Branch' of the Tamil Nadu police swung into action. Koneswaran further confessed that the LTTE supremo Prabhakaran had sent him to India to kill Sri Lankan leader Varadaraja Perumal, who was exiled in the country. Indian intelligence agencies had kept Perumal in a safe house in Bhopal after the assassination of EPRLF leader Padmanabha in Madras in 1990. The SIT came to know of Koneswaran's detention and flew him to Madras in a helicopter.

Koneswaran turned out to be a good catch. He further told the SIT that he had moved to Madras and stayed at the Esware Lodge. There he had met a fellow LTTE cadre, Murugan, who gave him a chit containing his name as 'Das' and another name, 'Nalini', along with her contact number, 419493. The investigators were hearing Murugan's name for the second time.

Ragothaman, the IO of the case, placed the photographs taken by Haribabu in front of Koneswaran and asked him to identify the woman in the orange-and-green salwar kameez and the man in the white kurta pyjama. After trying to dodge his questions in vain, Koneswaran identified the man in the photograph as Sivarasan, alias Raghuvaran, and disclosed that he was a trusted soldier of Prabhakaran. This came as a breakthrough. For the first time since the assassination, an LTTE cadre was implicating another in the killing of Rajiv Gandhi and dropping the name of the militant outfit's supremo Prabhakaran. More interrogators joined in.

Koneswaran went on to divulge that Sivarasan had carried out the assassination of Padmanabha as well. Verma was watching the interrogation. The name 'Sivarasan' struck a chord—he had heard a similar name—Sivarajan—earlier. He asked Koneswaran if Sivarasan and Sivarajan were the same person. Koneswaran reluctantly confirmed it. The local police of Vedaranyam had rounded up more LTTE activists following the arrest of Koneswaran. They were all sent to Malligai. Ragothaman took Koneswaran to face them and talked about Sivarasan, aka Sivarajan. He knew that the LTTE often played with the spelling of names to confuse security agencies. Of the fresh arrivals at Malligai, one Jagdeeshan, also from Vedaranyam, identified the kurta-pyjama-clad man as 'Raghu', adding that he had travelled during the Padmanabha killing in his speedboat between Vedaranyam in Tamil Nadu and Point Pedro in Jaffna. The man had three names until then—Raghu, Sivarajan and Sivarasan.

Kanth was checking the notebook that was found on Koneswaran. Nalini, whose number was found in it, was the same girl the Q Branch had met in her office in Adyar, south Madras, and found clean. Ragothaman and Verma jumped at this revelation made by Kanth.

'They let her go? Oh no! Fake ID cards were made in their names. Also, in the name of one Sivarasan,' Verma said.

'Let me talk to the "Q Branch" about this,' Kanth said.

It certainly looked like the SIT was making good progress. During the investigation of Padmanabha's assassination, the IB had claimed that LTTE hitmen Raghu and David were behind the operation. However, the domestic spy agency had no photograph of either Raghu or David to offer. So the question of whether Raghu and David were the same person had remained unanswered. But with the arrest of Koneswaran, it was clear that Raghu alias Sivarasan alias Sivarajan was behind the killing of the EPRLF leader. Investigation later revealed that there was no 'David'. The information could not be verified by any source. Reportedly, Sivarasan never used that alias.

Thinking the IB would have more information on Padmanabha's killers, Anirudhya met his IB friend and asked about Nalini, Murugan, Raghuvaran, David, Sivarajan and Sivarasan. Did they ring any bells? Whatever Anirudhya had gathered from the SIT about the Padmanabha assassination case was confirmed by his IB source, except that it could not furnish a photograph of David or Raghuvaran. Also, the IB had no clue about Nalini, Murugan and Sivarasan, although the intelligence outfit knew that Raghuvaran was a top operative of the LTTE and had lost an eye in one of his missions. Ever since, he had been referred to as the 'One-Eyed Rajah' within his close circle. Could it be that Rajah, Sivarasan and Sivarajan were all one person? His IB friend could not confirm this but felt it was worth looking into. But what had made the IB not follow up and procure a photograph of David and Raghuvaran? There was no answer to that. The CID had investigated the Padmanabha case under IG R. Nagarajan. Everybody knew the investigation had come under the scanner. Nagarajan was suspected of having been in cahoots with the perpetrators of the crime. He was eventually arrested for botching up the investigation.

On 30 May the SIT released Haribabu's photograph of the female assassin and the mysterious kurta-pyjama-clad man in the newspapers. It asked people to contact the SIT on the telephone numbers given and share any information they may have on those seen in the photograph. The identity of the informant would be kept confidential.

The telephone lines did not stop ringing for the next forty-eight hours. A section of the CBI staff painstakingly noted down everything the callers had to say and read through all the letters and telegrams that came in. Some callers claimed they had seen the kurta-pyjama-clad man in an autorickshaw; some said he was spotted on a train; some said he had been seen travelling by bus; and some claimed he stayed in their neighbourhood. Some of the information received led to raids and detentions. But nothing significant came to light until a man in his forties arrived in Malligai and claimed he had come with 'concrete information'.

And what was that?

'On the afternoon of 21 May, my wife saw our neighbour, Nalini, with the girl in green-and-orange salwar kameez carrying the garland, and the short man wearing the white kurta pyjama, just like in the photograph from the papers. There was another woman with them. All of them went out together in the afternoon that day when Rajiv Gandhi was killed.' He paused and looked at everyone around one by one, as if trying to see if they believed his words.

It only took a second for Verma and Ragothaman to realize that the man had come with a very important piece of information. The name of Nalini had appeared in the notebook seized from the LTTE operative Koneswaran after his arrest from Vedaranyam, following which the 'Q Branch' had looked into her antecedents. Verma encouraged him to carry on.

'Who is Nalini?'

'My neighbour, sir. She is reserved by nature; she seldom speaks with the neighbours. I hear she was the private secretary of the managing director of a company in Adyar.'

He paused and looked around. He was shown the photographs taken by Haribabu. The man immediately identified Nalini sitting with another woman in the women's enclosure.

'Please carry on,' said Ragothaman.

'Another boy called "Das" would often visit Nalini.'

'Where is your house?' Verma asked.

'In Villivakkam, in High Court Colony, sir.'

'Any idea if Nalini was there when you left home to come here today?'

'No, sir, she left home on 26 May and has not returned since. Her office is in Adyar, sir.'

'Thank you so much. Please call us if you see something or someone suspicious.'

Ragothaman saw him off at the reception and returned to Verma.

'Bad luck, sir! Wish he had suspected Nalini before seeing our appeal in the newspapers.'

'We have a tail on the photographer Ravi Shankar, right?'

'Yes, sir, we do.'

'Let us pick up Ravi Shankar.'

'What about Shubha Sundaram?'

'First Ravi Shankar.'

Shankar was brought to Malligai within hours. The scrutiny of photographs recovered from his possession showed Nalini, along with a few others. During his interrogation, Shankar identified one of the characters in the photographs. It was Nalini's brother—Bhagyanathan. The name rang a bell. His name had figured in a note to Haribabu, where the former had asked to pay the electricity bill of Muthuraja and hand over the same to Murugan. And Murugan's name had already featured in documents seized from Koneswaran.

'Place Bhagyanathan under surveillance. Round the clock. No slip-ups,' Verma said.

'I am putting Chelladurai on the task right away, sir,' came Ragothaman's instant reply.

The 'Q Branch' had confirmed that Nalini was working in an adhesive-manufacturing company and drew a monthly salary of Rs 2,000. She had attended office until 6 June—a fortnight after the assassination. She had placed her resignation letter in everybody's absence in the office premises. Unconfirmed reports suggested she had used a duplicate key and entered her office on a Sunday to do that.

Armed with information on Nalini, Anirudhya dropped into the office of Anabante Silicon Pvt. Ltd in Adyar. It was about to close for the day. Just one person, Sujaya Narayan, spoke to Anirudhya. She said, 'Nalini was working here as a private secretary to the managing director. The girl took half a day's leave on 21 May, saying she wanted to go to Kanchipuram and purchase a sari. She left around noon.' A tailor close to her office said he had seen her attending office since the day of the assassination. 'Everybody was shocked to see her picture in the newspaper in connection with the assassination,' said the tailor. He lived on top of his shop. He claimed to have seen a woman getting out of an autorickshaw in front of the office around five in the morning on Sunday. But he was not sure if it was Nalini as he was still sleepy. When asked, Sujaya Narayan could not confirm if Nalini had sneaked into the office on Sunday.

Past midnight, Kaarthikeyan was going through the progress of the investigation with Raju and DIG Sri Kumar, another member of the SIT, in his cabin. He had a chart on the wall displaying the developments until then. It was already the end of May, and he only had a photograph of the human bomb and a man in a kurta pyjama as a suspect. Of the two, the human bomb was dead.

'We have information that they are associated with this Nalini girl we are looking for,' pointed out Raju.

'Yes, Raju, but she has fled from her Villivakkam house.' Kaarthikeyan said.

Sri Kumar joined in. 'We now know that the pellets used in the explosive device used by the human bomb were similar to the pellets found in the unexploded SFG-87 grenade recovered from the site of Padmanabha's killing. That links the two assassinations, sir.'

'Yes, and that's a fabulous job done by the NSG and our own SIT.'

Kaarthikeyan had gone back to his chart. He pointed to the place where two names were written—David and Raghuvaran. However, the slots of their photos were still blank. Referring to that, Sri Kumar spoke again.

'Sri, we do have the names of Padmanabha's killers, David and Raghuvaran. But we do not have their photographs. Their names are not of much use, as you know.'

'Agreed, sir.'

'We are still groping in the dark while expectations are rising.'

Later that day, a grey Ambassador drove Sri Kumar out of the building. As the tail light of the car diminished, a silhouette appeared from a bush in the front courtyard and quietly scaled the six-foot-high wall of Malligai. The two sentries posted at the main gate were oblivious to what was going on. The figure landed on the sidewalk outside. The streetlight that fell on the figure showed a man, probably in his twenties, frail of body, with a dark complexion. A lot like the LTTE boys whose photographs were seen in newspapers daily. A motorbike rider came and took the guy on pillion and sped away.

Shortly, the bikers reached a residential neighbourhood in the northern part of Madras —Kodungaiyur—and stopped in front of a house. A man opened the door and led them in. The bikers wanted to speak to someone.

'We have found a suitable spot where we can plant the device,' said one of the bikers.

'Good. We can treat SIT in the same way as we did Rajiv Gandhi,' spoke the man who was seen in Haribabu's photograph wearing a white kurta pyjama. While the SIT had just begun to sense a breakthrough in its investigation, an assassin was plotting to blow up its very office.

---

A superintendent in the Madras IB, Mani Shankar, intercepted a communication between a 'rogue station' somewhere within his city and another that he suspected to be in Jaffna. The communication was in alphanumeric codes. In the aftermath of Rajiv Gandhi's assassination, the IB was on high alert. He immediately got a colleague to crack the coded message. It said: 'Ready to strike in Malligai. Send boat for immediate return.' The intelligence officer understood it had to do with the LTTE. He immediately sent it marked 'Top Secret' to the SIT's office in Malligai.

Mani Shankar's colleague was Anirudhya's IB contact in Madras. After careful thought, he shared this intelligence with Anirudhya—the LTTE was planning to strike at the SIT. While it had been Anirudhya's dream to work for *India Today*, he missed his daily reporting job at the *Times*. This kind of explosive information would probably become stale by the time his story was published.

He called Badhwar and shared the message the IB had intercepted. Badhwar sounded happy to note that his new recruit was 'getting the hard news'. He encouraged Anirudhya with a 'keep it up' and hung up. For a reporter who had been groomed in 'daily' culture, this was a 'front-page exclusive'. But for the managing editor of one of India's most famous magazines, it was the sign of a reporter having access to hard news. And that was it.

Next, he called Verma. He came on the line immediately. Upon hearing what Anirudhya had learnt, Verma paused briefly to respond. 'Maybe you should call the boss and tell him. He would know you are resourceful and not just dependent on his team.'

Anirudhya said he already had, thinking his friend was referring to *India Today*'s editor-in-chief and publisher Aroon Purie. But Verma had meant his boss, Kaarthikeyan. He said he would drop in that night and disconnected the call.

Anirudhya sat on stacks of newspaper clippings, all of which were about 'who' could have killed Rajiv Gandhi. One newspaper wrote, 'PETN was used to kill Rajiv.' The report quoted a witness who claimed to have watched Rajiv approach the dais when a woman came forward and fished out a bomb that was detonated by another woman with a remote control. But a senior Congress leader had denied it in the same report.

*The Hindu* had accessed a Colombo-based report that quoted Sri Lankan government officials who claimed that 'the LTTE was behind the assassination' and that similar tactics had been used to blow a special task force patrol in Batticaloa two months ago. They produced proof of the use of a radio-type remote-control device to set off that explosion.[3]

Another article that caught Anirudhya's attention claimed that the 'assassin was a guest of Congress leader Maragatham Chandrasekar', who had stayed in her house before the assassination. Anirudhya felt it was a new twist in the case. The next was even more intriguing, which blamed the SIT: 'Attempts to suppress the identity of the assassin.' Then another report claimed 'the CIA's hand behind the dastardly assassination', since Rajiv Gandhi was clearly emerging as the next Prime Minister, which was not in America's interests.

Anirudhya called Kanth at the SIT and asked if they were aware of the rampant speculation in the media. The latter said they were, and the problem was that they could not 'ignore' any such report. 'The SIT has to get all such claims verified,' he said. 'I guess most of it is to sell news.'

Security in Malligai was beefed up under the supervision of Sri Kumar following the IB's reports of a possible attack on the building. The CRPF's Cobra commandos were stationed there; a fire engine and two armoured Jeeps had also been brought in. Sri Kumar and Verma tried to ease the staff, saying there was nothing to worry about. Additional security meant they had become VIPs. But inside, they were all tense. There could not be a bigger terror than the LTTE in the state. However, news of a possible strike on Malligai was kept only within the key members of the SIT.

The top three of the CBI—Vijay Karan, S.K. Datta and Kaarthikeyan—were headed for the airport to catch a flight to Colombo. Anirudhya had called the SIT office hearing the CBI's second-in-command, Datta, was also in Madras. But he was told that he was not in office. Actually, he had been seeking Datta's time the past few days. A second call to a 'friend' in Malligai revealed that Datta was going to Colombo with two others. Anirudhya's next destination was to catch Datta at the airport. He rushed for it.

Kaarthikeyan was going through the files one more time, sitting in the airport's VIP lounge. They contained photographs of the kurta-pyjama-clad man and a comparative study of the modus operandi of the assassins in both the Rajiv Gandhi and the K. Padmanabha cases pointed to links with the LTTE. Satisfied, Kaarthikeyan told his assistant he could leave. It seemed he had noticed Anirudhya's arrival but chose instead to focus on his files. He certainly didn't want to be pestered with questions in front of his bosses.

Datta, too, was not comfortable talking to a reporter with his boss around. However, the latter made it easy. Vijay Karan got everyone, including Kaarthikeyan, involved in a discussion of the details, which he knew would not hamper the investigation if out in the press. The topic was once again Haribabu's photographs. He didn't want to disappoint a reporter who had come all the way to the airport chasing a story. He was exactly the same in his previous assignment as the Delhi police commissioner. Karan knew how to handle the press without giving out too much.

The SIT had scrutinized the ten photographs again and again. Yet, the depth of the involvement of the photographer with the killers was unclear. The SIT was not sure if Haribabu was hired only for that assignment or whether he was part of the larger scheme of things. Their investigation into Latha Kannan and Kokila (from the photograph) had also drawn a blank. The second photo, of the 'women's enclosure', was shown to potential witnesses, but nothing really had come out. The third one, which showed the musician Shankar Ganesh speaking to a Congress politician and a real estate developer, was also of no consequence. Everyone heard him with rapt attention.

A lounge staff member informed Kaarthikeyan it was time for boarding the Colombo-bound Air India flight. The CBI chief's talk abruptly ended. He asked Anirudhya to wish them luck. He was hoping for something good to emerge from this visit to Colombo. Datta, on a lighter note, spoke in Bengali to Anirudhya, '*Dekhi Colombo giye jante pari ki na oi pyjama-punjabi pora bhadralokti ke* (Let's see if we can find out in Colombo the identity of the kurta-pyjama-clad gentleman).'

That afternoon, Chelladurai brought in information to Ragothaman that a day prior to the killing, a Sri Lankan Tamil had come from London and was staying in a five-star hotel in the city and was in touch with Shankar Ganesh. The suspect was leaving for Colombo that very night. Any Sri Lankan Tamil had become a suspect in the eyes of the investigators. Who knew if he would turn out to be the man in the white kurta pyjama? Verma took it up with Kanth and Raju. They got ready quickly. The CRPF commandos were on standby in armoured Jeeps. Everyone checked their weapons and took enough ammunition in stock. A total of sixteen officials left Malligai in Jeeps and Ambassador cars.

Raju and Kanth led the team and raided the hotel. All they found were people partying with liquor, film extras and wannabe actresses. Raju, Kanth and Verma took the 'Sri Lankan Tamil' in question aside and talked to him. He revealed he was a British citizen of Sri Lankan origin. Yes, he had come to Madras a day before the assassination to arrange a music concert in Sri Lanka and was therefore meeting artistes in Madras. The raid turned out to be a tame affair.

The next day Kaarthikeyan sent a message from Colombo that the 'human bomb' was reported to be one 'Sundari' from Jaffna and that her parents were staying at Kottivakkam on the way to the famous tourist destination Mahabalipuram. He gave the detailed address. A team led by Verma and Ragothaman swung into action and headed for Kottivakkam. CRPF commandos in armoured vehicles and a small backup team of the Tamil Nadu police rushed to the spot.

On reaching the coastal town 18 km off Madras, the raiding team found Sundari's parents had four sons and three daughters. The eldest daughter, who ran a garment shop, was in Jaffna at that time. The two younger daughters were present at home. Verma contacted Malligai on their wireless phone and sought verification of the said girl's presence in Jaffna. In about thirty minutes, the SIT's contact from Jaffna reported back confirming Sundari's presence there. Verma and the rest of the raiding team figured that Sundari could not be the 'human bomb' as she was alive. On the way back to Malligai, Ragothaman explained to Verma that usually the younger generation of Sri Lankan Tamil expatriates sympathized with the LTTE, but that did not necessarily make them militants. Verma's mood was still off. None of the raids till then had produced any positive result.

That night, Verma had a telephone chat with his wife, Shobhana, in Delhi. She tried to cheer him up by citing old cases where he had achieved a breakthrough only after crossing many hurdles. She wanted to come to Madras for a couple of days, but Verma did not sound very encouraging. He told her to wait. There was not a minute of free time available for the investigators. Anirudhya, too, kept trying his number, but it seemed to be 'busy' all the time. He and Verma had planned to catch up that night. He pulled out his portable typewriter and sat down to write whatever was pending from his usual handwritten notes. He wanted to return to Delhi with a clear picture of the investigation so far.

# 4

THE PRIME MINISTER'S OFFICE (PMO) CALLED VIJAY KARAN BACK after five days in Colombo. The CBI head stopped in Madras on his way back to Delhi. Raju, Kanth, Sri Kumar, Verma and Ragothaman were present at the airport for a closed-door meeting with him. Sources in Colombo had already confirmed that the kurta-pyjama-clad man had only one eye and his name was Packiaraj, one of his many aliases. Karan briefed his officers on everything he had been able to gather in Colombo, and they, in turn, reported their progress in detail. There was no new information except what the SIT had already learnt about the kurta-pyjama man—that he was an LTTE operative who was one-eyed and known as Sivaraja Master with possible aliases such as Sivarasan, Sivarajan and Packiaraj. But that was yet to be confirmed. The flight was waiting for Karan as the rest of the passengers were already on board.

After reaching home, Karan was told that Cabinet Secretary Naresh Chandra had called twice. He promptly returned

Chandra's call. He came on the line and said he was expecting Karan to reach his office straight from the airport. The CBI chief had not had a bath for the past two days and requested time for a quick shower. Chandra noted that Karan had better hurry since the Prime Minister was losing patience.

When Karan entered the cabinet secretary's room, the home secretary and the heads of IB and R&AW were already there. Karan took them through the progress made by the SIT until then and how it was suspecting the LTTE to be behind the assassination. His debriefing was backed by evidence and his latest findings on the kurta-pyjama-clad man. Karan emphasized that the man from Haribabu's first photograph had been identified by independent sources from both Tamil Nadu and Colombo, with clues that were far too specific to be ignored. His counterparts in the R&AW and IB shook their heads in disbelief.

The R&AW chief had always maintained that the LTTE was not behind the assassination. He stuck to his belief with 'don't get carried away by just one coincidental information' to Karan. But for the SIT, the jigsaw puzzle had started falling into place. Intelligence agencies, domestic and foreign, often lived away from the ground reality. They were still choosing not to see what was right in front of their eyes. Karan did not respond to them.

In Madras, the airport police had detained a suspect who was a Sri Lankan Tamil and was trying to flee the country. They called the SIT and informed them. The same team, consisting of Raju, Kanth, Verma and Ragothaman, along with CRPF commandos, rushed to Meenambakkam.

Seeing the same officials who had earlier raided his hotel, the detained Sri Lankan heaved a sigh of relief. The SIT discovered to their disappointment that it was the same 'Sri Lankan Tamil' they had spoken to a few days ago. The man under suspicion said he was returning to London after finalizing his concert. The raiding team looked sheepish. But the man was upset. He registered a protest in front of everyone present and threatened Raju that he would lodge a complaint with the International Human Rights Commission for harassment upon his return to London.

—∞—

Anirudhya was going through his findings so far. What emerged stronger than anything else was Haribabu's links with the LTTE. According to intelligence gathered by Chelladurai and his team, a young man named Santhan was brought home by Haribabu in the first week of May 1991. He had left after a week. He was suspected to be an LTTE cadre. That showed Haribabu was an integral part of the Tamil Tigers. But who was Santhan? Neither the SIT nor the intelligence agencies could throw any light on him.

He compared his analysis of Haribabu with a report earlier sent in by Kaarthikeyan from Colombo. It hadn't been easy to secure a copy, but his 'friends' in the SIT had helped. Kaarthikeyan's report had mentioned Madras-based publishers who printed LTTE material to brainwash the Tamil youth and get them to join the organization. The report had given details of LTTE literature that were pumped into Tamil Nadu to fuel hatred for the Indian government's handling of the Tamil Tigers in Jaffna following the signing of the Indo-Sri Lanka Accord in 1987. Incidentally, a few days ago, Ragothaman's boys had found more than 3,000 copies of a booklet titled *The Satanic Forces* from a printing press. It was a compilation of articles criticizing the IPKF and India's Sri Lanka policy from July 1987 until March 1990. It had clearly shown the LTTE's hatred of Rajiv Gandhi. By the time the SIT inquired further, the publisher of the booklet had gone underground.[1]

Verma and Ragothaman confronted Ravi Shankar with a copy of *The Satanic Forces* and asked who was behind its publication.

Shankar revealed that one Bhagyanathan was running a printing press called 'BPL Allrounders' in Madras and that he should be able to throw light on the publisher of the booklet. The SIT put Bhagyanathan under surveillance. Learning about this, Anirudhya requested information on Bhagyanathan from his IB contact in Madras. He also wanted Verma to allow him to talk to Haribabu's photojournalist friend Ravi Shankar in that connection. Shankar knew Haribabu and senior photojournalist Subha Sundaram, whose links with the LTTE were no longer a secret. Also, Sundaram had asked Haribabu's father to destroy all LTTE propaganda material left in his house. Since Sundaram never entertained Anirudhya's request for an audience, he thought he would check with Shankar about how the 'brainwashing' was done. But meeting a suspect in custody in a case as sensitive as this one was impossible. Verma had already expressed his helplessness. Anirudhya had thought of taking advantage of the situation when the top bosses were not around, but Verma had not agreed.

After his return from Colombo, Kaarthikeyan had confirmed that the man in the kurta pyjama was 'One-Eyed Sivaraja Master' with many other aliases. This fell in line with what Anirudhya had learnt from his IB contact in Madras. That Raghuvaran—who was involved in the assassination of EPRLF leader K. Padmanabha, was a senior LTTE operative who had lost an eye in an operation and was referred to as the 'One-Eyed Raja' by his peers—could be the same person as this Sivaraja Master. Anirudhya called and thanked his IB contact and asked if he could get more information on the man. It was increasingly becoming clear that Sivaraja, Sivarasan, Sivarajan, Sivaraja Master and Raghuvaran were likely the same person. Aliases were created to confuse the security agencies. Anirudhya was armed with the full information from the dossier on Raghuvaran that was available with the Colombo unit of R&AW.

A copy of that must have been with the agencies in India by then. The source told to wait before Anirudhya published anything.

Just around the same time, a woman dropped into Malligai in response to the public appeal by the SIT seeking information on the suspected assassins. She was volunteering information. The female constables posted at Malligai screened her and took her inside after due approval from Kaarthikeyan's office and made her sit in Ragothaman's cabin. Verma walked in. Ragothaman switched on the tape recorder.

The woman made sensational claims. She said she had witnessed the assassination of Rajiv Gandhi and recalled photographer Haribabu, the kurta-pyjama-clad man and the human bomb carrying the garland. According to her, they were moving about with two other women in Sriperumbudur. Verma showed her the enlarged copies of Haribabu's photographs. She identified the two women in the enclosure seen in one of the ten photographs and said she had seen them before the blast.

Verma had four faces before him that were now suspected to be involved in the assassination—the human bomb, the man in the kurta pyjama and the two women sitting in the women's enclosure. One was dead and the rest of the three were missing.

On the night of 11 June, Ragothaman and his team raided the printing press 'BPL Allrounders'. They picked up Bhagyanathan and brought him to the SIT office. He was shown the photo of the women's enclosure that Haribabu had taken. Bhagyanathan said he didn't know what the photo was about. Then Verma showed him the photo the SIT had seized from Ravi Shankar's album that had one of the two girls—Nalini. Bhagyanathan feigned ignorance once again. He also refused to acknowledge Ravi Shankar's name. But his clouded face did not escape the interrogators' attention.[2]

Bhagyanathan played the interrogation well, particularly for a person who did not have any known criminal past. He admitted to owning the printing press but refused any association with the LTTE's Baby Subramaniam. He claimed he never bought the press from him. Ravi Shankar was brought into the room with clear instructions that he would have to pretend to not know Bhagyanathan. The SIT would just like to watch Bhagyanathan's reaction on seeing Shankar in the room. But Shankar failed to act as instructed and Bhagyanathan did his best to maintain a straight face. Shortly, Shankar was taken out of the room. Ragothaman showed Bhagyanathan the photographs again. The two girls, earlier identified by the informant, were especially brought to his attention. Bhagyanathan claimed he had never seen them. Verma then showed him the first photograph with the assassin girl and the kurta-pyjama-clad man. Bhagyanathan again denied knowing either of them. Both Verma and Ragothaman asked him repeatedly, but Bhagyanathan stuck to his answers.

His repeated denial of everything raised suspicion in the minds of the SIT members. It seemed to them that he was trying to hide something. Verma showed him the photos again and repeated the questions. Bhagyanathan, gaining confidence after being able to survive the interrogation that long, told Verma the SIT was wasting its time on innocent people such as him. Verma lost his cool, slapped Bhagyanathan hard and told Ragothaman to pick up Bhagyanathan's family, whoever was available.

Within an hour, Bhagyanathan's mother Padma was brought to Malligai. In front of her, Verma and Ragothaman cornered Bhagyanathan with a series of questions and faced him with the odds that were going against him. After a point, she broke down. Padma admitted that the girl in the picture was none other than Nalini, her daughter and Bhagyanathan's sister. The interrogators looked at Bhagyanathan in disbelief. He had done extraordinarily well in hiding his emotions when they were showing him a picture of his own sister.[3]

Padma went on to reveal that Nalini had eloped with her lover Das, alias Murugan, who was also an LTTE cadre. The LTTE operative Koneswaran had mentioned Murugan earlier. Verma abruptly stopped Padma and turned to Bhagyanathan. He could not feign ignorance any more. Ragothaman asked the female staff to shift Padma to another room. The interrogation of Bhagyanathan was to continue. He finally opened his mouth. He said the kurta-pyjama-clad man was Sivarasan—the LTTE cadre with one eye. Bhagyanathan confirmed what the SIT had learnt from Koneswaran, who was earlier arrested by the Q Branch. What about the various aliases such as Sivarajan, Shivarajah and Raghuvaran? Bhagyanathan confirmed that all of them belonged to just one person—one-eyed Sivarasan. Bhagyanathan was another big breakthrough in the investigation.[4]

The questioning of Bhagyanathan continued till ten o'clock the next morning. He confessed that the human bomb was Dhanu and her female companion in the photograph was Subha. Both the women were members of the suicide squad of the LTTE called the 'Black Tigress'. He corroborated the revelation made by Koneswaran on Sivarasan's role in the assassination of Padmanabha—Sivarasan had masterminded it and carried it out with the help of his deputy, Santhan. Bhagyanathan's claim confirmed Raju's and Kanth's earlier suspicions that both the assassinations were the handiwork of the same group. Bhagyanathan confessed that Sivarasan was the mastermind behind the Rajiv Gandhi assassination as well and that his main assistant was Murugan alias Das. His sister Nalini and Murugan had escaped soon after the Q Branch had met Nalini in her office in Adyar. The Q Branch's reluctance in taking Nalini in for questioning baffled the SIT. After all, her name and telephone number had been found in possession of an LTTE operative who knew Sivarasan, Murugan and other members of the Tigers' hit squad.[5]

By the time Bhagyanathan's interrogation ended, both Verma and Ragothaman looked exhausted. They needed a quick shower before they got back to Bhagyanathan for further interrogation. They left instructions with the staff to not allow Bhagyanathan any rest while they were gone. Any relief to his mind or body would give him renewed strength to deal with sustained interrogations. Instead, he had to be kept 'tense'.

—ꝏ—

The Madras unit of the IB had intercepted a fresh message between the 'rogue station' in Madras and Jaffna, where the 'sender' was again asking for a boat. The sender had said he could not bomb the SIT without a boat waiting to sail him out of India. The security situation had changed after the assassination. Time was running out for him. Anirudhya's friend in the IB was rushing to Malligai with the latest intercepted message. Security in Malligai had been tightened following the IB's earlier intercept highlighting the LTTE's threat to the SIT. But this second message underlined the LTTE's threat and indicated that the sender had come from Jaffna and was looking for a quick escape route. After interpreting the new message, Kaarthikeyan decided to expand his network once again by inviting the public to look for the assassins.

Wall posters carrying photographs of Sivarasan, Nalini and Subha, along with a computer-generated image of Murugan, were plastered all over Tamil Nadu and thousands of prints were sent across India seeking information on them from the public. The hunt for Nalini and Murugan had been mounted. What Bhagyanathan had revealed about his sister was more like a backgrounder. A graduate in English literature from Ethiraj College in Madras, Nalini was the eldest of the three children born to Padmavathi and P. Sankara Narayanan. Neither Bhagyanathan nor Nalini had had a happy childhood due to marital issues between their nurse mother and police sub-inspector father. The couple had split when Nalini was fifteen. Nalini, too, had left home to live with a relative. She had had no political links until Bhagyanathan started interacting with the LTTE and brought home Murugan.[6] Bhagyanathan, however, refused to confirm his mother's statement claiming that Nalini had escaped with Murugan. He maintained that she often fought with her mother and had hence left home. Last he knew, she had taken a room in a women's hostel. Ragothaman asked Bhagyanathan about the house in Villivakkam where Nalini had stayed with Sivarasan, Dhanu and Subha. He looked through the interrogators. He said he wanted to collect his thoughts before answering. He pleaded for some rest. Ragothaman spoke to Verma and acquiesced. The SIT's strategy was to give him a bit of a break before they put him through a strenuous session of interrogation.[7]

In response to the latest public appeal by the SIT, an informer of Ragothaman claimed he knew someone in Madurai who had seen Nalini in the company of a young man with a tonsured head. It could be Murugan, but no one knew what he looked like without his thick, bushy hair and moustache. The informer further stated that Nalini had visited a house in Madurai, wanting to rent it. She had introduced the man with the tonsured hair as her husband's brother. What crossed Ragothaman's mind was that Haribabu's girlfriend, Sundari, lived in Villupuram, close to Madurai. Did Nalini visit her? The informer had no idea about that. Ragothaman suspected Nalini might not have known that Sundari was already in the SIT's custody following the discovery of the love letters. He rushed DSP Krishnamurthy to Madurai with a well-armed small team. The team left in a rented Maruti car as it moved faster than the CBI's official Ambassadors. They would first go to Sundari's house in Villupuram, which was on the way to Madurai.

—∞—

Krishnamurthy stood at the front door of Sundari's house. His teammates had taken up strategic positions at a distance. An elderly woman was taking off dried clothes from a rope that hung diagonally across the front courtyard. Krishnamurthy spoke to her. She told the DSP that a 'fair-looking girl and a young man with a tonsured head' had come inquiring about Sundari but had left immediately when told no one was there. She said she had offered them lunch but they were not interested. Apparently, they were talking about going to Madras and that they would eat on the way.

Krishnamurthy went to the nearest phone booth and alerted Malligai that Nalini and Murugan could be on their way back to Madras.

Malligai transformed into a war room.

A large map of Madras was laid out on the table at the centre, illuminated by a bright overhead lamp. A strategic meeting on how to catch the couple alive started with Kaarthikeyan, Raju, Kanth, Verma, Captain Ravindran of the NSG, Sri Kumar, Ragothaman and DIG Manoharan (of Tamil Nadu Police) in attendance. All they knew was Nalini and Murugan could be coming to Madras in a bus. The questions far outnumbered the answers. What if the duo switched to a train or a taxi?

Kaarthikeyan asked Manoharan what the possible alighting points on the Villupuram-to-Madras route were. Drawing their attention to the map, Manoharan said the first stop upon entry in Madras was Tambaram, by the city border. The bus picking up passengers from Villupuram originated from Madurai and terminated at the Saidapet bus terminus. Kanth's instant counter was, 'What if she gets off before the terminus? Somewhere in the middle of the city?'

'Villivakkam is further up north, sir. If that's where they're headed, they'll have to get off at Saidapet,' said Ragothaman. Kanth's next question was if that was close to West Mambalam, where Nalini and Murugan might have another possible hideout.

Kaarthikeyan, putting a bright red tack on the map marking Saidapet, said it was a distance of 18–20 km; he marked two more points on the map between Tambaram and Saidapet. Everyone appeared tense. Manoharan looked at the map again.

'We can deploy men at the bus stops that have wide, crowded terminals. It'll be easier to blend in with the crowd there. Apart from Tambaram, teams can be stationed at the Chromepet bus stand and at Alandur, before Saidapet,' he pointed out, adding one more point with a red felt pen.

His face showing intense concentration, Kaarthikeyan told Manoharan to deploy his teams to keep a strict watch on railway stations and taxi stands close to those points as well. Raju took another look at the map with the four bright red points—Tambaram, Chromepet, Alandur and Saidapet—and the roads snaking through them, and asked, 'What could be their possible location now? How much time do we have?'

Ragothaman said, 'Villupuram to Madras by bus is five hours. Krishnamurthy called me around seven on 13 June 1991. Presuming Nalini boarded by five, they should be close to Madras by now.'

Everyone present realized they were racing against time, with only two hours in hand.

Kaarthikeyan said, 'We have only an hour in hand to plan, prepare and take positions at strategic points. Our focus will be on Saidapet bus terminus.'

To begin with, he decided to send teams to Bhagyanathan's printing press, the Vilivakkam house where Nalini lived and her mother Padma's house in West Mambalam, where she lived earlier.

Kaarthikeyan underlined, 'We must catch them alive.' He turned to the NSG captain. 'Ravindran, your boys are trained in close-combat strategies—you have to stop them from biting the cyanide pills.' And then, in his inimitable style, added, 'Dismissed.' The officers split into multiple teams.

Verma and Ragothaman probed Koneswaran about the possibility of Nalini and Murugan taking cyanide. He confirmed that Murugan would have one on his person; however, he wasn't sure of Nalini doing the same since it required a certain mindset that, in his words, 'Only an LTTE cadre has.' Nalini's brother Bhagyanathan, now in custody, denied that his sister ever carried a cyanide pill. Ragothaman sat across from Nalini's mother Padma and asked her the same question. She echoed what her son had just told Verma.

Ravindran did a quick mock drill with omega-3 capsules with his Black Cat commandos—how to prevent a target from biting cyanide and preventing arrest. It wasn't easy, with the available time between two and three seconds.

Kaarthikeyan supervised the CRPF Cobra commandos as they stocked up on ammunition. Armed Tamil Nadu Police, led by Manoharan, geared up as well. While some men were uniformed in khakis and camouflage, others, including the Black Cats, had changed into plain clothes.

Nalini and Murugan's photographs were passed around. A team of more than a hundred officers, policemen, Cobra commandos and Black Cat commandos stood outside the SIT office building. At the helm of the briefing was Kaarthikeyan. In a booming voice, he addressed his men to boost their morale and wished them luck.

The SIT boss said, 'First thing, we have to catch them alive. No bullets to be shot as you will be looking for them in crowded places. A bystander's safety is important. None of you will be in uniform, so mixing with the crowd will be easy. Be very discreet in all your wireless communication. Is that clear?'

'Clear,' the men chanted in unison.

'Best of luck. Let's go and get them,' said Kaarthikeyan with conviction.

The tracking team left Malligai in several convoys, then split into three streams and headed in different directions.

A team of the Tamil Nadu Police in plain clothes, CPRF commandos and CBI staff led by Ragothaman kept watch as passengers got off a bus from Madurai that had just arrived at the Chromepet bus terminus. A well-built young man climbed down from its roof and peeped inside through one of the windows as if trying to look for an occupant. His head was shaven. Everyone in the team was immediately alert. Ragothaman's eyes were fixed on the young man when another bus arrived and stopped right in between him and the bus from Madurai. The terminus was crowded. There was noise and chaos all around. Ragothaman could not see the guy with the shaved head any more. He was lost in the crowd.

A CBI staff member tapped Ragothaman's back and drew his attention to a man walking away with a young woman. It was the same man. He instantly started following him while the rest of his team gradually formed a loose circle around the couple. All they needed was a signal from Ragothaman to pounce on them. Ragothaman was only a metre away from the couple, but he could not see her face. Suddenly the woman bent down to check her slippers—something seemed to have pricked her feet. The man, too, bent down to check what the problem was. But as she raised her head, it turned out that she was not Nalini. By now

Ragothaman was right in front of her, looking directly at her. The rest of the crew, too, had encircled the couple, leaving them baffled. A disappointed Ragothaman let them go and waved at his people to move away.

Kaarthikeyan and Raju monitored the operation from in front of a wireless station in Malligai. While Kaarthikeyan looked tense and stiff after learning about the 'false lead' at Chromepet and a similar dead end at the Alandur bus halt, Raju got Kanth on the line from the Tambaram check post.

Kanth and his team were painstakingly checking every vehicle that passed by. Their flashlights on the drivers and occupants of the vehicles, however, showed no sign of either Nalini or Murugan. The darkness, the indistinct chatter over the wireless sets, the flashlights searching the vehicles and passengers, the presence of plainclothes policemen and vehicles queued up for clearance had turned the atmosphere eerie. Kanth had nothing encouraging to offer Raju when he called. 'So far, two leads only,' he said. 'Both turned out to be false. We will continue looking, though.'

The place with maximum activity was the bus terminus at Saidapet. Black Cat commandos kept watch through binoculars from building rooftops surrounding the terminus. They literally checked from person to person, passenger to passenger. On the ground, Kanth sat in disguise as a bus driver parked alongside rows of other buses. Not very far was Ravindran, who was waiting inside the office of the terminus along with six Black Cat commandos strategically posted inside the depot. There was no sign of the wanted couple. Unable to deal with the mosquitos, Kanth once asked over the wireless set if anyone could arrange for a mosquito repellant. The last thing he wanted was to fall sick with malaria or dengue.

It was over three hours now. A dull hopelessness had seeped into the tracking team. Ragothaman was back in Malligai. Kaarthikeyan asked him and Raju if the duo might have got off somewhere before the terminus at Saidapet. What if they had cancelled their trip back to Madras? What if they had got off the bus before it entered the city? Questions were many but answers hardly in sight.

The road outside the Saidapet terminus was more or less empty. Shops, except those selling tea and food, were all shut. The crowd was much thinner. A column of autorickshaws waited for the last passengers. A drunk man staggered across the street. The CRPF commandos and Tamil Nadu Police personnel maintained their positions, but a sense of hopelessness seemed to have crept in. Suddenly there was a message on the wireless set, 'Suspect in sight, suspect in sight. Over.' The message was from a commando positioned on a rooftop. He was adjusting his night-vision binoculars to properly see the face of the 'suspect'. Everyone jumped into action. Ravindran spoke on the wireless next, 'Maintain calm, maintain calm. Position of suspect?'

A couple had just alighted from a bus. There were very few other passengers with them. The wireless said, 'Near the main exit, near the main exit ... a male and a female ... Male has head covered ... Male has head covered in towel ... Over.'

Ravindran wasted no time in approaching the couple, who were near the main exit by then. Verma was inches behind Ravindran. 'Watch out ... they may be carrying grenades ... I will tackle Murugan and my boys the lady. You stay behind,' Ravindran told Verma.

Ravindran picked up pace, and his plainclothes commandos followed suit. The Black Cats stationed inside the compound scaled the walls, landed on the road outside the depot and quietly encircled the duo headed towards the autorickshaw stand.

Ravindran was right behind the man. Seeing one of his commandos quietly walking next to Nalini, Ravindran signalled with a nod. In a fraction of a second, the commandos pounced upon Nalini, and Ravindran caught hold of the towel covering Murugan's head and pulled it over his face to avoid him taking a cyanide pill. Murugan struggled at first and then reached for Ravindran's throat. But Ravindran wound the towel tighter, incapacitating him.

Verma watched the Black Cats put Nalini into a car. A few metres away, Murugan managed to grab Ravindran's pistol and held the muzzle against his abdomen while Ravindran used his arms to restrain Murugan. Verma turned to Ravindran and found, to his horror, that Murugan had a gun pressed into the abdomen of the NSG captain. Ravindran tightened his chokehold on the towel and whispered into Murugan's ear, 'Killing me will not help you escape. My men will catch you and roast you, because your ticket to martyrdom—the cyanide capsule—is in my hand.'

After a tense second, Murugan let go of the gun. He was shoved into a waiting car. The vehicles disappeared within seconds even as people from the food joints and tea stalls tried to figure out what was happening.

The vehicles rushed back to Malligai. That this was a big breakthrough was clear on the faces of the members of the tracking team. The interrogation of Nalini and Murugan started in separate rooms. Raju and Kanth handled Murugan; Verma and Ragothaman spoke to Nalini.

Nalini was throwing up. The team doctor found her three months pregnant. Kaarthikeyan told the team to keep her health condition in mind but certainly not offer her any sympathy. Hours passed but Nalini and Murugan remained evasive and tight-lipped. If Murugan was quiet, Nalini was animatedly arrogant. She dismissed the SIT investigators as a 'bunch of enemies that were tutored by Rajiv Gandhi'.

After some time, the interrogators switched their subjects. Verma and Ragothaman took charge of Murugan while Kanth and Raju questioned Nalini. Female officers were brought in for Nalini. Photographic evidence, incriminating documents, intercepts of wireless communication, confessions of other accused and forensic findings were thrown at them. But neither Murugan nor Nalini opened their mouths—despite the application of all interrogation techniques the SIT officers had in their bag. When Ragothaman played 'good cop' and Verma 'bad cop', Murugan played 'good suspect' and Nalini 'bad suspect' in response. How far could the SIT go to secure a confession from them? Hardball tactics were not working on the couple that had committed one of the biggest crimes in Indian history.

They were shifted to a bare, gloomy closet with just one chair. Verma told Nalini her fingerprints had been lifted from the blast site. She briefly looked into his eyes and then turned away, choosing to remain silent. Verma turned to Murugan next and said, 'Yours too.' While Murugan, too, remained silent, Nalini looked at Verma again. Murugan then spoke softly, 'I was sleeping in my house and never went out.' Verma knew he was lying, but he was happy that Murugan had said something.

His answer, whether true or false, underlined Nalini's refusal to answer. Her lack of a vehement reply was an indirect admission that she was at the venue.

Verma then told the duo about witnesses who had confirmed their presence at the venue and their links with the human bomb. Kanth produced 'confessional statements' of those witnesses, where they had implicated Nalini and Murugan as co-conspirators in the assassination. The documents were fake, but, of course, neither of them knew that.

Raju and Kanth took over the interrogation. Kanth, who had rich experience in cracking Punjab terrorists during the Khalistan movement, tried every technique he had. So did Raju, who was known for compelling Kashmiri militants to talk during interrogation. Yet, there was no success with Nalini and Murugan. The couple just wouldn't admit they had anything to do with Rajiv Gandhi's assassination. Finally Raju confronted Nalini with the photograph taken at Sriperumbudur, hoping it would jolt her. It did not. Nalini told Raju her presence at Sriperumbudur was no proof of her being an assassin. She refused to identify the girl accompanying her (Subha) in the women's enclosure in the photograph.

Captain Ravindran had been watching the interrogation, which had led nowhere even after two days. He could not take it any more. The nature of his work required split-second decisions and split-second action. After convincing Raju to give him a chance to crack the duo, Ravindran entered the room where only Nalini was sitting and asked the two armed female constables to leave. He would handle her alone. Ravindran removed his belt and threatened her with something she would regret till the time she was hanged for murdering Rajiv Gandhi. Nalini didn't succumb to his threats. She shot back, saying IPKF soldiers had 'raped women in Jaffna'. She asked Ravindran if he was only following in the footsteps of the IPKF. Ravindran couldn't care less. He removed the first button of his jeans. Nalini shouted for husband Murugan. Getting no response, she started screaming, 'The atrocities of the IPKF are back! The atrocities of the IPKF are back!' Murugan heard this from the adjoining room and gave in. He shouted back from his room, 'Come here! I will tell you what you want to know. There is no need to harass a woman.'

Raju arranged the names of the assassins in order of their arrest—Ravi Shankar, followed by Haribabu's girlfriend Sundari, then Bhagyanathan, Padma, Nalini and Murugan. Verma and Ragothaman spoke to Ravi Shankar. Kanth and Raju took charge of Bhagyanathan. Over time, the four officers took turns to interrogate all the six with a clear-cut message—either they cooperated with the investigation or got killed in encounters. They might have succeeded in their mission of assassinating a world leader but they were very small when it came to the state machinery. The choice was theirs.

Sundari didn't have much to add. She had been in custody for more than ten days. Bhagyanathan and Nalini's mother Padma offered no resistance and answered every question. Ravi Shankar, too, came clean easily. Bhagyanathan had started cooperating, seeing his sister and mother in custody. It was Nalini who had asked for a lawyer, to which she was told it was not the United States. Murugan got the message before she did—he started answering the SIT's questions.

Even as the gang started spilling the beans, Anirudhya's contacts and friends in the SIT tried to piece together the outlines of the conspiracy that killed Rajiv Gandhi.

Ravi Shankar disclosed that key LTTE operative Muthuraja and ideologue Baby Subramaniam, both trusted lieutenants of Prabhakaran, met Bhagyanathan at photographer Shubha Sundaram's studio. Ragothaman and Verma confronted Bhagyanathan about it.

Bhagyanathan revealed that he wanted to edit journals voicing the Tamil cause and the policy of the Indian authorities that did precious little for Tamilians in distress in Jaffna. And most people who published such journals had their own printing facility, howsoever small. Printers, in general, didn't encourage printing LTTE literature. For that, he needed money. But his family was already in debt and he had no regular income. Arranging their daily meal had become a problem. His mother Padma worked in a middle-level nursing home called Kalyani Medical Centre.

His sister Nalini was employed as a secretary in a private firm on a small salary. While Bhagyanathan was looking for money to bring some financial stability to the household, Padma's employers asked her to vacate the quarter provided by the nursing home. Apparently, the quarter was not part of her employment deal. So the family was also looking for a roof over their heads.

Verma made Ravi Shankar sit in front of Bhagyanathan and speak. He claimed that Muthuraja and Baby Subramaniam had come down to Tamil Nadu from Jaffna those days with the responsibility of arranging shelter for the assassins and preparing a base for communication and finance in the city. They learnt about Bhagyanathan's severe financial problem, and they saw in him their 'first recruit' for the assassination plot.[8]

Bhagyanathan sat quiet for a while and then spoke again.

Baby Subramaniam was looking for an opportunity to trap Bhagyanathan emotionally. He casually mentioned to Bhagyanathan that he was contemplating selling off his printing press as he was exploring new business opportunities. He asked Bhagyanathan if he could find him a customer. Bhagyanathan opened his mind and said he didn't have enough money or else he would have bought it himself. The LTTE operative was waiting for that very moment. He asked if Bhagyanathan could pay him in instalments? Bhagyanathan agreed, and Subramaniam sold him the press for a mere Rs 5,000 payable in parts. The deal gave Subramaniam access to Bhagyanathan's family, which was desperately looking for shelter, and the printing press came along with a house. He met Nalini at the printing press and asked her to assist her brother, who was doing great work for the Tamils living in distress in Sri Lanka. The printing press soon turned into a hideout for LTTE members; meetings were also held there.

Raju, Kanth, Verma and Ragothaman stepped out to discuss the revelations from the interrogations so far. They deduced that the second stage of the assassination operation seemed to be recruiting and getting more local people into the team. Subramaniam's strategy of convincing Nalini to help Bhagyanathan run the printing press had paid off.

They went back to the interrogation room. This time Raju joined in. Bhagyanathan spoke about the book *The Satanic Forces*. The key message it carried was that Rajiv Gandhi was responsible for the 'crimes perpetrated by the IPKF in Sri Lanka'. *The Satanic Forces* did not carry any message from the LTTE itself but a subtle quote by Prabhakaran, 'Work is worship', which served the purpose. The publication was a compilation of photographs from the archives of the LTTE, a reproduction of reports in the Indian media that questioned Rajiv Gandhi's handling of the Sri Lankan problem and the actions of the IPKF.[9] Bhagyanathan's revelation helped the SIT understand Nalini's attitude towards the officers even as she kept abusing Rajiv Gandhi.

Raju and Kanth went to interrogate Murugan. Bhagyanathan wanted a break, but neither Verma nor Ragothaman would allow that—either he revealed everything then and there or they would subject him to torture that would be far more unbearable than what the LTTE did to others. The interrogators' idea was to drive Bhagyanathan to a point where he felt the only way he could survive was by telling them everything. Verma brought in Ravi Shankar again. He revealed that Prabhakaran had sent a message to photojournalist Shubha Sundaram asking him to assist Muthuraja in a covert operation of the LTTE—to catch more young minds for a task that the supremo would explain later. Sundaram chose him and Haribabu for the job. Haribabu, too, was in debt. Sundaram came to his help—he overpaid Haribabu for photo assignments.

Muthuraja met Haribabu, told him that a guest from Jaffna was going to arrive soon, so it would be great if Haribabu could convince his parents to accommodate him at their house for a week. Muthuraja gave a wad of hundred-rupee notes to Haribabu to meet the expenses. Ravi Shankar disclosed to the SIT that the guest in question was Santhan, who eventually did much more than give Haribabu the chance to earn some extra money. Santhan convinced Haribabu to believe that Rajiv Gandhi, as Prime Minister of India, was responsible for the mutilation of innocent Sri Lankan Tamils in Jaffna. Therefore, his return in the 1991 general election would result in the return of the IPKF, followed by fresh assaults on Sri Lankan Tamils.

The motive behind the conspiracy to kill Rajiv Gandhi was slowly emerging before the investigators.

In the other room, Murugan continued his story before Raju and Kanth. After assessing the groundwork done by Subramaniam and Muthuraja in Madras, Murugan thought it was time for him to enter the scene. He held meetings with Sivarasan in Jaffna and took the next step—sent two LTTE cadres, Jayakumar and Robert Payas, to Madras. Their primary task was to look for houses that could be used as hideouts. Murugan claimed that Jayakumar and Payas arrived in Madras in early February 1991 and stayed with Jayakumar's brother-in-law Arivu Peraribalan. He was a diploma holder in computer science and stayed in Sabari Nagar, Porur, a suburb of Madras. Although a dedicated member of the LTTE, Peraribalan had not taken part in any operation of the LTTE until Murugan approached him in the middle of February 1991. Murugan was impressed with his expertise in electronics.[10]

The assassins started getting to know each other. A sympathizer of the LTTE cause, Peraribalan was a little younger than twenty. In 1986 he had taken part in an anti-Rajiv Gandhi agitation and was imprisoned for fifteen days in Madras. Sundaram knew his father. The young boy had joined the Subha Studio in May 1989 when Muthuraja and Subramaniam used to frequent the place in search of fresh recruits for their operation. Peraribalan was exposed to the LTTE's plans for 'liberation' and started selling and distributing LTTE literature.[11]

He sold these books in public meetings. In Subha Studio he also came in contact with Bhagyanathan and Haribabu. He stayed with Bhagyanathan and Muthuraja for a short while. Soon he came in contact with a number of LTTE cadres who were all part of Prabhakaran's grand plan. As the situation in Madras turned hostile for the LTTE cadres after the assassination of EPRLF leader Padmanabha, Subramaniam took Peraribalan to Jaffna in June 1990. There he met Prabhakaran amid the bloodbath between the LTTE and the Sri Lankan army backed by the IPKF. Peraribalan turned against the IPKF instantly. He returned to India in the second week of October 1990 carrying loads of LTTE literature, propaganda films in video cassettes and photographs from his trip to Jaffna. He had the company of two important members of the LTTE's political group, Suresh Master and his assistant Irumborai, and two injured female cadres Jamuna and Jamila. Suresh Master looked after the injured guerrillas undergoing medical treatment in India. He had deputed Irumborai to take care of some of them. Irumborai was a name given by Prabhakaran—his real name was Duraisingam. Peraribalan, Suresh Master and Irumborai arrived at Vedaranyam port. Peraribalan and Suresh Master headed for Madras and Irumborai took Jamuna and Jamila to a hideout in Neyveli.[12]

Upon his arrival, Murugan's first move was to shift Payas and Jayakumar to a new accommodation. Peraribalan helped him find a house, though he wasn't told anything about the main assassination mission. Murugan's task was to give logistical and financial support to all of them. By shifting Payas and Jayakumar to a new residence in Kodungaiyur in the north of Madras, he also provided an alternative hideout for the team. He asked Peraribalan to arrange a fake driving licence for a two-wheeler.

During Nalini's interrogation, she told Ragothaman that at the end of February, Muthuraja had introduced Murugan to her family. By then, she had studied a great deal about the torture of Sri Lankan Tamils by the IPKF and how Rajiv Gandhi was playing with the lives of innocent Tamils. She disapproved of Rajiv's 'returning to power and committing further atrocities on Tamils'.

Ragothaman then accompanied Murugan to Nalini's room. Murugan had no idea what his wife Nalini had confessed to. However, he picked up where he had left off. He said he had no problem finalizing a third hideout. The plot was falling into place with three hideouts; an expert in electronics, Peraribalan, who was asked to design a bomb that could be hidden underneath clothes; three zealous recruits in Padma, Bhagyanathan and Nalini; and a mentor, Sundaram. The stage was set.

Suddenly Kaarthikeyan arrived on the interrogation scene. He shifted Nalini and Murugan to a bigger room, where all the key officers of the SIT—Kanth, Raju, Verma, Sri Kumar, Ragothaman and he—would jointly question the assassins. Bhagyanathan was also brought in. The officers made all three—Nalini, Murugan and Bhagyanathan—face one another. They might have been dedicated soldiers of the LTTE but were closely related to each other. Murugan was married to Nalini, who was Bhagyanathan's sister. Facing the interrogation together was going to be an emotional hassle too.

The interrogators changed their tactics. None of them acted tough. The shift in attitude confused the suspects. Why were Raju, Kanth and Verma asking them questions like if they had eaten properly or if anyone was feeling tired? Murugan, with this military training, understood the SIT was now applying new interrogation techniques. He knew he could not resist the interrogators beyond a point. And that time had come. So he tried to make it easy for the interrogators. He told them that Sivarasan had landed in

Madras in early March. The mastermind of the plot stayed at the first hideout run by Payas in Porur. Subramaniam and Muthuraja came there to greet him and brief him on the new recruits—Bhagyanathan's family.

This was the beginning of Sivarasan's mission of killing Rajiv Gandhi on Indian soil. He took charge of executing it. Things worked according to plan. Being an expert on arms and explosives himself, Sivarasan studied the design of the bomb and appreciated Peraribalan's work. He thanked Subramaniam and Muthuraja for finding the right recruits and advised them to return to Jaffna—staying in India would not be safe thereafter. They did as told.

Nalini added that Sivarasan moved to her place and discussed the plan with Murugan, her and her brother Bhagyanathan. Her mother Padma knew what was going on but didn't join the meetings regularly. Sivarasan told them that he had somebody in mind who could act as the human bomb for the final strike. He never mentioned the target, though.[13]

Bhagyanathan went on to add that Sivarasan had directed him to get a photographer who could be trusted. The photographer would have to record the proceedings of the covert operation. Throughout, Bhagyanathan stressed upon his lack of knowledge of what Sivarasan's actual mission was and who his target was.

Ragothaman brought Ravi Shankar into the room, who claimed that both he and Haribabu had started sensing they were being involved in a secret LTTE operation and that both realized it was already too late to back out.

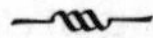

That night, Verma and Ragothaman raided a hideout where Sivarasan was apparently staying in Muthamil Nagar near Kodungaiyur and arrested Jayakumar for giving refuge to the killers of Rajiv Gandhi, which included Sivarasan. Jayakumar had visited India as early as 1984, when he had met Shanthi, an Indian Tamil who stayed in Madras, fallen in love and married her. Ever since, she was settled in Jaffna while he was serving jail time in Tamil Nadu. His sister Prema was married to Payas. Jayakumar and Payas were active during the IPKF operation in Sri Lanka. Impressed by their dedication to 'Eelam' (liberation), Pottu Amman had sent them to Madras in 1990 in disguise as 'refugees' and started setting up a base for the LTTE's INT (intelligence) group cadres. This was at a time when the Sri Lankan army was taking over the reins of battle from the IPKF. Pottu Amman could not lose his boys indiscriminately to the army's assault. He rushed hundreds of young minds from Jaffna to India to consolidate the support base being prepared by Jayakumar and Payas. But every decision of Pottu Amman's was taken in consultation with Sivarasan.

The officers continued their interrogation of the assassins. A clear picture was emerging about how mastermind Sivarasan set up the base for operation—three bases for three separate teams.

The first batch arrived on 12 September 1990. It had Perumal Vijayan, his wife Selvaluxmi and her father Bhaskaran. Bhaskaran and Selvaluxmi were Indian Tamils who had migrated to Jaffna years ago. No one but Sivarasan saw them off in Jaffna. They arrived at a refugee shelter in Tuticorin (now Thoothukudi) in Tamil Nadu. The next batch consisted of Payas, his wife Prema and sister Premlatha. Jayakumar with his wife Shanthi arrived a week later. They, too, came as Sri Lankan refugees and took asylum in a refugee camp in Rameswaram. The third batch, consisting of Ravichandran and Suseendran (part of the twenty-six-person assassination team) came on 17 December 1990. Murugan reached India in January 1991, and Radhayya (alias Chandralekha and Athirai) arrived in April 1991. The final arrival was of the most dedicated, hardcore members of the LTTE's hit squad, which included the human bomb Dhanu and Subha, on 1 May 1991. Sivarasan had arranged three hideouts in Madras. He placed Payas and gang in a house in Porur; Vijayan and family in Kodungaiyur; and Jayakumar in Muthamil Nagar adjoining Kodungaiyur. All three houses were equipped with ultra-high-frequency (UHF) wireless communication sets.[14]

Some of these names were still a mystery to the SIT. The road ahead to catch Sivarasan was getting longer and longer. On the very first day of office, Kaarthikeyan and many of his colleagues had sounded pessimistic about his being able to the case. They had thought the task the SIT had in front of them was impossible to accomplish. That very day, Kaarthikeyan had put up a handwritten note on the wall behind his desk, which read, 'Nothing is impossible. What is considered impossible takes more time, more effort and enormous risk.'[15] Every time a member of the team felt demotivated, Kaarthikeyan would draw their attention to that handwritten message. Losing was not an option for the SIT. Their mission was to catch the killers and put them behind bars—and nothing would stop them from doing that.

# 5

Kaarthikeyan was visiting Delhi to depose before the Verma Inquiry Commission. He had made it a point to visit Sonia Gandhi at 10, Janpath. Sonia could not hold in her tears. Her daughter Priyanka did most of the talking. Two years elder to her, Rahul Gandhi chose to hear the SIT chief debrief his mother on the progress of the investigation into his father's assassination.

The SIT was at working in a frenzy. Teams within teams were operating, as too many accused and suspects were being examined. They had to be seated across from each other and interrogated to check the veracity of their statements. And, above all, the SIT had to keep them safe. The judicial process was about to start. The investigation still had a long way to go.

If Raju and Kanth interrogated the accused, Ragothaman and Verma got busy decoding intercepted messages sourced from the intelligence agencies. And if Verma or Ragothaman took their turn at interrogating the suspects, Kaarthikeyan and Sri Kumar sat on the information sourced from the accused and analysed them threadbare. It brought out counter-questions too. And that brought out the story behind the assassination.

Another team of analysts and documentation staff went through tens and thousands of incriminating documents, literature, journals and photographs seized from various LTTE activists, cadres and sympathizers during raids across Tamil Nadu. The local police and 'Q' branch carried out raids whenever there were reports of any suspicious person or movements. Subsequently, they handed over the suspects to the SIT for further investigation.

In the meantime, Chandrasekharan's forensics team devised an electronic skull-identification method to identify the assassin with the help of earlier photographs of her, along with the skull and the head model of her.[1] The laboratory had constructed a model of the head using stone plaster after taking a mould from the human bomb Dhanu's severed head. It also identified Sivarasan and Subha by preparing models of their heads and then making a video comparison with their photographs. But that was that—they were often looking for that 'one more' clue, but it remained elusive. Chandrasekharan wanted to release this development to the media through a press conference, but the CBI got it scuttled in a clear message to him that it was not he who led the investigation.

Kanth examined surveillance reports from across India and overseas, particularly from Sri Lanka, the UK, France and the US, where there were many LTTE sympathizers. Besides, the SIT officers got 'unofficial' help from their batch mates posted in security agencies other than in the CBI.

Captain Ravindran was not into interrogation techniques that would take hours to secure a confession from the accused. Commandos were trained to swing into action in seconds and disarm the enemy in close-combat warfare. Therefore, he was not used to showing patience and sitting before an accused and questioning them endlessly. This was used as a tactic, as he, from time to time, would walk into different interrogation cells and play the 'bad cop'. It paid off.

Securing a confession from Nalini and Murugan still proved to be the toughest among all the suspects interrogated. They successfully adapted to the strategy of 'one step forward, two steps back'. Their 'passion for Tamil liberation' seemed to be winning over the team's interrogation tactics.

Both admitted they came close to each other within two weeks of Murugan's arrival. At that time, Nalini had walked out of her mother's house after a fight. Murugan had advised her to go back to her mother and brother but changed his mind, learning that Sivarasan was going to return with two girls (Dhanu and Shubha) from Jaffna, who might have to be put up with Nalini. This would not be possible if Nalini went to her mother's house. While falling in love with Nalini, Murugan admitted that he continued to apprise her of the 'sufferings of the Sri Lankan Tamils in the land of their birth and the atrocities committed by the IPKF' on them. Nalini started getting increasingly angry with Rajiv Gandhi. Murugan confessed this was how the LTTE usually made people bond with each other in their fight against New Delhi. Also, as Murugan revealed, this would have helped Nalini bond with the new girls coming to Madras as well.

At the beginning of May, Murugan revealed, Sivarasan went back to Jaffna to return with two members of the Black Tigress squad of the LTTE. Their task was to act as human bombs. Sivarasan met his bosses Pottu Amman and Prabhakaran and took them through the progress of work in Madras until then. It was at that meeting that Prabhakaran asked Sivarasan to undertake 'dry runs' before the actual operation. Amman instructed him to photograph the entire exercise and send the results to Jaffna. This was a shocking revelation for the interrogators.[2]

Kaarthikeyan asked Murugan to explain these 'dry runs'. The latter said they were basically rehearsals before the main act, where all steps were to be followed, barring the final act—the bombing itself. The human bomb would carry the bomb without the explosive device. His admission shocked everyone in the room. None of those investigation veterans and experts in understanding criminal minds had ever heard of such 'dry runs' where the intended target would have multiple security cordons around them.

Murugan must have enjoyed watching the shock on his interrogators' faces. He continued that Sivarasan returned to India with the two human bombs—Dhanu alias Gayathri, and Shubha. They reached Nagapattinam with the help of a local facilitator at night. Murugan was present with the local facilitator and received Sivarasan, whom he had 'immense respect and admiration' for. They all headed for Madras.[3]

Murugan's confession was revealing so much that the interrogators didn't want to leave the room. The tough-looking member of the LTTE's hit squad continued, for whom the next step was to procure the explosives—the C4 variety of RDX.

Kanth confronted him with their findings of the Padmanabha assassination case. He pointed out that the same variety of explosives and grenades were used in both the assassination cases. Murugan didn't deny having used RDX—the same green-coloured plastic explosive Sivarasan had used to kill Padmanabha. He admitted that the LTTE's network in Tamil Nadu made obtaining the explosive easy. He spoke with confidence and exuberance.

There was silence in the room after Murugan was done talking. It exposed how porous India's borders and its security system were. Murugan said that at that point, Sivarasan was set to execute his leader's directive—the assassination of Rajiv Gandhi.

The interrogation had run for more than thirty hours. Non-stop. Everyone needed a break. Kanth suggested that they resume with

Murugan after a gap of twelve hours and ask him to recall his story right from the beginning, so they could check for discrepancies. None of the interrogators were really interested in a break from Murugan's confession, but they saw Kanth's point and agreed.

Next morning, Murugan was again interrogated. He said he had taken Dhanu and Shubha to Nalini's house, where others were to join for a briefing from Sivarasan. Although, he added that Sivarasan did not want too many to attend his meetings. So he had asked Murugan to talk to Peraribalan, Payas and Jayakumar separately. Murugan explained to Peraribalan the specifics of the bomb in a separate meeting. Without disclosing the operation in detail, Murugan, at the behest of Sivarasan, asked for a bomb that could be comfortably hidden under clothes and fitted around the waist of a woman. Peraribalan was Sivarasan's and Murugan's latest addition to the list of operatives for the assassination.

The SIT laid a trap for Peraribalan with the help of a phone call from Ravi Shankar, who was in custody, and two other LTTE operatives who were cooperating with the investigation. Peraribalan was told to wait at a bookstore in Periyar Thidal in the city and that a rescue operative would go there and take him to a safer place. The tracker team of the SIT would already be both inside and outside the bookstore. The plan was a success, and Peraribalan was picked up within seconds of his arrival and brought to Malligai for questioning.

Raju confronted Peraribalan about him making the bomb. After denying the charge for hours, he was shown all of his former colleagues in custody. The sight jolted him. He finally talked. Peraribalan confessed to having worked out an original design for a vest bomb. In his design, six grenades could be fitted into it—the grenades would be made of less than 100 grams of RDX wrapped around 2,800 splinters adjusted within a casing of TNT. The six grenades would be wired in parallel and the circuit could be activated with two toggle switches, one for arming the system and the other for triggering the explosion. Peraribalan's ingenuity ensured that the device could be charged with a one-piece battery of 9 volts.[4]

Back in Murugan's cell, he added that empty grenade shells were procured from an LTTE operative in Coimbatore and given to Peraribalan. Some LTTE operatives had been given the task of manufacturing grenade shells in Coimbatore. They had sent over ten thousand shells to Jaffna. While two operatives, Raghu and Guna, looked after the manufacturing, another named Vicky managed the transportation in Maruti vans to Vedaranyam port. From there, another operative named Mahalingam shipped the shells to Jaffna.[5]

Names cropped up in dozens in each interrogation session. Digging up more information on them, tracking and arresting them was proving to be a gargantuan task for the SIT. They could not ignore any clue. But the ground reality was different. Many clues, leads or information could not be verified or followed up on. Part of the follow-up was shared with the local police, which did not yield much result.

The interrogation of Peraribalan, Bhagyanathan and Murugan continued with Raju, Kanth, Verma and Ragothaman; Kaarthikeyan would occasionally join in. Bhagyanathan had met Peraribalan, along with Haribabu, at Subha Sundaram's photo agency office in May 1990. Peraribalan's father was a staunch supporter of the DMK's ally party Dravida Kazhagam (DK), an organization that openly endorsed the LTTE's fight for Eelam and extended its support base for carrying out propaganda among the youth of Tamil Nadu. Subramaniam had taken Peraribalan to Jaffna through a secret route. Peraribalan's induction into the LTTE's violent battle took place at that time.[6]

He returned to India five months later and carried a sizeable quantity of the LTTE's propaganda material, including literature on how to train the LTTE cadres in arms in Jaffna. An album of photographs seized from Peraribalan's house in Madras had many pictures that showed him with Prabhakaran, Pottu Amman, military chief Mahathiya and other LTTE guerillas. Any Tamil youth who took interest in Eelam would be impressed with the political growth of Peraribalan and Haribabu.

—w—

In December 1990, Muthuraja had introduced Bhagyanathan and Arivu to an important LTTE operative in Madras—Nixon. He was an assistant to intelligence chief Pottu Amman. Nixon had given Peraribalan and Bhagyanathan the responsibility of providing logistical, political and medical support to LTTE operatives who were already functioning from different parts of the state. In February 1991, Nixon brought Murugan to them and asked them to arrange for his shelter. This happened a fortnight after the DMK government in Tamil Nadu was dismissed by the Centre in January 1991 over the state government's alleged links with the LTTE following the arrest of various cadres. Both Bhagyanathan and Peraribalan knew Prabhakaran would not take Rajiv Gandhi's role behind the dismissal of the DMK government in Tamil Nadu lying down. Prabhakaran had declared war against the Congress supremo.[7]

Peraribalan confessed that he had presented his design of the bomb to Sivarasan and got his approval. Satisfied, Sivarasan told him to look for a tailor who would stitch the vest that would hide the bomb. Nalini found a local tailor. Sivarasan pointed out that the fabric used should be heavy enough to support a bomb close to a kilo in weight. So the vest was made of denim. After the vest jacket was ready, Peraribalan fit the bomb into it. Both he and Murugan felt the bomb was ready for use. They made another presentation to Sivarasan. He approved of everything. Murugan admitted that Sivarasan was not happy about his relationship with Nalini, but seeing the progress in work, he realized that work was worship for Murugan and that he would not allow his personal matters to come in the way.[8]

Murugan said Sivarasan was now ready to conduct the dry runs ordered by his boss Pottu Amman. The first was conducted on 18 April on the crowded Marina beach in Madras, a location frequently used for holding political rallies. Reportedly, Nalini added here, Sivarasan had information suggesting that Marina beach was the venue for Rajiv Gandhi's rally in Tamil Nadu. The same meeting, according to some newspaper reports, was to be jointly addressed with the Congress party's ally, AIADMK supremo J. Jayalalithaa. The assassins thought the Marina beach venue would be reused when Rajiv visited Tamil Nadu next. This dry run was photographed by Ravi Shankar.[9]

Ravi Shankar was brought in before Nalini. He confessed he had photographed the meeting and was paid by Subha Sundaram's agency. The agency also took a video recording but he did not know who shot it. Kaarthikeyan asked his team to launch a hunt for the video recordings of the dry runs. Murugan further revealed that they did not get too close to the two leaders on that dry run. Haribabu was also present but was not asked to photographically record it. Ravi Shankar said it was Haribabu who told him later that the target was going to be a politician. For the first time, Ravi Shankar said he was scared by the thought of what they were getting into. But Haribabu was unruffled about it, he claimed.

Verma next brought in the drawing experts and got sketches of the dry run made while Murugan spoke about the event again. He claimed that the next dry run was carried out on 12 May at the political rally of V.P. Singh and DMK supremo M. Karunanidhi in Nandanam near Madras. The exercise was more advanced and closer to success this time as Dhanu was able to penetrate the security details around the former Prime Minister V.P. Singh and touch his feet. Exactly nine days later, Dhanu repeated the act with Rajiv Gandhi.

Once the meeting was over, Murugan pointed out to Nalini that she had missed photographing the event and that it had made Sivarasan angry. However, this time Haribabu recorded the session on video for Sundaram's photo agency, which would have sent it to Jaffna for scrutiny at the behest of Sivarasan.[10]

After back-to-back successful dry runs, Sivarasan looked for the right opportunity for the assassination—it was a task he was determined to accomplish at any cost. But time was running out. On the morning of 19 May, newspapers reported that a political rally by Rajiv Gandhi was to be held in Sriperumbudur on 21 May. Sivarasan told Murugan this was their chance.

The interrogation team decided to split again. Kanth and Raju sat with Bhagyanathan and Peraribalan. Verma and Ragothaman sat with Murugan and Nalini. Sri Kumar and Manoharan sat with Padma and Ravi Shankar.

Murugan talked about how Sriperumbudur was finalized as the venue. There wouldn't be another opportunity to strike at Rajiv Gandhi after that. Sivarasan made it clear that failure was unacceptable in the LTTE, to which the human bombs said they could not wait any longer to kill Rajiv Gandhi.

On the morning of 21 May, Ravi Shankar called Haribabu and asked him to buy a sandalwood garland and meet Sivarasan and the others at Nalini's new house in Lawyer's Colony, Villivakkam. A sheepish Haribabu told him that his camera was not working properly and asked if Shankar could lend him one. The latter told the interrogators that he didn't want to give one of his own cameras, since they were expensive, so he borrowed a cheaper model from a friend and gave it to Haribabu, along with a Kodak colour roll.

The interrogators deduced from the confessions of Murugan, Nalini, Bhagyanathan and Ravi Shankar that the night before the assassination was a relaxed one for everyone as they watched a film on VHS. There was no sign of tension or nervousness in Dhanu when Shubha, the substitute human bomb, helped her wear the denim vest with the bomb. Dhanu also wore a pair of spectacles for disguise. All was well and nobody noticed Dhanu quietly slip out—she went to the roof of the house.

Nalini said after a while, when there was still no sign of Dhanu, she and Shubha went looking for her and found Dhanu looking up at the sky and the stars in it. Dhanu was mumbling to her 'martyred colleagues' that she would soon join them, after she had taken revenge. Dhanu expressed her gratitude to Prabhakaran more than once for this opportunity to exact revenge for her fallen colleagues. Nalini admitted that she was left speechless by Dhanu's composure.

Dhanu had got it from her family. On 10 June, when Prabhakaran made his first public appearance since the assassination, eight eminent Tamils were honoured by the LTTE for their contribution to the Tamil Eelam. Among those honoured were Kasi Anandan, Prabhakaran's political adviser, and, posthumously, Rajaratnam, a Sri Lankan Tamil who, according to many, was like a mentor to Prabhakaran—he had died in 1975. At a function in Jaffna, Prabhakaran gave away gold medals and cash rewards for each of the eight. According to reports confirmed then by the Sri Lankan army and R&AW's Colombo desk, Dhanu was Rajaratnam's daughter. Dhanu's family performed her last rites a day after Rajaratnam was honoured posthumously; no one but Prabhakaran attended the ceremony.[11]

Nalini had managed half a day's leave from office on the pretext of going to Kanchipuram to buy a sari. However, she went to her mother's house, where Murugan was waiting. Sivarasan wanted the 'human bombs' to get ready for the final strike. At the Kodungaiyur hideout, the women sat together and offered a little prayer in an inner room of the house. Dhanu wore the explosive-laden vest and slipped on the loosely stitched salwar kameez over it. Sivarasan was waiting in the living room. After taking a careful look at Dhanu, he led them to an autorickshaw waiting some distance from the house. Sivarasan didn't want the rickshaw to stand in front of their hideout. He dropped Subha and Dhanu at Nalini's house.

Nalini revealed that Dhanu again said how grateful she was to her leader Prabhakaran for giving her this opportunity to kill a 'traitor'. She then turned to Sivarasan and expressed the same gratitude with a promise that she would not let him down on this mission and that she would not come back alive. Subha expressed gratitude to Nalini for everything she had done for them and noted that Dhanu was going to create history.[12]

Sivarasan and the women visited a temple in the neighbourhood. Dhanu offered a last prayer. Once done, the four left for Parry's Corner to meet Haribabu and take a bus to Sriperumbudur from the terminal.

Where was Murugan, Verma asked. Murugan said he saw them off at Nalini's Villivakkam house and left for the hideout in Porur, where Jayakumar was waiting with Peraribalan. The two of them in custody confirmed the same.[13]

Sivarasan, Shubha, Nalini and Dhanu got out of a taxi at Parry's Corner. Haribabu was waiting there with a khaki-coloured envelope marked 'Poompuhar'. Sivarasan asked him what it was. Haribabu said it was the sandalwood garland he had bought an hour earlier from the state emporium named Poompuhar. Sivarasan handed the envelope to Dhanu. All five boarded a state transport service bus for Sriperumbudur. They reached their destination around eight in the evening.

The assassins gathered at the venue. The moment had come. It was time to make the final strike.[14]

—∾—

Kaarthikeyan gathered all the key accused in the same room for a joint interrogation. All the officers were there to listen to how the final moments of Rajiv Gandhi's assassination transpired. Much to the SIT's surprise, none of the accused spoke until asked a question. Kaarthikeyan watched them for almost ten minutes; he had a few words with his colleagues but paid no attention to them. The accused sat motionless, unruffled. They were waiting for the next question. It was a game of nerve between the accused and the accuser.

Among the assassins present in the room, only Nalini had been present in Sriperumbudur. The others looked at her, but she kept mum. Murugan looked at her and nodded. Nalini took a deep breath and started talking.

Dhanu, carrying the garland, positioned herself around the VIP enclosure. Sivarasan and Haribabu were hanging around her. Sivarasan stood slightly away from them, posing as a press reporter. Nalini and Shubha headed for the women's enclosure and watched everything from there.

Soon, a policewoman (sub-inspector Anusuya) began speaking to Dhanu. She and Dhanu were worried. What if they were caught? Yes, Sivarasan was carrying a gun as the lone backup person, but Dhanu getting caught would fail the mission completely. Even if she managed to detonate the bomb instead of getting caught with it, the target (Rajiv Gandhi) would escape. And it could take

Sivarasan's life instead. That would be a disgrace to Prabhakaran's fight against New Delhi.

Nalini, standing at a distance, did not know what the policewoman was telling Dhanu. But from the policewoman's hand gestures, it seemed that she was asking Dhanu to leave the place. At that point, Haribabu intervened, and the policewoman told him to leave as well. Both Dhanu and Haribabu left the spot. Sivarasan was still around. The policewoman also left, as Rajiv Gandhi had just arrived. Many people were heading in the direction where Rajiv was coming from. Dhanu and Haribabu took the opportunity to go back to their earlier positions. Nalini and Shubha heaved a sigh of relief. When Rajiv Gandhi came near Dhanu, she motioned to Sivarasan to move away—she must have pressed the first toggle switch to activate the bomb's system.

Nalini stopped speaking. She seemed to have been overcome by emotion, by the 'sacrifice and dedication' of Dhanu. Kanth noticed a fire in her eyes. He certainly didn't want to give Nalini a break at this juncture. He screamed at Nalini to speak. She turned to him with the same fire in her eyes and resumed talking.

Nalini said that a girl (Kokila) was reading something to Rajiv. Dhanu was standing very close to her. The policewoman (Anusuya) again tried to push Dhanu away, but Dhanu didn't budge, and as soon as the girl finished reading, put the garland around Rajiv's neck. Then Dhanu bent down.

Nalini stopped again. Kanth urged her to continue. She looked straight into his eyes and said, 'Then there was an explosion and Dhanu became a martyr.' She didn't say 'Dhanu "killed" Rajiv'. Kanth insisted that she admit to the word 'killed', but Nalini remained defiant. Silent. Kanth lost his cool and shouted at Nalini and asked if she wanted the company of Captain Ravindran again. At that, Murugan turned furious and threatened Kanth that if he took one step towards Nalini, he would kill him. And Murugan looked like he indeed would. The security guards encircled Murugan in seconds, with their guns aimed at him.

After a moment of tense silence, Nalini resumed the confession.

The sound of the explosion was deafening, she said. Shubha and Nalini ran out of the women's enclosure and reached the statue of Indira Gandhi that Rajiv had garlanded just about twenty minutes ago. Sivarasan was waiting for them there. Sivarasan confirmed that Rajiv Gandhi was dead, Dhanu was martyred and so was Haribabu. They had to leave the place right away. Nalini was panting. Sivarasan and Shubha, trained in coping with such situations, dragged Nalini away from the scene. A little ahead, Sivarasan knocked on the door of a house and asked for some water for Nalini to drink before they could escape in an autorickshaw.

They changed the autorickshaw at Poonamallee and continued their journey until Jayakumar's house in Kodungaiyur. Sivarasan immediately called Subha Sundaram and informed him that Haribabu had died in the blast as he had got too close to Dhanu. Along with Haribabu, the camera was lost too. It had to be retrieved, Sivarasan told Sundaram. At any cost.

After overcoming the initial shock, Sundaram called a fellow photographer, Ramamurthy, and asked if he was still at Sriperumbudur and if he could collect the camera. Ramamurthy said he hadn't gone to Sriperumbudur.

On 24 May, when *The Hindu* published the picture of Dhanu wearing an orange-and-green salwar kameez and holding a sandalwood garland at Sriperumbudur, in the company of Sivarasan, news of the picture spread like wildfire. From Jaffna, Pottu Amman sent a wireless message query to Sivarasan about whether Dhanu could be identified in the photo. But that very day, Murugan, Nalini, her mother Padma, Shubha and Sivarasan left for Tirupathi to offer thanks to Lord Venkateshwara and returned to Madras the next day. On the trip, Murugan reportedly asked Sivarasan why Dhanu and Shubha were chosen and not him. Apparently, Murugan had expressed his willingness to act as the human bomb. Sivarasan was aware of that, besides Pottu Amman and Prabhakaran. Sivarasan revealed it was Prabhakaran's decision to assign a woman to retaliate against Rajiv Gandhi because the IPKF had perpetuated many atrocities on women. Sivarasan, Murugan and Shubha sought Lord Venkateshwara's blessings for their safe return to Sri Lanka.

Knowing the situation would eventually turn against them, Sivarasan advised Nalini to cross over to Sri Lanka with Murugan. But she turned down the idea. The couple went back to Tirupati even as Murugan got his head tonsured to honour his vow to kill Rajiv.

Anirudhya was back in office after eight days. He wanted to debrief his editors on his investigation in Madras. But all of them seemed busy. And Shekhar Gupta was off to Colombo. Dilip Bobb called him on the intercom and asked him how it had gone in Madras. Anirudhya started narrating what he had uncovered so far. 'Just write down everything,' Bobb said.

By the time he finished writing down 'everything', it was four in the morning. The only break Anirudhya took in between was to briefly speak to his wife on the phone twice. He sent the story to Bobb and Inderjit Badhwar through the office system and left for home.

The next day, he didn't hear anything from either Badhwar or Bobb. He hung around their cabins, but there was nothing. Senior cameraman Pramod Pushkarna stopped by at his desk in between asking him if he needed any photographs for his Madras assignment. Anirudhya said he was waiting to hear back from the editors. Pushkarna wished him luck and left.

Anirudhya could not wait any longer. He checked with Harpal, who coordinated copies for the entire editorial department about what was happening to his story.

Harpal spoke without raising his head, 'No idea. Have you checked with Dilip?'

'Not yet.'

'Inder?'

'Nope.'

'Wait till the evening. They must be busy.'

'I see.' Anirudhya was a little nervous.

'Relax, brother. I shall try and find out.'

Anirudhya went back to his desk and could not sit any longer. He went to the cartoonist Ninan, who was in the middle of sharing a joke with his colleague Subodh. They sat in the same cabin. Ninan didn't miss the look of uncertainty on Anirudhya's face. He waved at him to have a seat and asked if he would like some coffee. What was intriguing was that Ninan didn't ask about his Madras trip at all. Something was wrong. Anirudhya shared his feelings with Ninan. The famous cartoonist and a key member of the magazine laughed out loud. Before Anirudhya could figure out what had made Ninan laugh like that, the receptionist peeped into the cabin and told Anirudhya to see Bobb in his cabin. Ninan winked at Anirudhya.

Anirudhya stood in front of Bobb and counted his moments. Bobb was printing out a copy, so, naturally, he paid no attention to him. The wait seemed never-ending to Anirudhya. Once it was done, Bobb clumsily wrapped up the metre-long printout and gave it to Anirudhya. 'You read it first. See if it's all right.'

Anirudhya didn't even ask what it was. He went straight to his desk and had a look at the first paragraph of the copy. It was his

Madras datelined story on Rajiv Gandhi's assassination. He started reading it and felt that Bobb had done sheer magic to the story he had filed.

'THE INSIDE STORY OF RAJIV GANDHI'S ASSASSINATION'[15]

Determined to prevent Rajiv Gandhi from returning to power fearing the reinduction of the IPKF, the LTTE supremo Pirabhakaran [sic] ordered the killing of Rajiv at a meeting held in Jaffna in October 1990. An exclusive investigation on the people involved and how the plot was hatched and executed. One month after the brutal assassination of former Prime Minister Rajiv Gandhi, the crack special investigation team (SIT) has managed to edge considerably closer to unravelling the complex plot behind the shocking crime that stunned the nation.

The exhaustive investigation process and interrogation of key suspects picked up so far have established that the plot to kill Rajiv Gandhi was first hatched in October 1990 deep in the jungles of Jaffna. The motive is now understood to have been related to the political tremors then emanating from New Delhi. The then Prime Minister V.P. Singh was battling for survival following a threat by the BJP to withdraw support to his minority National Front government.

Across the Palk Strait, in the forest hideouts of Jaffna in north-eastern Sri Lanka, the LTTE leadership met for a crucial assessment of the situation. The meeting decided that the chances of Congress (I) president Rajiv Gandhi returning to power were now almost certain. For the extremist organization struggling for Tamil Eelam, this meant a possible re-induction of the IPKF in Sri Lanka and a certain crackdown on the elaborate LTTE network established in Tamil Nadu.

> Even before the National Front government finally collapsed, the LTTE had made up its mind to prevent Rajiv Gandhi from regaining power even if it required the ultimate deterrent - his assassination. By early November 1990, the V.P. Singh government was voted out and Rajiv Gandhi was virtually back in power, shooting from behind Chandra Shekhar's shoulder. The possibility of a mid-term poll loomed ever larger. The LTTE was getting desperate.

Estimating it would be next to impossible to target Rajiv once he becomes the Prime Minister, the LTTE decided to strike before that, at a time when security status was much lower and what could be a better location than an election rally where Rajiv will be surrounded by crowd leaving him more vulnerable. By the end of November 1990, Prabhakaran called a meeting of four key people who he thought would be best to carry out the task of Rajiv's assassination. He summoned four key operatives – Sivarasan, Murugan, Muthuraja and Baby Subramaniam and finalized the outlines of the plot.

Prabhakaran, in consultation with the Pottu Amman, cut out the task for the above four. Baby Subramaniam, an ideologue of the Tamil Tigers, would go back to Madras, increase the production of LTTE literature spewing venom against Rajiv Gandhi and rope in local, young people to distribute them. The same set of recruits would then be used to set up hideouts in Madras where the assassins could be sheltered before and after the assassination. Muthuraja too would go down to Madras along with Baby and prepare a support base in and around the city, set up UHF communication facilities, hire couriers for messages and create a channel for distribution of money to keep the assassins up and running. Murugan, an expert on explosives, will take over mission once Baby and Muthuraja had accomplished their tasks and returned to Jaffna. Sivarasan will enter the scene with the human bombs once the key assassins are in place in Madras.

The motivation behind Prabhakaran's plot gained momentum with New Delhi dissolving the DMK government led by M. Karunanidhi in Tamil Nadu. Reports filed by the state unit of the IB had suggested that the powers that be gave indulgence to indulgence to free movements of the LTTE in the state. One may recall here that Karunanidhi had repeatedly described the fellow Tamil's cause in Sri Lanka as just and noble.[16]

Someone tapped on Anirudhya's shoulder as he was lost in his own story. It was Bobb. Anirudhya stood up in a second, like a soldier at 'attention'. Bobb asked if the story was reading fine. Anirudhya fumbled. Bobb hung around a bit in the newsroom, checking with other reporters what they were up to and left. Special Correspondent Harinder Baweja, or Shammi as everyone called her, leaned over his copy. She said Bobb's body language suggested he was happy with the story.

Finally, Anirudhya felt relieved. His strength was not in 'language' but in gathering hard information from sources, contacts he had cultivated over the years. He was apprehensive about catering to *India Today*'s style of writing. That didn't seem to be a problem. Shammi said a reporter's job was to get the story—the rest, the 'desk' would take care of. Anirudhya took everyone's leave. He had taken the copy along to share with his wife.

Badhwar stopped him as he passed by his cabin. 'Your story is reading great, sonny. I am putting it on the cover.' *India Today*'s managing editor was all smiles and looked happy.

'The Inside Story of Rajiv Gandhi's Assassination' took everyone by surprise. Not that everyone was praising it, but no one had quite expected a newcomer to steal the show, where scores of good stories were being killed on a regular basis for want of space, where special reports had ended up as half-page box items, and where it took years for a reporter to see his or her first story on the cover of the magazine. Suddenly, Anirudhya felt he was getting paid extra attention.

Of course, his friends in the industry called and congratulated him when the Associated Press (AP) wired the story and every single newspaper worth its salt carried it on their front pages—in most cases with his byline. Anirudhya's in-laws called from Calcutta (now Kolkata) and inquired if *that* Anirudhya Mitra was their son-in-law. While some felt euphoric about it, some felt the story reminded them of 'sensationalized reporting'. *The Hindu* called the story 'yellow journalism' in one of its opinion pieces. The paper's crime reporter even snidely remarked that it seemed Anirudhya was reporting right from the jungles of Jaffna and not from Madras.

Chief editor Aroon Purie was curious about why *The Hindu* was choosing to attack its reporter. Shekhar Gupta had just returned from Colombo. Purie asked him to cross-check with his sources if something was wrong in Anirudhya's story. Gupta spoke to his contacts in the CBI and got back with 'every CBI officer had vouched for the authenticity of the story'. A joint director had told him the 'story read like a charge sheet'.

Then the former Prime Minister V.P. Singh called Purie. He was shocked to read about the dry run conducted at his public meeting on 12 May in Arkonam. Singh wanted to know if the magazine was sure about the information. Purie put Singh on hold, called Anirudhya and asked if he stood by his story. Anirudhya said he did.

By then, the story had become a sensation in Tamil Nadu. The staff of *India Today*'s Madras bureau were scared to go to work, fearing an attack by the LTTE on the office. The head office from Delhi intervened and made them feel safe. Yet, the Madras bureau had two police constables for security for the next few weeks.

Amid all this, two entities registered their disapproval of the story. SIT boss Kaarthikeyan thought *India Today* had published 'too much too soon'. He had to face awkward questions from other publications about how the SIT was favouring a particular magazine with so much exclusive material. Charges of favouritism were levelled against him. The editor of a Delhi-based daily taunted Kaarthikeyan in his Sunday column that it was not clear if the SIT chief was 'working for a magazine' or for the CBI. Kaarthikeyan stopped taking Anirudhya's calls. When reporters questioned him about 'why the SIT was giving *India Today* preferential treatment', he flatly denied any such thing. Some photojournalists asked Kaarthikeyan to clarify why one of their profession's stalwarts, Subha Sundaram, a man of repute, was getting dragged into the case. The SIT chief, in response, observed that a lot of the information printed in *India Today* had been 'a reporter's imagination'. But within four days of *India Today*'s story, Sundaram was arrested, belying Kaarthikeyan's claim that most of the *India Today* story, including that Sundaram's studio was a hub of LTTE activities, were 'a reporter's imagination'. Two others—photographer Ramamurthy and a colleague Vijay Sadasiva, who had been sent by Sundaram to the blast site to look for the missing camera—were also arrested. Why did the SIT arrest people earlier accused in the story if they were innocent and their role in the operation was 'a reporter's imagination'? However, Kaarthikeyan refused to comment on their arrest in spite of repeated queries from the media. The arrest of Sundaram, a giant in the journalism world, had put a lid on the trolling.

# 6

After Sivarasan returned from the blast site, which was past midnight, the first thing he did was make a call to Subha Sundaram, asking him to retrieve Haribabu's camera at any cost. Accomplishing the task would be child's play in normal times. Since that was not the case, Sundaram dialled a VIP number straight away the next morning—that of the state Congress president Vazhappady Ramamurthy—and sought his help. Ramamurthy had reached Delhi by that time, accompanying his leader's coffin. Sundaram had called around 10 in the morning. 'My boy, one Haribabu, had been to Sriperumbudur to take photographs and has not returned. Don't know what happened to my camera.' He asked the Congress leader if he could make an inquiry into the same.[1] 'Where is your boy Haribabu?'

'He is dead. The camera must have been seized by the police.' Sundaram requested Ramamurthy to use his influence and get him the camera. Being in Delhi and amid a disaster, Ramamurthy was not able to look into such a request. 'The matter is under investigation. The camera you are looking for must have been collected by the police. I should not be asking them to part with it.'

Next morning, news published in *The Hindu* implicated Haribabu in the assassination and referred to his ties with the LTTE. Sundaram swung into action and summoned Haribabu's father Sundarmani to his studio. He asked the father to immediately issue a denial and counter the story linking his son with the Tamil Tigers. Sundaram had the statement ready and typed. He took Sundarmani's signature on it and made over a hundred photocopies. Sundarmani took the copies and distributed them in media houses.

The second attack on Anirudhya was from the DMK supremo M. Karunanidhi. He called the journalist an agent of the CBI in his weekly column in *Vikatan*, where he rubbished *India Today*'s 'inside story of the Rajiv assassination' and called for the boycott of the writer of the story in question. Editors at *India Today* advised Anirudhya to ignore what the DMK supremo had to say. Politicians had compulsions to speak, they said. Karunanidhi eventually would do no harm. Badhwar asked Anirudhya to get ready for his next trip to Madras and dig up more on the DMK's stand on the LTTE. The party was maintaining a premeditated silence on its links with the Tamil Tigers, but history would throw light on their relationship of convenience. The matter was highlighted later in 2005 when the Jain Inquiry Commission, set up to investigate the larger conspiracy behind Rajiv Gandhi's assassination, released its findings. It said inter alia that the party had openly encouraged various activities of the LTTE even after Rajiv Gandhi signed the peace accord with the Sri Lankan government. While Prabhakaran had openly shared his opposition to the accord, Jaffna sent fillers to Karunanidhi seeking his support. However, the author of this book could not find any record of Karunanidhi's response to the emissaries.[2]

*India Today* broke a story on the indictment of the party, quoting from the findings of the Jain Commission report. Prabhu Chawla wrote:

> The LTTE was getting its supplies, including arms, ammunition, explosives, fuel and other essential items for its war against the IPKF from Tamil Nadu. That too with the support of the Tamil Nadu government and the connivance of the law enforcement authorities. Antagonism was evident between the DMK government in Tamil Nadu and the Rajiv Gandhi government at the Centre.[3]

But it was also true that the Jayalalithaa government, which had returned to power with a landslide victory in the assembly election post the assassination, was trying to pressurize the SIT to implicate the DMK and the DK in the case. A senior bureaucrat from the state secretariat had asked Kaarthikeyan when he was going to arrest Karunanidhi for insinuating the LTTE to kill Rajiv. Whatever might have been the source of the bureaucrat's claim, Kaarthikeyan didn't pay heed to it. He knew the politics behind such queries. However, he also knew the sensational claim one of the assassins in custody had made during interrogation—that on 17 May, four days before the assassination, Sivarasan had met a person at the hideout in Jayakumar's house in MR Nagar at Kodungaiyur. Sivarasan had introduced the guest as Srinivasa Aiyya. After an hour-long talk on the open terrace, Sivarasan had come down to see off his guest. The guest had expressed his hope that Sivarasan would help them see Vaiko as chief minister of Tamil Nadu soon. To that, Sivarasan had said, 'Once this mission is over.'

Anirudhya tried to meet Karunanidhi again with a written questionnaire that his Madras office had already made available to the politician's office. But citing ill health, the leader had stayed away from answering *India Today*'s questions. Once he returned to Madras, Anirudhya sensed a clear polarization of opinions brewing in the SIT. Officers such as Kanth, Verma and Ragothaman felt the direction of their investigation was being influenced by an agenda. The probe was being remote-controlled to ensure it was a case of one victim and one murderer. The victim was Rajiv Gandhi and the murderer the LTTE—and that would be the end of the story. Any other complicity and angle of conspiracy had to be kept aside. And if anyone was clear about it, it was the boss, Kaarthikeyan.

The SIT had not explored several leads, including the ones that had pointed to a nexus between the assassins and certain members of the DMK. Anirudhya asked Kaarthikeyan about it and his reply was instant: 'Some with vested interests have been trying to derail the remarkable job done by my men by planting stories about a larger conspiracy. The SIT is investigating a murder case. The accused have been produced in court, taken on remand and further investigation to prove the murder is on.' New Delhi had set up separate inquiry commissions to look into any such allegation that fell outside the purview of his team. 'The SIT will prove the charges in court and secure the conviction of the accused,' he added. 'The SIT need not be taught its role.' He did not see the SIT ignoring any avenue that could establish the charges.

Technically speaking, it was a case of 'murder', but the assassination of a world leader who was set to return to power in the world's largest democracy was not just a case of 'murder'. Kaarthikeyan was well aware of that. Yet his denial to look beyond was inconceivable. He was once again more than happy to offer evening tiffin served at Malligai than discuss the course of the investigation. He might have thought it was not obligatory on his part to answer certain questions, but the world was raising them. Charu Lata Joshi from *India Today* raised the issue of what prevented the investigators from probing leads directing them to a link between Rajiv Gandhi's assassins and some DMK members. Or why intelligence reports exposing an international angle to the conspiracy remained unexplored. And, very importantly, why 'portions of the case diaries [were] deleted from investigation records when presented at the time of production of the assassins before the court'.[4]

According to Joshi's story, Kaarthikeyan had written to his director, Vijay Karan, that certain case diaries recorded on 23 June 1991, be expunged from the records. These diaries contained a statement made by Thomas Charles, an independent witness, on 29 May 1991, eight days after Rajiv Gandhi's assassination, to Kanth, Verma and Ragothaman. On the basis of photo identification, Charles had singled out Sivarasan, one of the key conspirators in the assassination case, as also being one of those involved in the assassination of EPRLF leader K. Padmanabha in Madras on 19 June 1990. Escaping to the coast after Padmanabha was killed, the LTTE hit squad had hijacked Charles's car the same night.[5]

But Kaarthikeyan refused to pay any heed to the controversy as he saw it as more of an ego clash between some officers. Reportedly, Vijay Karan wrote to Kaarthikeyan after some officers took exception and said the matter should have been referred to the CBI's legal adviser, which was not done. But the SIT's investigations had confirmed the link between the two assassinations and had been very well appreciated by Kaarthikeyan. So how crucial was Charles's statement that Sivarasan was the same person who had made off with his Maruti van, implicating him in Padmanabha's assassination? He was an 'independent witness', and therefore his statement had strong evidentiary value as compared to what was claimed by an accused in custody. Many experts were of the opinion that Charles's statement should have been taken more seriously. Charles was the only witness to Sivarasan and the other assailants fleeing after killing the EPRLF leader K. Padmanabha in

Madras in June 1990. They had stopped Charles in the middle of the road and forcefully taken his Maruti van as a getaway vehicle. The sloppy investigation into the assassination of Padmanabha at that time was seen as collusion between the investigators and the assassins. And the same mastermind of Padmanabha's killing had returned to India and killed again, this time a world leader and India's former Prime Minister Rajiv Gandhi. Yet, the SIT did not consider it important to investigate the LTTE's nexus with politicians in India.

Even the arrest of R. Nagarajan, who was the home secretary at the time of Padmanabha's assassination in Madras, did not shake the SIT. The investigators tracking the Tamil Tigers' trail believed they had unearthed a massive conspiracy linking militants with politicians who had facilitated the escape of the killers of Padmanabha.[6] According to sources in the CID,

> After two slips, the police had one entire day, during which the militants freely moved in and around Trichy. But the police chose to ignore, or maybe did not know of, the militants' activities. The Tigers not only switched cars but also parked at Santhan's house in Trichy for a night.
>
> On June 14, while the militants waited for three hours on the Ramnathapuram coast for a boat to take them to Jaffna, the locals even provided them rice and fish. The police arrived on the scene but only an hour after they had left and made a token arrest of two local fishermen who had cooked for the LTTE men. When the then DGP appeared on television that night to announce the arrests, he chose not to mention the identity of the two prisoners. The case was reopened only after the Sivarasan nexus was discovered.[7]

It was strange that the SIT never bothered to interrogate Nagarajan even after he was put behind bars. By the same yardstick, the SIT was not pursuing the trail that could have led them to the RDX supplier Murugan had sourced from, in spite of reminders from the CBI's second in command, S.K. Datta. The SIT reported to Datta and Karan. According to sources, the denim vest bomb carried six grenades.[8] From the remnants of the blast, the explosives expert of the NSG had identified SFG-87 made in Singapore, clearly establishing the foreign links of the assassins. Yet Datta's reminder was not considered. Detection of the supplier of the explosives would have only added value to the charge sheet.

Based on inputs from the intelligence agencies, Datta had given a list of individuals whose role in the conspiracy warranted investigation. One of them was Kumara Padmanabha, popularly known as KP. He lived in Switzerland. Reportedly, Interpol had shared a report on KP's activities with the SIT that underlined his role in acquiring logistics for the LTTE, including procurement of arms and ammunitions, and means of transport, including a ship called *Tong Nova*, which he had sent to ensure safe passage to Rajiv's assassins. The ship was intercepted by the Indian navy off the Karaikal coast near Pondichery (now Puducherry) and blown up mid-water when the occupants of the ship refused to surrender. Kaarthikeyan later wrote in his book that the SIT had information that 'KP had telephonically intimated to a Sri Lankan Tamil based in India in November 1990 that the LTTE would attack the Indian leadership. Based on this vague information, it was not possible to charge KP in the Rajiv Gandhi case.'[9]

But stories of people pulling strings from beyond Jaffna were gaining ground even as the divide within the SIT was becoming clear. A couple of members started looking for KP, who, besides handling money and arms purchases, held accounts in at least four branches (London, Cayman Islands, Panama and Frankfurt) of the BCCI, and another bank in Singapore was used regularly to pay off arms dealers operating from Panama, Cyprus, Honduras and Singapore.

Anirudhya learnt that a CBI team would be visiting these countries to further probe the matter. Inquiries were also being made with banks to ascertain the LTTE's financial reach. Two senior officers of the SIT were coordinating with other agencies to get a handle on the enormous scale of the LTTE's international dealings.[10] But every time it came to the top brass of the SIT, the mandate was to work on the LTTE and secure the conviction of the arrested assassins in the court of law. It was not only the SIT—strangely, the R&AW also did precious little to be on KP's trail. If one dug into the archives of the same R&AW, one would find a dossier on the jetsetter LTTE operative. Serious allegations were levelled against him, indicating his links with international arms dealers, including an infamous operator from Saudi Arabia. The allegations gained significance as the Saudi Arabian arms dealer was known to be close to New Delhi. But a thorough probe to establish his links with Sivarasan was overlooked for reasons best known to the powers that be.

When Anirudhya tried to check with his sources in the R&AW for KP's links with the Saudi arms dealer, he was redirected to the SIT, since the R&AW was 'not investigating the assassination case'. Exactly in the same fashion, when Anirudhya asked Kaarthikeyan about the same, he said, 'Please ask agencies that are responsible for intelligence gathering from foreign sources.' He was referring to the R&AW without taking its name. However, what one could not take away from Kaarthikeyan was the way he remained focused and forged ahead with the investigation to secure the conviction of the assassins.

—ɯ—

Anirudhya ran into a mine of information on Sivarasan. Details around Sivarasan were pouring in from multiple security agencies as the SIT focused on the trail of the mastermind of the assassination. He had planned the assassination and directly supervised its execution on the ground. A member of the LTTE's intelligence wing, he used many aliases, including Sivarajan, Rajan, Rajah, Raghuvaran, Raghu, Raghuappah, Arumai and Aravinth. His peer group called him 'Ottraikkanna', which meant a one-eyed person, and the Indian press referred to him as 'One-Eyed Jack', from a classic Western movie by Marlon Brando.

His real name, however, was Chandrasekharampillai Packiachandran, and he hailed from Udupiddy, a small town 32 km from Jaffna city and about 3 km off Prabhakaran's home town, Valvettithurai, the epicentre of Tamil armed militancy. His father, Chandrasekharampillai, used to teach the English language in a missionary school in Udupiddy. His mother, Sivapackiyam, also hailed from the Jaffna peninsula. He was named after his parents—'Packia' from his mother and 'Chandran' from his father. He inculcated Tamil nationalist feelings at a very young age, thanks to his father, as per reports by the Sri Lankan military. He started supporting the Tamil United Liberation Front (TULF) from that time.[11]

He was known to be a smart student with an aptitude for languages. He passed examinations with flying colours. The early death of his father in 1977 compelled him to drop out of school and take on the family's financial responsibility. Among his jobs was a stint with the state electricity board in Trincomalee and another at Batticaloa in the Eastern Province. Around that time, he was arrested for distributing leaflets with pro-Tamil sentiments. In jail, he had reportedly painted prison walls with slogans demanding Tamil liberation. His prison term was extended and he was shifted to the Jaffna Fort Camp prison. Soon, he joined the Tamil Eelam Liberation Organization (TELO).

After joining TELO, Packiachandran left for India to receive training in Kumbakonam, Tamil Nadu. Posted in the propaganda unit of TELO, he interacted with students in Tamil Nadu, Kerala, Andhra Pradesh and Karnataka. Besides his fluency in the English language, Packiachandran became conversant in other south Indian languages and Hindi. He could even speak Tamil with a Tamil Nadu accent. He returned to Jaffna and joined the LTTE, where he was rechristened 'Raghuvaran', or 'Raghu'. His initial job was that of a money collector. According to some reports, he wouldn't mind extracting money from people at gunpoint, which led to rising terror around him. On one occasion, according to reports, he snatched dowry money from a wedding and decamped with a large portion of the food meant for the wedding guests. Was he trying to be Robin Hood? No one could say, because he had also earned the wrath of a section of the villagers from Uduppiddy, where he was reported to have ordered the killing of an informant of the IPKF. Residents of the village said he had not even spared his own cousin who had refused to join the LTTE from a rival group.[12]

Raghuvaran was wounded in an ambush when the Sri Lankan army tried to recapture a part of Jaffna called Vadamaratchy, in May 1987. He lost an eye in the operation. Around the same time, the then Indian Prime Minister Rajiv Gandhi signed the Indo-Sri Lanka Peace Accord with the Sri Lankan President J.R. Jayawardene, paving the way for the IPKF to take temporary control of Jaffna, leading to an all-out war between the LTTE and the IPKF. Many injured cadres of the LTTE were taken to India for treatment. Sivarasan was among them. He was hopeful of getting his eye injury fixed, but that didn't happen and he was compelled to replace his lost eye with a plastic one. Raghuvaran returned to Jaffna in early 1988. It was from that time that he got into the habit of wearing sunglasses most of the time.

Raghuvaran fought the IPKF and earned the attention of the top commanders of the LTTE. Reportedly, it was he who launched the first rocket-propelled grenade on an IPKF sentry post. He was soon promoted to the post of commander and given temporary charge of Vadamaratchy.

Raghuvaran was then transferred from the military wing to the LTTE's intelligence wing, which functioned under Pottu Amman. He was promoted to captain and given a new name—Sivarasan. Captain Sivarasan of the LTTE's intelligence wing was entrusted with specific assignments, to be undertaken clandestinely in India. Among these were the expansion of the LTTE's intelligence network in India and the setting up of hideouts in Tamil Nadu. Significantly, he was tasked with carrying out the assassination of EPRLF leader K. Padmanabha.

A blueprint to assassinate Padmanabha on Indian soil was devised by Sivarasan in consultation with Pottu Amman. This entailed the deployment of a 'spy' in Madras to monitor the EPRLF's movements. Sivarasan handpicked the LTTE operative Suthenthiraraja for the mission. The EPRLF had an office in Kodambakkam in Madras, where he was stationed. He certainly didn't disappoint Sivarasan and led to fruition the LTTE's first operation on Indian soil—the assassination of Padmanabha and eleven of his followers. The entire operation was devised by Sivarasan, along with a deputy, Santhan. Both Prabhakaran and Pottu Amman were impressed by his work. Seeing promise in him, Prabhakaran thought Raghuvaran was destined for bigger assignments in India.

—ᴡ—

Even as the legend of One-Eyed Jack grew in the Indian media, the progress of the investigation was failing to match up to the expectation of Prime Minister Chandra Shekhar. He called Vijay Karan and Kaarthikeyan to Delhi and made that clear. He was surprised at the fact that the mastermind behind the assassination was nowhere to be seen. He asked both of them if any support was lacking from New Delhi. Kaarthikeyan thanked the PM for his support and tried to explain the manhunt his team had launched to catch the mastermind. But like the legendary Scarlet Pimpernel, in Baroness Orczy's novel of the same name, the one-eyed fugitive seemed to be everywhere at once. One day he was seen in Madurai, the next he was supposed to be in Visakhapatnam and the next he was 'spotted' near Bangalore. Sivarasan had become an enigma.

In a meeting with Prime Minister P.V. Narasimha Rao (who became Prime Minister on 21 June 1991), the CBI boss Vijay Karan tried to explain that the investigation into Rajiv Gandhi's assassination had fanned out into remote corners of the country while following several leads. A major outcome of the CBI investigation, Karan reportedly told the Prime Minister, was that it had exposed the network the LTTE had successfully established in Tamil Nadu. Many of the organization's hideouts were hit and cadres put behind bars. He told him he was sure that the mastermind of the assassination was holed up in India.[13] Reportedly, the Prime Minister was not satisfied with Karan's submission. He reminded the CBI boss of the SIT's mandate—to catch the killer and not write a thesis on the LTTE in India.

A critical element established by the SIT was that Sivarasan was not only in India but had come very close to falling into the net of the SIT sleuths more than once. Anirudhya was writing a story on the acceleration of the manhunt for 'One-Eyed Jack'. He wrote:

What enabled the sleuths to track his movements was the high-frequency communication device Sivarasan carried to keep in touch with Jaffna. The SIT managed to intercept coded communication between 'Jack' (his codename) and the LTTE in Jaffna.

The investigators were expecting the information gathered on the LTTE'S contacts and activities abroad would be used to test the theory that a foreign hand might have been behind the plot to assassinate Rajiv Gandhi, with the LTTE as a willing tool. Though at that stage it was comparatively a long shot. Closing the case would have been impossible till Sivarasan was caught and questioned. Which is why the manhunt had assumed such overriding importance.[14]

After returning to Madras, Kaarthikeyan directed his people to take the initiative of collecting intelligence rather than just wait for various agencies such as the R&AW, IB and the JIC. It was better for the officers to check with the intelligence agencies on a regular basis to see what was available. Kaarthikeyan entrusted Sri Kumar with the responsibility.

A mole from within the LTTE informed Ragothaman that 'Jack' was armed with an ultra high frequency (UHF) transmitter. Sri Kumar immediately asked the Tamil Nadu Police that was keeping watch on the coasts along the state, the Indian Coast Guard and the Indian navy patrolling the waters between the north-eastern part of Sri Lanka and Tamil Nadu to be on the lookout for any high frequency communication. But nothing much came to the fore as the navy and the Coast Guard did not take orders from the CBI. After repeated tries, Sri Kumar suggested that Kaarthikeyan take up the matter with New Delhi.

Kaarthikeyan went to Delhi and pressed the government for procuring more sophisticated VHF (very high frequency) and

UHF direction finders to be able to compete with the highly sophisticated communication facility of the LTTE. The system available to the Indian intelligence agencies was outmoded. Getting caught up in bureaucratic tangles would not expedite the investigation, he said, therefore New Delhi should treat the matter as very urgent. Kaarthikeyan's pressure worked.

A breakthrough happened in the first week of June, when a naval vessel intercepted a communication to Jaffna from somewhere in Tamil Nadu. The problem was in cracking the code. Neither Ragothaman nor anyone in the SIT was equipped to crack alphanumeric codes. Verma had an idea—Arivu Peraribalan, who had innovated the vest bomb to kill Rajiv Gandhi and was already in their custody. He got Peraribalan to decode the intercepts. At first, Peraribalan feigned ignorance but finally decoded the messages and showed how Sivarasan had modified the use of alphanumeric codes to maintain greater secrecy. Sivarasan's message was an urgent request for a boat to ferry him across the Palk Strait.

But Jaffna was not responding to such messages positively. It baffled Verma. He took up the matter internally. Was the LTTE supremo Prabhakaran trying to dump Sivarasan? Why, then, would he not help his most prized soldier out? The assassin's utility might have been over for Prabhakaran but Sivarasan being in police custody could not have been good news for the LTTE boss either. However, it confirmed one thing— Sivarasan was still in India.

The next day they intercepted another message that indicated that Sivarasan could be somewhere near Anna Nagar in Madras. The tracking team led by Raju and Kanth, along with NSG commandos, raided the suspected hideout. But there was no sign of the fugitive. He seemed to have used that hideout only to send out messages and never lived there.

Based on another tip-off, the tracking team, consisting of Verma, Ragothaman and Ravindran, and his Black Cat commandos in plain clothes, kept watch on a house in Kalpakkam, south of Madras. They had information that Sivarasan was inside the house. The house was locked, but the flickering of lights suggested there were people inside. It was the season of mangoes. The Black Cat commandos hung around the house in disguise as mango sellers and hid their arms and ammunition inside the fruit baskets. Adding to their inconvenience, people would often approach them to buy mangoes. But the commandos in disguise could not afford to sell the fruit, as it would have exposed the hidden arms.

There was no movement around the house, except for one woman who came out of the house twice to buy something from a shop nearby. After a little over three hours of waiting, Verma and Ravindran broke into the house. They discovered it was a studio for making pornographic films. Hundreds of porn cassettes were stored inside. Sivarasan wasn't here either. Everyone was disappointed. Ravindran tried to boost their morale saying this was their job—to check out every single place or person they were tipped about. A commando quietly asked if he could take one or two cassettes back with him. Ravindran first made a face and then said, 'After everyone has exited.'

Before twenty-four hours were over, another intercepted communication indicated that Sivarasan would be near Peraribalan's house in Kodabakkam. Around the same time, someone called the SIT and claimed that his neighbour had spotted Sivarasan in the house next to his own. The man had tried contacting the SIT but didn't have a phone at home and was too scared to go out, fearing Sivarasan would attack.

Again a large team headed by Kanth, Verma and Ragothaman launched a combing operation in the suspected area before dawn broke. And once again they saw no sign of Sivarasan. While Kaarthikeyan's strategy of the SIT taking the initiative of gathering intelligence and decoding them had paid off, Sivarasan was still proving to be one step ahead.

Sivarasan did not prove to be a slippery fugitive for nothing. The enthusiasm in the SIT camp had started fading away. Verma started suspecting that Jack had realized his messages to Jaffna were being intercepted and decoded. So it was possible that he had chosen not to stop transmission. Could he be faking the messages to divert the SIT to different directions, so they always ended up drawing a blank? He shared his apprehensions with Raju and Kanth. They told him not to lose hope. Sivarasan had been ahead in the game so far but they had to beat him at his own game.

In another operation past midnight, the SIT rushed a sixty-man force led by Raju, Kanth, Verma and Ragothaman, along with a thirty-member squad of the NSG led by Ravindran, to Pulicat lake on the Tamil Nadu–Andhra Pradesh border. It was a massive operation following intercepted messages indicating that Sivarasan was camping out in a boat in the lake. The massive tracking team combed every inch of the 600-plus sq km lake in the dead of night only to find that they had been handed another red herring. Sivarasan had used that hideout only to transmit a message to attract the SIT's attention.

On the morning of 29 June, an interstate service bus coming from Thiruvanmiyur stopped at Royapettah in Madras and picked up a man who looked to be in his thirties and who carried a bag. He had a startling resemblance to Sivarasan. He got into the bus, kept his bag under the conductor's seat at the rear and moved up. Passengers rushed out of the bus fearing a blast. Some were heard shouting, 'Sivarasan! Sivarasan!' The passenger stood inside the bus for a while and then asked the driver why he would plant a bomb in a bus that he was travelling in himself.

There was no end to such stories. If a tip-off about Sivarasan's charred body being found in New Kalpakkam reached the SIT one day, the very next day he was spotted in Porur in Madras. It was true that Sivarasan had stayed in a house in Porur with Robert Payas, but the place had been raided much earlier, leaving no scope for Sivarasan to revisit that hideout. Then came the news of Sivarasan and Subha Sundaram being seen boarding an autorickshaw near the Vaigai river in Madurai. The local police had sealed off a large part of the city in search of the assassins. That tip-off, too, turned out to be false.

In a joint operation, the Indian navy and the Tamil Nadu Police launched a massive hunt for the fugitive on the Rameswaram coast following a tip-off that LTTE operatives had arrived in speedboats to take Sivarasan back to Jaffna. A house-to-house search was carried out in Rameswaram and Dhanushkodi. All the jetties were closed in the region to check any boat sailing out.

Around 9 a.m., the local police alerted the naval ship with a message that said a Yamaha speedboat named *Karainagar* with multiple engines was seen speeding towards Casuarina Grove with militants on board. The ship altered its course and headed in its direction. It could not spot any such vessel, though. A naval chopper that was carrying Kanth and Verma to Rameswaram picked up the radio message and also looked for the speedboat. It was shortly found abandoned in the shallow waters near the grove. But there was no one in it. A passport-size photo of Sivarasan was found in the boat, indicating that it had indeed come on a rescue mission.

The police sent out a red alert in the areas where there were chances of the militants mixing with the local crowd. Among the hundreds of calls the SIT received, one call that should have been responded to with alacrity was ignored. And that proved to be the SIT's undoing. A woman called twice and said that Sivarasan and Sundaram were her neighbours. The caller didn't divulge her name and address, but she did tell them the name of the locality she lived in—Kodungaiyur in north Madras. In her second call, she asked the SIT to meet her at a restaurant in the area, after which she could lead them to the house where Sivarasan had been staying. For reasons best known to the SIT, the call was ignored for want of a specific address, though the caller had given the address of the restaurant where the SIT could meet her. The SIT insisted on the address of the house where the caller claimed Sivarasan had been living.[15]

The caller was Esylen Mantel. She and her family lived in the house right next to the assassination hit squad in Everready Colony, Kodungaiyur. Had the SIT acted fast that day, it might even have caught the entire gang. The house was Sivarasan's base, from where he kept in touch with Jaffna through the UHF set. The Mantels were the only neighbours the gang used to interact with. However, it had all come to a halt when Sivarasan's photograph was published. Mantel had asked the landlord of the house, Bhaskaran, if his tenant was wanted for Rajiv Gandhi's murder. She was told to 'mind your own house'.

Sivarasan did not suspect that the Mantels had recognized him and the gang. But the Anglo-Indian couple had become suspicious of what was going on in the house. They not only made inquiries with Bhaskaran and his son-in-law Vijayan, Esylen's daughter Merry also tried to peep into the house more than once to see if she could spot Sivarasan. Thereafter, Esylen made those calls to the SIT. However, when no one turned up, the Mantels decided to make no further moves, fearing Sivarasan might come to know and kill them.

In the meantime, the media picked holes in the SIT's investigation. Questions were raised in Parliament about the less-than-desired progress in catching the assassins. Even many questions from Anirudhya posed directly to the SIT members went unanswered. Pressure mounted on the SIT, and on Kaarthikeyan in particular. The theory of a larger conspiracy had started floating with a number of speculations. Kaarthikeyan advised his men to not take the media seriously and to ignore their speculations as 'baseless'. He suspected it was a way to demoralize the SIT. He stood firm in his conviction that he would eventually crack the case. All he wanted from his men was to gain greater momentum in their chase of the 'mastermind' and catch him.

# 7

THE DRAMA HEIGHTENED FOLLOWING AN INTELLIGENCE MESSAGE from the Colombo unit of R&AW. It said that two LTTE operatives were reported to be active in Delhi. Kanth was rushed to the capital and arrested two Sri Lankan Tamils—seventy-year-old Kanagasabapathy and his teenage daughter Athirai—from a hotel in Paharganj. They were brought to the CBI headquarters in Delhi's Lodhi Estate and interrogated.

At the age of thirteen, Athirai had joined the LTTE movement. She was taught how to prepare code sheets for clandestine communication, how to make bombs and drive vehicles through forests, and was even trained to fire AK-47 rifles in military camps of the LTTE's shadow squad. And once she was ready, they brainwashed her into agreeing to bite a cyanide capsule if the need arose. Better bite the cyanide than be arrested, was the LTTE's belief. She had successfully made it to the suicide bombers' group in the LTTE, called the Black Tigress. Her siblings were settled in Switzerland.[1]

In her confession, Athirai spoke with pride. She claimed that the LTTE did not tolerate any kind of opposition within its ranks and that the undisputed leader of the organization was Velupillai Prabhakaran. Disclosing the names of the LTTE leaders she had worked with, Athirai confirmed that Pottu Amman headed the intelligence wing and had been directing Sivarasan and Murugan in the Rajiv Gandhi assassination operation.

She recalled that her friend and an LTTE wireless operator had died in 1988 in a fight with the IPKF at the age of twenty-four, followed by her boyfriend's death within a year, again, in a raid by the IPKF. Besides this, countless LTTE soldiers had fallen to IPKF attacks, she added. She talked about how Prabhakaran was 'compelled' to sign the Indo-Sri Lanka Accord and 'how the IPKF, instead of protecting Tamils in Sri Lanka, actually fought against them and committed atrocities on the innocent lives in Jaffna'.[2]

She talked about the Black Tigers and the Black Tigresses, where members would be ready to die for the Eelam at any moment. Speaking of Dhanu, Athirai said the 'human bomb did not wear spectacles but for the purpose of hiding her identity in the operation', she did. She also identified Shubha as belonging to the group of human bombs in the LTTE. She, Dhanu and Shubha had been trained together. In Rajiv Gandhi's assassination plan, Athirai claimed that Prabhakaran had chosen Dhanu from day one. Shubha was only a backup, in case something happened to Dhanu, and also to boost Dhanu's spirit from time to time.[3]

Kanagasabapathy, a Sri Lankan national, had been frequenting India since 1986. His latest entry into the country was through a secret sea route, to escort Athirai from Jaffna to Madras and then all the way to Delhi. Pottu Amman had introduced Athirai to Kanagasabapathy in March 1991. Kanagasabapathy was an old hand of the LTTE and was to help her settle in New Delhi. He kept shifting Athirai from one hideout to another in Madras before catching a train to Delhi with her. Neither Kanagasabapathy nor Athirai had ever visited Delhi before. The old man took Athirai and left for Delhi on an Indian Airlines morning flight. The understanding was that she would go to Delhi apparently to learn Hindi and how to operate a computer. She was given to understand that the duo would gather information about certain 'marked places' and 'marked Congress politicians' who would be of use in an operation later. Those who were to join her later from Sivarasan's team would stay in her Delhi house and work as her support system in liquidating the main target. The old army veteran bought a road map of Delhi and guidebooks to acquaint the girl with the city. Athirai, too, usually kept quiet in front of guests and strangers, pretending to be in mourning after her 'mother's death'.[4]

In the first week of May, Sivarasan handed Kanagasabapathy a list of VVIPs and their contact details in Delhi. The LTTE had penetrated the Indian capital. This was the most alarming revelation since Rajiv Gandhi's ghastly murder.

During interrogation, the old man and the teenage girl disclosed that their task was to contact a fellow LTTE operative, Thyagarajan, in Kathmandu and work out an escape route for Sivarasan. After much persuasion, Kanth cracked the old man and made him call Thyagarajan in Kathmandu and fix an appointment. Thyagarajan obviously had no clue that Kanagasabapathy had been arrested.

In Kathmandu, Thyagarajan was waiting to receive Kanagasabapathy. Instead, he met Amod Kanth from the CBI, along with the local police. Thyagarajan was arrested and brought to Delhi for questioning. It had been established from their collective interrogation that Nepal was the planned escape route for Sivarasan and Shubha, and had been decided at a meeting of the

Tigers in the first week of May 1991 in New Delhi. This indicated the presence of several LTTE cadres in the capital.

CBI chief Vijay Karan took up the matter with the commissioner of Delhi Police. The police immediately increased security in the city, with special emphasis on VIPs' security. But Kanth was not satisfied with the outcome of their interrogation. He suspected they were hiding something. He decided to shift them to Malligai at the earliest. NSG commandos flew the trio and Kanth to Madras in a special plane. Kanth interrogated Thyagarajan on the flight. The dossier sent by Malligai showed Thyagarajan was known for havala dealings and carrying out money laundering for the LTTE in Nepal and Madras. He confessed to Kanth that he was handling the flow of funds from Singapore, Thailand and Malaysia to the LTTE and was not involved in any kind of violence. But Kanth did not take his words at face value. Soon after he landed in Madras, he tried finding out if Nepal really was the escape route all three of them had claimed or whether it was another red herring. Was Thyagarajan talking about Nepal to divert their attention, even as Sivarasan took another route out of the country?

New communication devices had been installed at Malligai. A fresh intercept revealed a sensational conversation between Sivarasan and Pottu Amman. It appeared that Sivarasan had begun suspecting that his arrest was imminent. He was drawing Pottu Amman's attention to the news reports of heightening security at airports, railway stations, bus terminals and ferry stands, besides strict vigilance on the waters of the Indian Ocean—this had already led to arrests of many LTTE cadres. All this, he knew, could eventually lead to him too. He drew Pottu Amman's attention to the cash rewards of ten lakh and five lakh rupees for information leading to his and Shubha's arrests, respectively. He was asking his boss to get him out of the country. Sivarasan sounded upset over the lack of response to his earlier messages for a boat.[5]

Pottu Amman's response suggested that the LTTE's political group leader, Gundu 'Trichy' Santhan, would help him out. But Santhan had gone underground, so Pottu Amman was waiting for communication from him. Sivarasan insisted on faster action. To that Pottu Amman said he would organize a meeting for them in the house of an LTTE sympathizer who was an engineer and lived in Eldams Road, Madras. Pottu Amman ended the conversation by telling Sivarasan to shut down the current communication set-up as it was becoming risky to use it. Amid the numerous dead ends the SIT was meeting, this seemed to be a solid opportunity to catch the mastermind. The SIT swung into action. Karan and Datta flew down from Delhi and camped at Malligai.

Round-the-clock surveillance was mounted on the Eldams Road area where the LTTE sympathizer was supposed to live. It was a posh locality with very few pedestrians—a quiet area, which made it easy for the sleuths to monitor it undercover. It was the biggest operation to nab One-Eyed Jack since the failed Pulicat lake operation. Many extra precautions were also taken to avoid any slip-up.

Verma was keeping watch from inside a van parked about a hundred yards away from the building. Ragothaman was watching from the window of an adjoining building. Kanth and Raju monitored the operation from inside a makeshift surveillance van. Others, including the NSG commandos and the Madras Police special task force, all in plain clothes, kept watch on the apartment from rooftops of neighbouring buildings, from the streets, from inside a parked truck and a black-and-yellow taxi. Some others kept an eye on the area from autorickshaws plying around Eldams Road.

But there was no sign of either Sivarasan or Santhan. More than six hours passed and the situation remained calm. Coordinating with the rest on wireless, Kanth sent Chelladurai and Krishnamurthy disguised as Madras Water Supply servicemen to peep into the flat where Sivarasan was to come and meet Santhan. But the officers returned without any information or clue to their whereabouts. After another hour, Ragothaman went in disguise as a technician from the local telephone exchange to check the connection of the flat. But he, too, got nothing as the woman in the house told him her telephone line was working fine.

The whole day passed without any sign of Sivarasan and Santhan. Around eight at night, Verma and Raju knocked on the door of the flat and spoke to the engineer and his wife. The wife admitted that a young man, 'Dixon', had visited their apartment. An hour later, a Sri Lankan woman had dropped in asking for 'Trichy Santhan'. She said she was carrying a letter for Dixon. Immediately, Dixon had sent a reply through her. A little later, a young man, Raja, came to meet Dixon. Both left together shortly thereafter.

It was clear that Dixon and Raja had come in place of Santhan and Sivarasan, respectively. But the SIT was not looking for them. The SIT only had a photograph of Sivarasan. They had no photograph of Dixon. Santhan and Sivarasan were never to visit the apartment in person. The intercepted message had actually thrown a smokescreen around the sleuths. Sivarasan had fooled the SIT once again.

Ragothaman had managed to get a photo of Dixon from a studio in Madras, where they also found a photo of Sivarasan without his false eye. Raju was the senior-most after Kaarthikeyan. He asked the members not to feel demoralized. They were dealing with super intelligence in Sivarasan and Prabhakaran. To counter that, the SIT had to up their ante, and had to be as cunning and as ruthless as them. He advised Kaarthikeyan that the team members needed rest and should take breaks in turns.

Kanth's wife, Rekha, visited Madras but fell sick within a day. A worried Kanth spent two days with her in the city, dropped her back to Delhi and took the return flight back to Madras. In the meantime, Verma went to a friend's house and tried his hand at cooking while taking instructions from Shobhana over the phone. Kaarthikeyan visited his family in Hyderabad for a day on his way to Delhi. Ragothaman slept for an entire day and night at home and returned to work fresh. Sri Kumar stayed back while his colleagues were away, keeping communication alive among the officers and Malligai. Information poured in round the clock at Malligai about Sivarasan—it seemed he was everywhere at once and nowhere.

For some, the short break afforded an opportunity to introspect. To begin with, there was the chief investigation officer Ragothaman's take on the much-awaited 'videotape' that had recorded the tragedy at Sriperumbudur. The Congress candidate from Sriperumbudur, Maragatham Chandrasekar, and state Congress chief Vazhappady Ramamurthy had hired the services of a videographer to record the event on the night of 21 May. 'Imagine visuals of Sivarasan, Dhanu, Haribabu, Shubha, Nalini and Santhan loitering around the venue of the rally! Who were they talking to? Whether a party functionary granted them access to the VIP enclosure or if they did everything on their own will be clear from the video,' Ragothaman had said.

It was widely believed that Dhanu, along with a Congress worker Latha Kannan, had talked to Latha Priya Kumar, daughter of Maragatham Chandrasekar, and obtained permission for garlanding Rajiv Gandhi. The information should have been confirmed by the video cassette. Latha Kannan had died in the blast. And Latha Priya Kumar had denied giving them permission.

The recordings in the video cassettes could have been vital, but the IB was sitting on it and Kaarthikeyan had not bothered to get them back, much to the dissatisfaction of Ragothaman.

The videographer, hired by Maragatham Chandrasekar, was shooting Shankar Ganesh's music performance and activities at the site, of the movements of the people in and around the stage. The other one, engaged by Ramamurthy, was covering the events around Rajiv Gandhi from the moment he had landed at Meenambakkam airport and gave press interviews to the *New York Times* and *Gulf News* on the way to Sriperumbudur. The SIT had collected the cassettes from Ramamurthy at the beginning of the investigation. The crime branch of Madras Police had taken the cassette from Maragatham Chandrasekar's videographer. The head office of the IB from Delhi had sought the cassettes on the pretext of making a presentation to the PMO. But neither of the cassettes had been returned to the SIT.

Anirudhya had spoken to Kaarthikeyan about the cassettes. His candid reply was, 'The videotape was hazy.' Apparently, it was not going to add any value to the SIT's probe. According to him, shortly before the blast, Dhanu, along with photographer Haribabu, had been seen talking to Latha Kannan. One man, probably a party worker, presented a shawl to Rajiv Gandhi and then posed for a photograph, all the while holding him with both arms. Rajiv Gandhi was struggling to move through the crowd of admirers. The videographers were shooting from the stage, which was not very close to where Rajiv was standing. It was a makeshift stage and had only one source of power for the cameramen. Even as Rajiv Gandhi got closer to the stage, the crowd swelled. They hovered around the videographers, who had no choice but to disconnect from the power source and switch off their cameras.

Going by what Kaarthikeyan told Anirudhya, the contents of the video cassettes were of no value. Why would the IB sit on them, then? After a series of phone calls, director of the IB, M.K. Narayanan, granted Anirudhya audience at the India International Centre in New Delhi. Rushing to the city for just one meeting and then going back to Madras by air was difficult for Anirudhya to explain to the bosses at *India Today*. The Madras office could not book his flight for want of approval from the Delhi office. As luck would have it, Narayanan was to visit Madras. Anirudhya caught up with him at the Trident hotel two days later.

The IB chief was clear. However, it was not possible to establish whether the woman made her way into the sterilized area only after Rajiv Gandhi arrived or if she had been waiting there as one of the guests whose names were cleared by the authorities to greet him. Video recordings of this part of the meeting were being scanned to identify the woman, he said. This was a very diplomatic answer. The super sleuth of India was merely repeating from his letter marked 'Secret', dated 22 May 1991, to the Prime Minister. The world by then knew the identity of the 'lady' who had killed Rajiv Gandhi. But Narayanan chose to remain silent. His focus seemed to be on the filter coffee in front of him.

After a lot of coaxing, the bespectacled, soft-spoken sleuth told Anirudhya that certain parts of the video cassettes were 'blurred', echoing Kaarthikeyan's earlier statement. But who would have blurred the contents? There was no reply. The coffee was over. But the seasoned spy in Narayanan could evade answering a critical question even when he had no coffee to use as an excuse. He looked straight into Anirudhya's eyes and said, 'You find out.' Anirudhya was not willing to quit. He asked, 'Do you think the cassettes were tampered with?' Narayanan, a veteran at handling such questions, shot back, 'Why don't you find out? I will be happy to know your findings.' But Anirudhya was not an investigator. He did not have the power to get hold of the tape. Narayanan then added, 'Your stories on the assassination suggest you sometimes know more than the SIT. I would appreciate it if you enlightened us.' Anirudhya understood that India's intelligence head was upset with the questions and that he was in no mood to cooperate any further.

—∞—

A section of the press was catering to the LTTE. In a damaging indictment, the SIT's investigation had dug up how Sivarasan, who had masterminded the assassination, had, in fact, been 'trained in handling sophisticated arms and ammunitions, explosives and telecommunication work and close combat warfare at a training camp in Kumbakonam in Tamil Nadu in 1983 by certain intelligence organizations'. Significantly, this was the first time a government agency was admitting the existence of training camps on its soil. The revelation also came in handy for those who sympathized with the Tamil Tigers.

Likewise, the sudden discovery of a taped telephone conversation between Prabhakaran and his political adviser Anton Balasingham sent shockwaves through the security agencies. In the conversation, Prabhakaran is heard telling Balasingham that Rajiv Gandhi should be 'fixed' once he (Prabhakaran) gets off Indian soil. It was June 1985 when Prime Minister Rajiv Gandhi had Prabhakaran as a visitor at his 7, Race Course Road residence. The R&AW had chosen New Delhi's prestigious Ashoka Hotel for Prabhakaran's stay. The LTTE supremo had come with his military chief Mahathaya and Balasingham. The meeting took a dramatic turn even before it could start. When Prabhakaran and his companions arrived at the security-check area at Rajiv Gandhi's residence, the security staff raised objections to the trio entering, since they had cyanide capsules hanging around their necks. While cyanide capsules were mandatory for marked LTTE cadres to avoid arrest, the Special Protection Group (SPG), specially created for protecting the Prime Minister, could not allow anything around the Prime Minister that could pose a potential threat to his life.

A commandant of the elite force asked them to remove the capsules. Mahathaya and Balasingham obliged but Prabhakaran refused. He was not ready to take off something that worked for his protection. Prabhu Chawla wrote in his story in *India Today*,

> SPG and the IB feared that the mercurial leader could use the lethal capsule to kill Rajiv Gandhi. An IB officer tried to persuade Prabhakaran, but the rebel leader simply refused to budge. A compromise was reached. Prabhakaran could wear the cyanide capsule, but he would be escorted by two SPG guards to ensure that he made no sudden moves. Rajiv Gandhi was kept at a certain distance from him. The SPG joined two tables together to ensure that Prabhakaran would never come within handshaking distance of Rajiv Gandhi.[6]

The episode had soured Prabhakaran's mind even before the meeting could begin. A former diplomat and a loyalist of the Gandhi family, Natwar Singh, was a special invitee to that meeting. He later told the media that the Prime Minister should not have met Prabhakaran in the first place. Apparently, Natwar Singh had asked Rajiv Gandhi later if he had got anything in writing from the LTTE chief. The PM had apparently got irritated and said that the rebel leader had given him his word. Natwar Singh had to say that Prabhakaran's word, to him, meant nothing as he had done it more than once. He later told Anirudhya that the LTTE boss should have been asked to give his 'consent in writing' as 'he would double-cross us when it suited him'.

Two years later, in July 1987, Prabhakaran visited Delhi again in connection with the finalization of the Indo-Sri Lanka Accord. He was again staying at the Ashoka Hotel, although he felt he was put under house arrest. Prabhakaran, in a telephone conversation with Balasingham, was heard saying that he would teach Rajiv Gandhi a lesson if they let him go. He was of the view that New Delhi would arrest him during that visit. Six years later, Prabhakaran used a human bomb to kill his former host at a political rally. The unexpected discovery of the telephone tapping was good for proving the LTTE's motive behind killing Rajiv Gandhi but was of no help when it came to tracking Sivarasan, which was a priority at that time.

Stories to divert the attention of the SIT were continuously being planted in the media, both national and foreign. Even before the phone-tapping controversy—when the Indian security agencies had tapped Prabhakaran's phone when he was staying at the Ashoka hotel—had settled down, a report from the R&AW surfaced. It highlighted that the head of R&AW's counter-terrorism division, B. Raman, had sent a secret assessment to then Cabinet Secretary Vinod Pandey on the 'likely threat' to then Opposition leader Rajiv Gandhi. The veteran sleuth had stated that 'there was a greater threat to the security of Rajiv Gandhi as the leader of the Opposition than to the security of V.P. Singh as the Prime Minister'. The report also stated that the main threats to Rajiv Gandhi were Khalistani terrorists in the north and the Sri Lankan Tamil terrorist organizations in the south. The report made a strong case for the continuation of the security cover of the SPG to Rajiv.

Anirudhya's source had refused to share anything more, fearing a story in the press would refresh the debate about whether withdrawing Rajiv Gandhi's SPG cover when he was the leader of the Opposition had been a legitimate move. Politics aside, the truth had to be reported. Anirudhya tried for an audience with the person behind the sensitive report, B. Raman, but in vain.

Kondath Mohandas, former director general (intelligence) of the Tamil Nadu Police, was feeling out of the limelight. Raman had worked under him at some point in the state intelligence department. He agreed to convince Raman to speak to *India Today*. However, he laid a condition for Anirudhya—the meeting had to be held at his apartment. Anirudhya agreed. The Madras bureau of the R&AW had earlier aired similar concerns about the LTTE's attitude towards Rajiv Gandhi, that the Sri Lankan Tamils were the biggest threat to him. Then why did the R&AW chief G.S. Bajpai deny the LTTE's hand in the assassination?

Bajpai's denial was an open secret by then. The fact that this had drawn flak from the IB, the CBI, the Tamil Nadu Police and other security agencies was no secret either. Raman claimed later that even shortly after the assassination of Rajiv Gandhi, at a meeting of concerned officers, he was asked for his views about who might have killed Rajiv Gandhi. Raman's instant reply was the LTTE. But his view was dismissed, Raman said. The problem was that the security agencies in Delhi and the security experts from the JIC had got it into their heads that the Tamil Tigers wouldn't strike at Rajiv Gandhi since his Sri Lankan policies and his mother's had actually helped the Sri Lankan Tamil struggle more than anything done by any other Indian political leader. New Delhi never looked deep into the making of Velupillai Prabhakaran, and therefore didn't anticipate what he was capable of.

A study of what had shaped Prabhakaran was therefore becoming necessary. To his followers, Velupillai Prabhakaran was a revolutionary fighting for the liberation of the Tamils in Sri Lanka. To his critics he was a narcissist with an obsession for power who had no regard for human life. Someone who had reportedly killed the mayor of Jaffna at the age of nineteen and who eventually led the LTTE to become the deadliest guerilla force in the world, with experts calling it more fearsome than the militia of the Colombian drug lord Pablo Escobar. The LTTE's 10,000-plus members swore by Prabhakaran and were ready to bite cyanide than be taken into custody. Such was his charisma.

Born in a fisherman's family on 26 November 1954 in Valvettithurai, Jaffna, Prabhakaran was known as an introvert who preferred spending most of his time buried in books in junior school. By the time he reached senior high, he was drawn to Tamil movements. Right from an early age, Prabhakaran refused to accept the discriminatory treatment meted out to Tamils by the Sinhalese in Sri Lanka. Claiming to be an admirer of Subhas Chandra Bose and Bhagat Singh, he disagreed with his seniors in the Tamil movement and made it clear that an armed struggle was the only way to win freedom and not through dialogue, which had failed to produce any results for the Tamils in northern Sri Lanka.

Soon after Rajiv Gandhi's assassination, the *India Today* magazine wrote about how Prabhakaran picked his recruits young, predominantly in the age group of twelve to thirteen. These children were already aware of the hardship and the atrocities inflicted by Sri Lankan soldiers. Training would be completed by an oath of personal loyalty to Prabhakaran and the gift of a cyanide capsule to the new guerrilla on his behalf. In the quest for supremacy, which began nearly eight years ago, Prabhakaran's men devoured the frontline leadership of all the other major Tamil guerrilla groups to emerge as the unchallenged rulers in Jaffna. His funds came from drug smuggling, havala rackets, extortions and donations from expatriate Tamils. Investigations conducted by Interpol had revealed that 80 per cent of the Sri Lankan nationals sent to jail abroad for drug trafficking were reported to be Tamils. *The Washington Post* and Bogota's Spanish paper *El Tiempo* first busted the Tigers' links with Colombia's notorious Medellin Cartel.[7]

The BBC, in its obituary of Prabhakaran, wrote that the rebel leader lived in secrecy all his life. Despite becoming known to the world, he rarely appeared in public. It said,

> His movements between his various jungle hideouts were carefully planned to avoid capture or assassination. At the height of its powers at the end of the 1990s and the early years of this decade, the LTTE controlled nearly one-third of Sri Lanka. But Prabhakaran was unable to translate this authority into his dream: an autonomous Tamil homeland in the north of the country. His single-minded determination in pursuit of his goal never wavered: he once claimed he had ordered his own men to shoot him if he ever gave up his demands for a Tamil state.[8]

But Raman's warning and reports from the IB's Tamil Nadu unit were not taken seriously. Only after the photographs taken by Haribabu became public did R&AW chief Bajpai and his loyalists stop denying the LTTE's role in the assassination of Rajiv Gandhi.

# 8

ALTHOUGH THE ELDAMS ROAD OPERATION TURNED OUT TO BE A smokescreen, Verma instinctively knew that this was the thread the SIT needed to follow to track Sivarasan. He and Ragothaman met the engineer's wife again. They learnt about an elderly Sri Lankan lady, 'Aunty', who was instrumental in Raja's visit to her apartment to meet Dixon. Apparently, she lived with her daughter in Royapettah, Madras. The officers' next destination was Aunty's house. When brought to Malligai for questioning sometime in July, the SIT realized the importance of the lady in the investigation. Aunty claimed that 'Thambi Anna' had brought Sivarasan to her house in the first week of May. He carried an introductory letter from her mother, who lived in Valvettithurai in Jaffna—a place where the LTTE's armed struggle had taken birth under Prabhakaran. Apparently, Aunty's mother had asked her to extend whatever help was necessary to Sivarasan.[1]

Sivarasan had become a regular visitor to Aunty's house. He particularly enjoyed her sour fish curry with rice. One day he brought a young girl, 'Gowri', and asked Aunty if she could keep her for a week. Aunty was planning to go on a tour of south India with her family. She was sceptical about Gowri staying alone at the house. Sivarasan assured her that Gowri was smart and could look after the place. After Aunty left, Sivarasan brought over more guests. First, it was Raja and then Kanagasabapathy. Gowri gave her real name to the old man. She was Athirai, and part of the hit squad of the LTTE. This was the first time Kanagasabapathy and Athirai had met. It was planned for him to take her to Delhi. But with Thambi Anna, another LTTE operative close to Sivarasan, getting picked up by the Q branch of the police, Sivarasan did not think it was safe to keep Athirai there any more.

The SIT received an anonymous call towards the end of June. The caller refused to identify himself. There were instructions that any such call would have to be entertained, irrespective of whether the caller was willing to give his/her name and contact details. Incidentally, the anonymous caller had a long story to share, which allowed the SIT communication experts to trace the caller. He was picked up within two hours with the assurance that his identity would never be disclosed. The caller had no choice. He told them his story all over again.

The caller, from Saidapet, had an unexpected guest, Bhaskaran, from Jaffna. They had met at a refugee camp in Vellore, Tamil Nadu, sometime in 1987. Bhaskaran said he was looking for a house on rent but facing problems because he was a Sri Lankan citizen. Would he be able to help? The natural query from the Saidapet man was, 'Who will be staying in the house? Another Sri Lankan?' Bhaskaran, he claimed, was not comfortable answering the question. But he appeared desperate to get a house on rent.

But the caller said he was not willing to help until he knew the identity of the tenants, particularly after the assassination.

Bhaskaran finally gave in. He reluctantly said his daughter and son-in-law were being held hostage by Sivarasan and his gang in a house at MR Nagar, Kodungaiyur. The Saidapet man could not believe what Bhaskaran had told him. However, he soon realized that Bhaskaran was in a soup. He told him to go to the police and report this. Bhaskaran left and, unfortunately, the caller didn't think of asking for the address of the house where Bhaskaran's daughter and son-in-law were being held hostage. After discussing the matter with his family, he picked up the phone and called the SIT.

Murugan was asked to give details of the hideouts in MR Nagar. He could not describe the location. The SIT took him to the area in one of the bulletproof cars used by the Cobra commandos of the CRPF. But even that didn't work. However, he revealed that Bhaskaran could be traced to a refugee camp in Tuticorin. Luckily, the Tuticorin Police found him there and brought him to Malligai. In his interrogation, he gave the SIT the address of Sivarasan's hideout—in Everready Colony in Kodungaiyur. That was the house where Sivarasan had brought the human bomb Dhanu and Shubha after the hit squad arrived in the country on 1 May.

The tracking team got ready to strike. Raju, Kanth, Verma, Ragothaman and Ravindran, along with the Black Cat commandos, broke into the house. But Sivarasan and gang had managed to flee again. The only person found was Bhaskaran's son-in-law Vijayan and daughter Selvaluxmi. The mastermind of the assassination must have suspected afoul when Bhaskaran had not returned home for over two days. The SIT found the container of the explosives suspected to be used in the assassination, some components of the UHF transmitter Sivarasan was using for communicating with Jaffna and a spare glass eye, audio cassettes containing LTTE songs, detective novels, a Kawasaki Bajaj motorcycle key, and photos of Sivarasan with Jayakumar's family. The SIT painfully realized it should have acted upon the anonymous caller's alert about Sivarasan's presence in her neighbouring house around the time Athirai and Kanagasabapathy were caught in Delhi.[2]

The revelations made by Vijayan, Bhaskaran and Selvaluxmi were stunning. The SIT got first-hand information on the mastermind, someone they had lived with before and after the assassination. Vijayan used to be a lorry driver in Sri Lanka. By the end of 1989, he had started repairing damaged vehicles of the LTTE and risen in its ranks. His business took a hit when the IPKF began driving out the LTTE and started cleaning the jungles of Jaffna of the LTTE's hideouts and bunkers. Vijay, his wife Selvaluxmi and father-in-law Bhaskaran relocated to India on 12 September 1990. But before that, Sivarasan asked him to rent a house in Madras where he would have to accommodate a few LTTE activists. In the first week of May 1991, Sivarasan came to his Madras house with Shubha and Dhanu. Besides some daily essentials, Sivarasan carried only a wireless set. Vijayan had to procure a car battery from the local market to activate the wireless set. Sivarasan brought in more communication instruments within two days. He also got LTTE activist Nero to operate the UHF communication set.[3]

One day, Sivarasan bought Vijay's wife a television set. She was pregnant then. Sivarasan told her television programmes would keep her entertained when she felt unwell. Normally, Sivarasan would connect with Jaffna at night. Nero usually spoke on the wireless transmitter starting with '910 to 91' and then connected. But after that all communication would be in alphanumeric codes, which Vijayan had no clue how to read. What intrigued Vijayan about Sivarasan and the two human bombs was that they always kept their things in black duffel bags and carried them around whenever they would go out. One day he asked Sivarasan about it. Instead of answering his direct question, Sivarasan gave him Rs 10,000 in support of his kitchen.[4]

But more surprises awaited Vijayan. Sivarasan had asked him and Nero to dig up a pit in the kitchen, where he hid the wireless set and a gun. On the morning of 21 May, Sivarasan asked Nero to send a message to Jaffna. Vijayan said he distinctly remembered that Nero appeared nervous when sending the message—and that Sivarasan did not like it. He suddenly got Dhanu there and asked Nero to look at her. Dhanu did not know what the message was about but could guess. She tried to boost Nero's morale and asked him to take pride in sending out that message. Sivarasan asked the girls to have lunch and be ready by noon. He left after that.[5]

The mastermind came back half an hour later wearing a kurta pyjama with a camera in hand. Shubha and Dhanu came out of their room, ready. Shubha was wearing a sari. Usually, Vijayan's wife would help Shubha wear a sari, but that day she managed it on her own. Dhanu was dressed in an orange kurta with a green dupatta. She was also wearing spectacles and had put on make-up. By that time, Selvaluxmi had appeared on the scene and asked Shubha why she hadn't called her before wearing the sari. Sivarasan handed the camera to Vijayan.[6]

A photo session started after that. Vijayan clicked about ten photographs of Sivarasan, Dhanu and Shubha—some solo, some in a group and some in pairs. Sivarasan had asked Nero to get an autorickshaw and wait near the bus stand. Neither Vijayan nor Selvaluxmi found that unusual. The idea was to keep the driver from identifying the house later.

With Vijayan and his father-in-law Bhaskaran, no coaxing was required and no admonishment was necessary. Both spoke to the SIT as if getting a weight off their chests.

Vijayan resumed talking after a pause. The morning after the assassination, Sivarasan came in very early with the news of Rajiv Gandhi's death. He had stayed the previous night in a different hideout. He scribbled something on a piece of paper and gave it to Nero to communicate to Jaffna. Did that mean Prabhakaran did not know about the outcome of the operation the previous night, as soon as Rajiv Gandhi was killed, the SIT asked. But Vijayan could not vouch for that. He didn't know what Sivarasan had written on the paper. His messages were coded, both when transmitted and when written down.

Sivarasan left after lunch. To Vijayan's surprise, Nero carried an AK-47 even inside the house. He looked tense. He said that the police would be coming. The next day, on 23 May, Sivarasan returned on a bicycle. He picked up his motorcycle and left again. The same evening, he returned with Shubha. And that night onwards, all three—Sivarasan, Shubha and Nero—did not sleep peacefully. They would be alert for any police action. Sivarasan would keep his 9 mm pistol under his pillow. He said he would kill at least a dozen policemen before getting caught. On 25 May, he and Shubha left for Tirupati, only to return the next day.[7]

Vijayan used to buy at least ten newspapers every morning, which Sivarasan and Nero would read, trying to figure out how far the investigation had progressed. Towards the end of the month, Sivarasan's photograph appeared in the newspapers. The first thing Sivarasan did after that was shave off his moustache. He also reduced the number of times he went out. Nero told Vijayan that Jaffna was going to send a boat in which Sivarasan, Shubha and he would escape from India. But it didn't happen while Sivarasan was still at the house. In fact, Nero sounded upset when there was no sign of a boat from Jaffna. And then came the next surprise. Photographs of Shubha also appeared in newspapers. Nero's name as Sivarasan's wireless operator had been doing the rounds in the media.[8]

Bhaskaran, mustering up the courage, asked Sivarasan if the buzz around them was getting hot. The mastermind agreed. What if some of their neighbours barged into their house and caught them? Even though Sivarasan assured him nothing of the sort would happen, he made some changes in the set-up of the house to pre-empt any intruder from finding out anything suspicious. He asked Vijayan to put up photo frames of Rajiv Gandhi, MGR and Jayalalithaa on the walls, get some musical instruments and place them around, and add more calendars of Hindu deities that local Tamils worshipped. Sivarasan didn't want to take any chances. He had also asked Bhaskaran to arrange for another house. But no one was willing to rent Sri Lankans any place.

Sivarasan might have kept his cool on the exterior but his mind was not at rest. An instruction that came from Jaffna through a wireless message was a big jolt to him. Pottu Amman had instructed Nero and Sivarasan to stop messaging Jaffna as all their messages were being intercepted by the Indian security agencies and decoded. Earlier, Sivarasan had succeeded in confusing the Indian security forces with his messages, but not any longer. The Indian navy, the Coast Guard, the Tamil Nadu coastal police and the SIT were now working together and kept strict vigil on any coded communication. Jaffna turned down Sivarasan's request for more time to figure out an escape route from the country.[9]

—ww—

The Congress party's medical cell head, Dr Chokalingam, took Anirudhya to the house in Kodungaiyur, where he met the Anglo-Indian Mantels who lived next door to Sivarasan. 'Had the SIT acted fast they would have caught the gang,' regretted Robert Mantel, a retired employee of the Indian Railways. His wife Esylen added that she was always sure of the tenants' identity, but nobody listened to them. The house was Sivarasan's base, from where he kept in touch with Jaffna through his VHF device.

Esylen claimed that Vijayan and his wife would often drop in for a chat. But slowly their attitude changed. Robert Mantel recalled, 'Sivarasan used to ride a Kawasaki. He would often wear jeans, a khadi kurta and a Panama cap while riding it. He was not too particular about hiding his glass eye until it became an identifying mark. And maybe when my wife asked Selvi about his eye, Sivarasan became suspicious. And he would always carry a black duffel bag with him. Dhanu and Shubha would rarely step out of the house, except to go cycling on their BSA SLRs in the evening dressed in churidar kameez. They would never go shopping. The broker who got them the house would buy them the things they needed.'

Esylen said that one day four people—two men and two women—came in two autorickshaws to her neighbouring house. She learnt then that they had taken the house on rent and that their names were Dhanu, Shubha, Nero and Sivarasan. They had brought a TV with them, the antenna of which they fixed on the terrace. However, they also put up two casuarina tree posts connected with a black wire. This raised her suspicions. Why would an ordinary family require such things? On the fateful day, Esylen claimed to have seen Sivarasan, Shubha and Dhanu waiting at the bus stand in her colony. And the very next day, Esylen watched the news of Rajiv Gandhi's assassination on television. She caught a glimpse of her new neighbours again after five days. But she could not spot Dhanu among them. She was looking for her in particular following the publication of her photograph in newspapers that morning. She understood it was the same girl she had seen at the bus stand. Esylen saw Sivarasan's photograph in the newspaper three days later. She immediately understood that her neighbours were the killers of Rajiv Gandhi. She said that she was scared to even think about it. Her hands had started shaking when she found out. About one week after that, Vijayan came to her house and borrowed a driller. He said he wanted to fix a fan regulator.

Esylen, scared yet curious, went to her neighbour's house to ask for the driller back.

She saw Sivarasan standing in the hall. This time he was not wearing his glasses. He stood there with his left eye shut. But Esylen, whether in person or in photographs, had always seen him in glasses. She dared to ask Selvaluxmi what happened to his eye. She said he had lost it while playing. Esylen again realized she was shaking as she realized she was looking at one of the world's biggest fugitives standing right in front of her. If she was terrified on the one hand, she also could not resist finding out more about him on the other.

Esylen saw Sivarasan again the next day when he was sitting on the steps. Mustering up the courage, as such an opportunity she realized may never come again, she asked if he was employed somewhere nearby. The fugitive reportedly said no, and that he was trying to land a job in Dubai. At that time, Esylen noticed he had two eyes. One looked artificial. It was at that moment that she thought of going to the CBI office and telling them everything. But nobody in her family agreed because it was not safe.[10]

Anirudhya stepped into the hideout after the raiding team had left. In the living room, where the assassination was planned, photographs of Rajiv Gandhi, Jayalalithaa and M.G. Ramachandran, the founder of the AIADMK, still adorned the walls.

He rushed back to his hotel to call the Delhi office. A message from Harpal was left below the hotel-room door. It said, 'Hey, got your last filing. Thanks. Bobb was asking for info on Shubha, the other human bomb. Asap.' True, anyone had hardly written about her. The limelight had been stolen first by Dhanu and then by 'One-Eyed Jack'.

Shubha was no less important a target in the manhunt—she was proving to be just as elusive as Sivarasan. Verma, from the confession of Murugan, felt the two were not together. No one in their custody could give them any information on Shubha's whereabouts. Murugan claimed that even if Shubha was caught, chances of getting anything from her were remote. Being a member of the LTTE's suicide squad, she always carried a cyanide pill as a pendant around her neck. Murugan said they took pride in biting the cyanide capsule. It was his misfortune that he could not.

While the investigators were getting closer to catching Sivarasan and gang, the courtroom battle was intensifying. IO Ragothaman spent more time in court, responding to petitions filed by Peraribalan, who designed the bomb, and Padma, Nalini's mother, who claimed to have no knowledge of any assassination plot. They were asking for access to legal assistance, citing it was their constitutional right. Their petitions were prepared by lawyers from the DK, an ally of the DMK. The court had rejected both the petitions—it was clear that the lawyers had filed those petitions without actually having taken written consent from the so-called petitioners. Peraribalan and Padma were in the SIT's custody and had no access to legal consultations under the TADA.

LTTE cadres Jayakumar and Robert Payas, who were already in the SIT's custody for giving refuge to Sivarasan, told Ragothaman that one Sivaruban alias Siva was given the task of retrieving Haribabu's camera from the site. To do this, he had to ensure that he was close to Haribabu and Dhanu. Though it contradicted the confession of Murugan and Nalini, which said that Sivarasan had asked Subha Sundaram to retrieve the camera, the revelation of a new accomplice to the crime was significant.

When Nalini took Shubha and Dhanu to a tailoring shop in Purasawakkam in Madras and purchased clothes, including the orange-and-green salwar kameez, the same day, 17 May, Sivarasan and Santhan sent Sivaruban to Jaipur to finalize a hideout for the conspirators and to take one on rent under a cooked-up name.[11] The next day, when Peraribalan purchased a 9-watt golden power battery and met Sivarasan, the latter was deputing Kanagasabapathy to be ready with all arrangements in the newly acquired hideout in Delhi, which would be the pit stop for Sivarasan on his escape route to Nepal. The mastermind was setting up multiple hideouts across the country for the assassins to evade the police.

Kanth swung into action with the assistance of Jaipur Police and arrested Suresh Kumar aka Sivaruban, and his uncle Meghaja from Hotel Vikram in the city. Sivaruban, who had only one leg, had told the hotel management that he was visiting Jaipur to get an artificial limb fitted from internationally famous surgeon Dr P.K. Sethi. The SIT thought he had lost his leg in the Sriperumbudur blast and therefore was suspected to be one of the nine-member hit squad that had arrived on 1 June to kill Rajiv Gandhi and was now working on an escape route.

Kanth didn't buy Sivaruban's artificial-leg story. The other assassins in the SIT's custody had told him that Sivaruban had lost his leg in an ambush in Jaffna when he was sixteen. But he continued to be an active soldier of the LTTE. He had reached Jaipur on 19 May, two days before the assassination, with the task of fixing hideouts for the assassins. He could not produce a single piece of evidence to link his artificial-leg problem with Dr Sethi's medical facility. Neither did anyone from Dr Sethi's office remember any inquiry ever being made by him. He had stayed at the Golden Hotel, Jaipur, from 19 to 23 May, before shifting to Hotel Vikram, where he was arrested.[12]

Instead of any evidence that could indicate his arrival in the city for medical treatment, what the SIT found was a small notebook containing the phone numbers of Payas, Peraribalan and Thambi Anna; and a letter from Santhan asking him to keep changing hotels after the assassination. The SIT asked why he, not a senior leader of the LTTE, had to be sent to a specialist in Jaipur when his artificial leg could have been fixed at any other place, say Madras and Bangalore, which also had many surgeons of repute. And why was he in Jaipur for so long and still not had his leg operated on? Sivaruban had no convincing replies to those questions. It only made the SIT's beliefs stronger that he had been deputed to Jaipur to find a hideout for Sivarasan and Shubha to help them escape.[13]

When Anirudhya contacted the clinic, they requested their name to be kept out of it.

It looked like the SIT was being able to arrest everyone connected to the assassination except Sivarasan and Shubha. Kaarthikeyan sat with the team and asked who, from those in their custody, was still withholding information about Sivarasan. He asked all the officers one by one. The most common reply was Jayakumar. He was brought to the interrogation room. After a while, he revealed that something belonging to Sivarasan was concealed in a 'hole' in the kitchen of the house in MR Nagar. He assumed it was something 'very important', as Sivarasan would always send him out of the room before looking at it. Within hours, Jayakumar was guiding Verma and Ragothaman to the house. He took them straight to the kitchen, where he said there was a hole below the floor tiles. The raiding team ripped up the floor and discovered, to its shock, a damp three-foot-deep trench under a two-by-two-foot kitchen tile.[14]

What the raiding team of the SIT found was a Tamil-to-English dictionary. When opened, they found a cavity inside that could conceal a pistol. It was immediately confirmed with the recovery of fifty-three live rounds for a 9 mm gun, an artificial eye made of glass, some eye-cleaning liquid, a notebook and two small diaries. The content of the diary gave them telephone numbers, addresses, code names and details of payments, which didn't make much sense to the SIT initially. There was a passport with the diaries that turned out to be of one Suthenthiraraja, aka Raja.

Further investigation revealed that Raja was none other than Santhan, who had played a vital role in the Padmanabha assassination and then in killing Rajiv Gandhi. For Sivarasan, he would pass information from one cadre to another; he would carry cash and distribute it among them; he would handle relocation of operatives between hideouts; and he would arrange meetings and carry instructions from Sivarasan to others. He had a sharp mind and knew what his boss wanted. It could be debated that he was of greater significance than Murugan as far as Sivarasan was concerned, although Murugan had played a deputy's role in the assassination of the former Indian Prime Minister.

Athirai confirmed Suthenthiraraja (who later turned out to be Santhan) was the same person who had moved her out of Aunty's house in Royapettah to another in Meenambakkam. But she didn't have its address. All she could remember was that she had crossed the airport. And that there were two girls in the house Suthenthiraraja was operating from—she gave the SIT their names, their class and what their school uniforms looked like. Armed with those details, the SIT found the address of the house quickly enough from the school authorities.

In an early-morning operation, Verma, Ragothaman and the Black Cat commandos nabbed Raja while he was fast asleep. He tried to reach his cyanide pill kept under his pillow but was quickly overpowered by the Black Cats. He was brought to Malligai. His interrogation began with the excitement of catching probably the last obstacle in their path to Sivarasan. One puzzle had been solved—Santhan was Suthenthiraraja, who was also Raja.

—∾—

Twenty-two-year-old Santhan was a member of the intelligence wing of the LTTE. Records earlier supplied by Colombo showed he had studied till the fifth standard in a government school in Jaffna. He had come in contact with Sivarasan in 1986 and soon earned the latter's confidence. Two years later, Sivarasan sent him to Madras for further study funded by the LTTE. Santhan took admission in the Madras Institute of Engineering and Technology.[15]

Officers of the SIT took turns to hear Santhan's story from the man himself. Sivarasan had persuaded Santhan to join him in killing Padmanabha, then considered to be the arch-rival of Prabhakaran. Santhan started following the movements of Padmanabha and kept Sivarasan posted. His groundwork eventually led to their success, with the assassination of the EPRLF leader in June 1990. He left with Sivarasan the very next day and returned to Jaffna. Prabhakaran and Pottu Amman lavished praise on him for his work in the assassination.

By the last week of April 1991, Amman had assigned Santhan to the team Sivarasan was going to lead to Tamil Nadu. It included Shubha, Dhanu, Sivaruban and Nero. Later, they all took shelter in the infamous Kodungaiyur house. Sivarasan introduced him to the rest. On the evening of 9 May, he introduced Santhan to Haribabu, Murugan and Peraribalan at the Marina beach political rally. That same night, Sivarasan took him to his Porur hideout and introduced him to Jayakumar. But his accommodation was arranged with Haribabu. Over the next seven days, Haribabu took Santhan for shopping essentials. Camaraderie developed between them instantly. Haribabu was always thrilled meeting an LTTE cadre. Reportedly, he wanted to become one of them. Santhan's statement corroborated what Haribabu's father, Sundarmani, had earlier claimed. Haribabu had to coax and cajole his mother to accommodate Santhan in their house. There was no space to accommodate a stranger, especially when there were other female members staying under the same roof.

On the night of 15 May, Santhan met a top LTTE leader, Kanthan, and handed him a letter from Sivarasan. Kanthan gave him five lakh rupees, which might be required by Sivarasan from time to time. Santhan was asked to keep it safe. Next day, Sivarasan went to pick up twenty thousand in cash from Santhan. He told him about Prabhakaran's increasing confidence in the boy, particularly after the killing of Padmanabha. Sivarasan told him about the purpose behind getting human bombs such as Shubha and Dhanu—and that's when Santhan heard about the LTTE's plan to assassinate Rajiv Gandhi for the first time.

Santhan met Sivarasan regularly thereafter. Sivarasan had to collect cash in instalments, and the operation started unfolding before Santhan. On the morning of 21 May, Santhan witnessed Sivarasan preparing himself for the final execution. He was facing a mirror and checking if his pistol, concealed beneath his kurta pyjama, could be seen from the outside. He had taken Santhan's observation on that too. Santhan assured him that the pistol was not visible. This was right before Sivarasan went to the Kodungaiyur house to pick up Dhanu and Shubha a little after noon.

That night, after returning from Sriperumbudur, Sivarasan told him that Rajiv Gandhi was dead. And that Haribabu, too, had died in the blast. Thereafter, Santhan kept moving from place to place until he got settled at the Sundara Lodge. Sivarasan met him there to discuss his next move. Santhan noticed his boss had shaved off his moustache. Sivarasan told him that Murugan was going to look after Sivarasan's work in India and that Santhan should extend to him all the support he needed. Santhan, as per earlier instructions, handed over twenty-five thousand in cash to him and three bus tickets for Coimbatore, purchased under fictitious names. Before leaving, Sivarasan told him about his plan to murder a person named Chandrahasan—Santhan had to coordinate with Murugan to execute the job. The murder was being planned to divert the attention of the CBI from the assassination.

Verma had a feeling that Santhan was applying the same strategy now to divert their attention from Sivarasan. He was put through a gruelling interrogation. But he claimed he knew nothing more about Sivarasan's 'likely whereabouts'. When his interrogation had started, Santhan had spilt the name of someone who could be helping Sivarasan—Dixon, the same LTTE cadre who had met Santhan at the engineer's apartment on Eldams Road on 22 June. From there, Santhan had taken Dixon to Sivarasan's hideout in Everready Colony, where the assassins were staying with Vijayan and his family. Santhan had introduced Suresh Master from the political group to Dixon and others later, a move that indicated that the entry of the political group's head, Gundu 'Trichy' Santhan, was imminent. Jaffna was considering handing over Sivarasan to Trichy Santhan for further action. Suthenthiraraja alias Santhan clarified that Suresh Master was Trichy Santhan's number two, who looked after wounded LTTE cadres undergoing treatment in LTTE hideouts across Tamil Nadu. Pottu Amman's assurance to Sivarasan, when the latter had sounded sure he would be arrested, was taking shape. The SIT had released a photograph of Dixon in the newspapers, and the CBI's staff had pasted flyers with Dixon's and Sivarasan's pictures in autorickshaws. The flyers mentioned Dixon's role in helping Sivarasan and gang move to a hideout, underlining how crucial his arrest was to the investigation. The assassins were believed to be commuting in autorickshaws.

The manhunt for Sivarasan had by now extended beyond India. The CBI had enlisted the services of Interpol, the Narcotics Control Bureau (NCB), the Royal Canadian Mounted Police and Scotland Yard in London, seeking help in identifying some of Sivarasan's associates who had operated from foreign soil. Interpol was concentrating on finding out more about the LTTE's international links.

Verma claimed before Kaarthikeyan and Raju that information gathered so far on the LTTE's contacts and activities abroad could be used to test the theory that a foreign hand might have been involved in the plot to assassinate Rajiv Gandhi, with the LTTE as a willing tool. Kaarthikeyan straightaway refused. He said that was comparatively a 'long shot'. Closing the case would be impossible unless Sivarasan was caught and questioned. And the SIT boss was unwilling to look beyond that. Verma acknowledged his argument. However, he felt there seemed to be more to the assassination than just the LTTE.

The limelight had by now again fallen on *India Today*'s coverage of the assassination case. Anirudhya was expected to entertain his 'sources, contacts and friends in high places' with the latest updates on the progress of the investigation. Lunch, high tea and dinner invitations were on the rise. He was getting caught between office and the world outside. Shekhar Gupta made it easy for him. 'Anirudhya, remember your only allegiance is to your stories, your readers and your editor. Rest everything can wait.'

Gupta was teaching him how to say no to invitations.

'But Shekhar,' Anirudhya spoke hesitatingly. 'How do I ignore my sources?'

'They can wait. They give you stories in their own interest. As long as you are in a position of power, at least in their perspective, they won't turn their back on you.'

'I hope so.'

'Relax. Go home after office. You look washed up.'

'Thanks, Shekhar.'

The assassination plot continued to thicken even as the number of potential targets multiplied. Fresh intelligence reports from the IB suggested that the LTTE had bigger plans in place, with a long hit list. The assassination squad wanted to eliminate at least three more VIPs—Tamil Nadu Chief Minister Jayalalithaa, the state Congress President V.K. Ramamurthy and the director general of Tamil Nadu Police, S. Sripal. The Q branch had picked up some suspects in that connection and handed them over to the SIT for further investigation.

The conspiracy appeared to have had international links. Interrogation of suspects and documents seized indicated that Sivarasan, the man who wove the complex web of the assassination and its aftermath, was in regular contact with people in London, Sweden, Singapore, France, Saudi Arabia and the UAE. All these countries had been bases to key members of the LTTE. Kittu, the head of the international wing of the LTTE, was in London. Anton Balasingham, Prabhakaran's political adviser, was in Sweden. Naydu Raghavan, an explosives expert with the LTTE, was in Singapore. Pushparaj, an LTTE operative who reportedly coordinated with Sivarasan's overseas contacts, was in France. And Peniyapann, reportedly a fundraiser for the LTTE, was in the UAE. Could it be that Sivarasan was seeking their help for his escape after Jaffna had ignored his calls for a boat? Having said that, Kanth felt that it was too early to deduce that Prabhakaran had removed the cover of protection from Sivarasan and gang, leaving them to fend for themselves.

'That he and Shubha have still managed to evade the SIT is nothing short of amazing,' he said.[16]

Anirudhya wrote in his next story, titled 'Rajiv Gandhi Assassination Probe Casts Its Net Wide',

> The flip side to that was [that] the carefully built network of over a decade was collapsing like a house of cards; the lynchpin of yesterday had now become a liability. Major LTTE establishments in Tamil Nadu had been wiped out, while there had been a rich haul of arms, explosives, high-powered communication gadgets and money. Also over 30 of their members were either dead or cooling their heels in prison. Little wonder that Sivarasan's SOS for a boat to Jaffna had failed to elicit a response. There was another apprehension that might have been keeping the Tigers from having him picked up from the Tamil Nadu coast. The Tigers probably feared that if Sivarasan was arrested or killed by the Indian or Sri Lankan security while being pulled out from India, the involvement of the LTTE in the killing of Rajiv would be established beyond doubt.[17]

But it was an IB report that rocked the SIT. It claimed that Sivarasan was actually not trying to escape, despite the manhunt launched to catch him—he was getting ready to strike at more VIPs. Both the VIPs were to pay a visit to the Prime Minister later in the month. Some of the assassins in custody revealed that Sivarasan was supposed to visit New Delhi and meet two LTTE members, Kanagasabapathy and Athirai (now already in custody). The latter was a human bomb and the head of the Black Tigress group of the LTTE. Dhanu and Shubha were trained under Athirai. Multiple sources confirmed the duo's visit to the Indian capital.

Further interrogation of the assassins led the SIT to believe that the duo had gone to Delhi as part of Plan B—killing Rajiv Gandhi in India's capital if the LTTE's Tamil Nadu mission failed. Although the SIT was not bound by the IB's 'findings', such claims did create confusion in the government that the investigators were accountable for. Some in the government, and at least two officers within the SIT, believed that Kaarthikeyan was 'determined to hold the LTTE as the lone and sole executor of the assassination, prove that in the court and secure the conviction of those already in his custody'. Therefore, anything outside the Tamil Tigers would not fall in his list of priorities. Naturally, forces that didn't see eye to eye with the SIT boss had started making noise. For Anirudhya, the source of the report was more intriguing. Both Athirai and Kanagasabapathy, being LTTE cadres from Jaffna, should have been on the radar of R&AW. Yet, their movements were tracked by the IB, and R&AW was nowhere in the picture.

When Anirudhya met the former director general (intelligence) of state police, Kondath Mohandas, at his apartment in Madras, he pointed to the 'intriguing circumstances' in which Sriperumbudur was added to Rajiv Gandhi's itinerary without consulting the state party chief Vazhappady Ramamurthy. He also mentioned the snag in the aircraft from Visakhapatnam, which was rectified immediately, making sure he made it to the rally. But these events were interpreted as 'destiny' by the SIT and Anirudhya's sources in the IB. It was clear from sources in the Congress party that Rajiv Gandhi was genuinely interested in campaigning for his 'Aunty (Maragatham) Chandrasekar'. But the former director general went on to cite more instances of 'oversight'. 'Yasser Arafat's warning to Rajiv Gandhi,' he said, 'should also be looked into. I strongly suspect that the LTTE was used as a front for some other organization.' However, the same Mohandas remained silent when asked why the LTTE was handled softly during his tenure as the state police chief under MGR's rule. Multiple sources, agencies and the media were accusing the SIT of a 'partisan probe', but nobody came up with any proof. Too many conjectures were doing the rounds. At least at that point of time.

A section of the investigators increasingly claimed to have definite knowledge of Sivarasan's visits to Sweden, Singapore and

France to procure arms and explosives and his jaunts to Saudi Arabia and the UAE to raise funds. What they were baffled about was why a functionary not very highly placed in the organization had been sent on missions that were always handled by top-level functionaries such as Kittu Anandan, Anton Balasingham and military head Mahathaya. While Kaarthikeyan had his reasons to ignore such intelligence on the fugitive, at least two senior members of his team—Kanth and Verma—came up with a new hypothesis that Sivarasan might have been acting on his own in liaising with groups other than the LTTE.

Multiple intelligence agencies, including those from other countries, backed his communication with sources other than Jaffna. It was a complex issue. The pressure to catch the mastermind was mounting. Persuading leads pertaining to his foreign links were left for future action—at least till after Sivarasan had been caught. Also, even as ramifications of the case widened, one could see the relationship between the SIT, the state police and the IB turning cold. While the SIT accused the state police of non-cooperation in private, the state police resented the SIT's high profile, which was consciously trying to hog all credit.[18]

# 9

A STANDARD PRACTICE FOLLOWED IN THE INTERROGATION OF criminals is asking them the same question over and over again. Besides applying other tactics, the SIT asked the same question to all the assassins and tallied their replies to see if there were discrepancies. Ragothaman was interrogating Robert Payas and Jayakumar probably for the tenth time. He was deliberately asking hypothetical questions. One of them was what would have happened if the assassins had failed to kill Rajiv Gandhi at Sriperumbudur. Neither had any answer to offer. Ragothaman already knew about the LTTE's plan B to eliminate Rajiv in New Delhi using the human bomb Athirai. Ragothaman wanted to know if Payas and Jayakumar were aware of it. That would have defined their role in the conspiracy to kill the former Indian Prime Minister, besides corroborating the confessions made earlier by Athirai and Kanagasabapathy.

After a while, both Payas and Jayakumar revealed that the LTTE's intelligence chief Pottu Amman had a plan B in case his plan in Madras failed. Then the place of strike would be Delhi. Pottu Amman had sent another human bomb—Sonia alias Athirai alias Akila—along with an old man, Kanagasabapathy, posing as her grandfather to the Indian capital. The next step for Ragothaman was to make Athirai and Kanagasabapathy sit face to face with Jayakumar and Payas. With an increase in the number of the subjects, Ragothaman had asked Verma to join in. Eventually, the four confessed to their roles in the grand operation of the assassination of Rajiv Gandhi.

Payas and Jayakumar told the SIT what they knew about plan B. Sivarasan had devised a plan to infiltrate a travel agency named M/s President Travel Services in the capital that was run by V. Kalyanasundaram. He was related to a senior Congress politician and a close aide of Rajiv Gandhi.

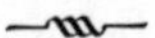

When Anirudhya heard the name of the Congress politician, he ran a quick check on the travel agency through *India Today*'s Delhi office. Kalyanasundaram denied any links with Sivarasan or the LTTE, but various media reports indicated that the LTTE had got his contact details from Kalyanasundaram's uncle, Jagadeesan, a retired army man who ran a rice mill in Thopputhurai.

When contacted, the Congress politician categorically denied any knowledge that 'President Travels' had links with the LTTE and said he had never used the agency for any of his or his family's travels. Was the SIT being misled again? Knowing how the LTTE would have used the lead, the SIT questioned Payas and Jayakumar on whether they had used Maragatham Chandrasekar, the Congress candidate from Sriperumbudur, to get Dhanu close to Rajiv? There were reports of Latha Kannan and Kokila, who were seen flanking Dhanu in Haribabu's picture, getting their VIP passes to greet Rajiv through Chandrasekar's daughter Latha Priya Kumar, also a Congress worker. However, with both Kokila and Latha dead, the reports could not be verified. Both Payas and Jayakumar claimed they knew nothing. It would have suited them to implicate a Congress politician, that, too, someone as close as Maragatham Chandrasekar to Rajiv. But they refrained. The duo was sent back to their cell even as the interrogation of Athirai and Kanagasabapathy continued.

According to unconfirmed reports, Sonia, alias Athirai, was chosen because she had a fair complexion, which they thought would allow her to mix better with the Delhi crowd. Pottu Amman told her that Kanagasabapathy would be accompanying her to the Indian capital and arrange for her stay at a place where a few more LTTE cadres would also take shelter. Their task would be to collect information about the movements of certain VIPs in the capital. Athirai would be informed when the time was right to strike. Athirai did not admit that the target was Rajiv Gandhi at that stage of her interrogation. The place Kanagasabapathy chose was:

> [A two-room] Central-government quarter, illegally rented out by its government servant, had made it the perfect cover. It was located in a sprawl of single-storey government accommodation in north Moti Bagh in south Delhi. It was just eight kilometres away from Rajiv Gandhi's 10 Janpath residence. Kanagasabapathy had paid Rs 5000 as advance to the broker, claiming his granddaughter would come and stay there very soon to study Hindi and computers.[1]

Jayakumar was brought back into the interrogation with Athirai and Kanagasabapathy. He confirmed that while Sivarasan was confident of accomplishing the task of killing Rajiv Gandhi in

Tamil Nadu, his immediate boss Pottu Amman preferred the Indian capital. 'Why don't we try Delhi?' Pottu Amman had asked in a coded message in March 1991. 'I am confident that I can do it here [in Tamil Nadu],' Sivarasan had replied in a coded message. Pottu Amman had insisted he continue with Delhi as the backup plan. The Delhi plot was, naturally, abandoned after the LTTE's success in Sriperumbudur.

Sivarasan's stories had made him an almost cult figure in the eyes of the investigators. He was proving to be too smart for the sleuths. The best and worst part was that the more the interrogators heard about the one-eyed mastermind, the more mesmerized they got.

Jayakumar further claimed that Sivarasan, not getting any help from Jaffna despite repeated calls for a boat, sent Athirai and Kanagasabapathy off to Delhi to escape through Nepal. If that would have been a success, he, too, would take the same route out of the country. Thyagarajan was all set for that.

Verma asked Kanth to join the interrogation at that point, since it was he who had arrested Kanagasabapathy and Athirai from a hotel in Paharganj in Delhi. Earlier, Payas had confessed to Kanth that Kanagasabapathy and Athirai had made two trips to Delhi—first, to assassinate Rajiv Gandhi in case their plan in Madras failed, and second, when they were trying to figure out an escape route via Nepal.[2]

Parallel to these revelations, Radhavinod Raju was studying the diary of Sivarasan found in the kitchen hole of his Kodungaiyur hideout. At first, the tiny pages, with Tamil and English notes scrawled all over in Sivarasan's handwriting, hadn't thrown much light on events. It appeared to be a mix of telephone numbers, addresses, contact persons, aliases, code names and payments. Instead, the two pocket diaries were turning out to be the key to unlocking the conspiracy.

Raju had brought to Kaarthikeyan's notice that the notebook and the pocket diaries could be crucial evidence to proving the link between Sivarasan and the other assassins. After landing at Vedaranyam with the hit squad on 1 June, Sivarasan started jotting down the progress of work in these pocket diaries. A scrutiny of dates recorded indicated that he maintained them until two days after killing Rajiv Gandhi. He hid them in his Kodungaiyur hideout but it seems like he forgot to take them along when fleeing the place.

Sandeep Unnithan reported the details of the diary in a story in *India Today* much later. A salient part of his story was:

Dhanu wore a green-and-orange salwar kameez. During the journey to Sriperumbudur, Nalini recoiled in horror when Dhanu asked her to feel what was under her clothes. There were no metal detectors and no frisking at the venue. Nalini and Shubha escorted the human bomb Dhanu.

At 10.20 p.m. Rajiv Gandhi walked down a red carpet laid out at the grounds at Sriperumbudur. Rajiv, who looked tired, was welcomed by an enthusiastic crowd. Dhanu garlanded Rajiv and bent down as if to touch his feet. She flicked a switch on the right side of her garment to trigger off explosives in her bomb jacket. The blast instantly killed Rajiv Gandhi and seventeen others. In the melee, Sivarasan and his hit squad melted away.[3]

After going through Sivarasan's diary, it wasn't difficult for Raju and Kaarthikeyan to understand that the mastermind didn't want to be captured while in possession of incriminating documents that would link him to the assassination. Yet he left it behind for the SIT? IO Ragothaman was of the opinion that the LTTE believed in publicity and that Sivarasan leaving his diary behind was proof of that. Sivarasan knew that the contents of the diary would not lead the sleuths to him. It would, however, link him to the assassination. But he perhaps didn't care.

—~—

Raju went through the diaries of Sivarasan for days and deciphered how Sivarasan had masterminded the assassination with meticulous planning and executed it with clockwork precision. It revealed the network of the LTTE that worked on the assassination, right from Jaffna to Tamil Nadu to New Delhi to London. From plan A to plan B to even a plan C. From critical information on Tamil Nadu politics to who all from among them could be of help—the DMK and its ally parties. From friendly pressmen to those who were hostile to the LTTE's cause. The diary also confirmed his other name—Packiachandran. It also showed that the LTTE supremo Prabhakaran liked to address him by a shorter version—Pakia. One part of the diary corroborated what Athirai and Kanagasabapathy had said in their confessions to Kanth. Sivarasan had indeed noted down an alternative plan to killing Rajiv. In fact, Athirai was the first human bomb to have landed in India, more than a month before the arrival of Dhanu and Shubha. The curly-haired young girl made a clandestine arrival at Kodikkarai in Vedaranyam. This was the same place where Sivarasan had arrived with his nine-member hit squad. The girl was taken to a hideout in Madras, where Sivarasan had introduced her to Kanagasabapathy. They were to go to Delhi together by train.

Raju confronted Kanagasabapathy with the entries Sivarasan had made in his diary. The old man admitted that he had visited the capital and met a fellow LTTE member, along with a politician from Tamil Nadu. They had introduced him to a real estate broker who got him a house that would substitute for a hideout if and when Sivarasan arrived—the same two-room government quarter in south Delhi's Moti Bagh that was only eight kilometres from Rajiv Gandhi's official residence at 10, Janpath Road in New Delhi. It also worked because no one would view the occupants of a government quarter with suspicion.

Three sources confirmed the same crucial piece of information—Jayakumar and Payas, entries from Sivarasan's diary and Kanagasabapathy. The perfect murder was turning out to also be a perfect thriller for the SIT.

It was time to confront Athirai and Kanagasabapathy with the contents of the diary. Raju got Kanth in on the interrogation. The duo revealed that following instructions from Pottu Amman, Sivarasan set up a separate team to execute the assassination, in case he failed to strike at Rajiv Gandhi in Tamil Nadu. This was another stunning confirmation of what Jayakumar and Payas had revealed earlier. Athirai had shocked her interrogators by saying how much she regretted that another suicide attacker had succeeded in killing Rajiv Gandhi, depriving her of the chance of martyrdom. But Athirai maintained that she didn't know who could have been her target in Delhi. 'It was clear after what happened in Sriperumbudur,' she added.

Kaarthikeyan had stepped in at that moment and interchanged the interrogation teams. He asked Verma and Ragothaman to question Athirai and Kanagasabapathy and see if they could get a clue about what Sivarasan's next move would be. Likewise, he put Raju and Kanth before Payas, Peraribalan and Jayakumar all over again to see if they could dig up more on Sivarasan. Catching the mastermind was of paramount importance. Everything else could wait. And he took the responsibility of talking to Nalini and Padma himself to learn more about Sivarasan and the other human bomb, Shubha.

Athirai disclosed that the suicide-attack squad of the LTTE had carried out more than twenty-five suicide attacks, all within Sri Lanka. Rajiv Gandhi had been its first operation on foreign soil, for which three Black Tigresses were chosen—she, Dhanu and Shubha. She was the first of the lot to have been taken into custody by the Indian authorities. She gave them a name—Jagadeesan—whom, she said, had been assigned the task of collecting information on the Congress-party members in Tamil Nadu and Delhi by Sivarasan.[4]

Another name that cropped up during the interrogation was 'Mahalingam', a Sri Lankan Tamil who had stayed in Kodiakkarai and organized the movements of Jayakumar, Athirai, Kanagasabapathy and Payas after their arrival from Jaffna. Was he also responsible for the movements of Sivarasan? No one seemed to know. Murugan was brought in and asked the same question. He did not implicate anyone, but, instead, said, 'Yes, Mahalingam had taken Sivarasan once from Madras to Coimbatore and back.' Anyone who had come in close contact with the mastermind was considered a prize catch. He was picked up in the wee hours of the next day from his house near the Kodiakkarai beach. Verma understood Murugan was trying to mislead the interrogators. At his behest, two CBI constables gave Murugan a piece of their mind. Murugan kept quiet for a while and then admitted that he knew Mahalingam and that the latter knew Sivarasan well. In fact, Murugan implicated everyone present, as it was common knowledge among the INT group.

After he was picked up, Mahalingam promptly admitted that he knew Murugan, Santhan, Payas and Jayakumar. He could not remember if he had ever seen Sivarasan, though. He had read about Sivarasan in the newspapers but claimed to have had no knowledge of the LTTE's plan to kill the former Indian Prime Minister. He said he didn't know if it was the LTTE who did it. But that was the standard offering of everyone when they were caught.

Around the same time, an IB report assessed that the movements of LTTE militants and their landings took place mostly in Nagapattinam, about 300 km from Madras. Nagapattinam was crucial because of the presence of a top-notch smuggler, Shanmugham, who carried out major transportation work for the LTTE.

Criminals, hardcore political activists and rebels can all be dedicated to their causes but facing interrogation by seasoned police officers requires different skills. Very few can withstand their gruelling methods. From his initial denial of ever knowing Shanmugham, Mahalingam eventually confessed to having assisted him often, including the time when Sivarasan had arrived in India with the human bombs. Likewise, Santhan also eventually spoke. He disclosed to Verma that Shanmugham could throw light on Sivarasan's movements. Upon inquiry, Manoharan of the Tamil Nadu Police (attached to the SIT) figured that Shanmugham had gone underground. Verma realized that he would have to crack Mahalingam to get to Shanmugham.

He offered Mahalingam a barter deal. The SIT would set him free in exchange for Shanmugham. Mahalingam knew it was a trap. He did not give in and kept denying he knew his whereabouts. A rich overlord who was rolling in money, courtesy of the LTTE after years of penury, Shanmugham had the reputation of having the local police and politicians on his payroll. Verma gave Mahalingam a break and had a small chat with Ragothaman on the side.

A little later, Mahalingam was put through the same drill of interrogation and this time it yielded some results. He revealed that he had ferried Sivarasan and the entire gang, including Dhanu, Shubha, Murugan, Nixon, Neru, Suthenthiraraja, Athirai and a young man with one leg, on 1 May and landed at Kodiakkarai. While Sivarasan still remained elusive, the role of the INT group under Sivarasan's leadership was getting substantiated by all its members.

Suddenly Ragothaman walked into the interrogation room and disclosed that Shanmugham had been shot dead in an encounter by the Tamil Nadu Police. However, the local police were unable to identify the body. He asked if Mahalingam could. Verma took Mahalingam along for identification. They landed up in a dilapidated building. But there was no sign of an encounter having taken place there. And neither did Verma and Ragothaman seem bothered about Shanmugham's body not being there. There were no police personnel there either. Mahalingam sensed he had walked into a trap and that his time was over. Verma pointed his gun at him. It worked. Mahalingam broke down and agreed to cooperate with the SIT in tracking Shanmugham.

—∞—

Kaarthikeyan took the help of the Tamil Nadu Police to get Shanmugham. Sending the tracking team to Nagapattinam would alarm the locals, including the local police, who were on the smuggler's payroll. Instead, Kaarthikeyan and Raju used their connections with the top brass of the state. A stern message was sent to Shanmugham: Cooperate with the investigation or face arrest. Shanmugham chose the first option. However, he filed for anticipatory bail before surrendering. He was a man of connections and arresting him in his den would not have been easy.

Shanmugham tuned out to be valuable to the investigation. The dark, curly-haired smuggler, aged forty, had direct links with the LTTE's top bosses. He made money smuggling gold. The LTTE gave him the freedom of movement on the Palk Strait in exchange for him ferrying arms and ammunition, explosives, communication instruments, gold biscuits, etc., for them between Jaffna and Tamil Nadu. The SIT knew he was the key to uncovering the nexus in Tamil Nadu between arms dealers, smugglers and terrorists.

It would also reveal the shipping routes for arms being sent to India. Another crucial revelation Shanmugham made before the SIT was that it was he who had received Sivarasan, along with eight other assassins, in Kodiakkarai on 1 May. Mahalingam's claims corroborated what Koneswaran's testimony earlier to the Q branch of Tamil Nadu Police had revealed. The group consisted of Sivarajan, Dhanu, Shubha, wireless communications operator Nero, Santhan, Koneswaran, Vijayanandan, Sivaruban and the 'driver' Anna.

The thin man came in perfectly ironed, all-white clothes, in stark contrast to the glitter of his gold wristwatch, sunglasses and neck chain. Shanmugham seemed to have realized that it would be dangerous for him to implicate the LTTE or reveal his role in establishing the organization's activities in Tamil Nadu. Therefore, he chose not to cooperate any more and tried to evade every question thrown at him. The SIT believed some very important documents, which could get them fresh leads in the investigation, were in the smuggler's possession. Shanmugham was the man who had arranged Sivarasan's transportation from Jaffna to India twice; he had also done so once for his nine-member hit squad and on another occasion for Athirai and Murugan. He was thus a mine of critical information. But he wouldn't admit to anything. Once again, Kaarthikeyan's connections came in handy. The CBI's lawyers managed to get Shanmugham's petition for anticipatory bail rejected in the Madras High Court.

The SIT made his arrest official, produced him before the magistrate and took him into custody. Then they flew him to Vedaranyam in a chopper. With no other option left for him, Shanmugham started cooperating. He disclosed that the LTTE had stashed a large number of transmitters for communication, explosives, arms and ammunition under the forest floor in Kodiakkarai. He claimed to know the exact spots where the

LTTE's possessions were buried—in deep pits dug by his own men. He revealed there were hideouts in the coastal town where LTTE cadres would stay upon arrival and before departure to Jaffna. He had been providing them lodging and boarding. He confirmed Mahalingam's claim about the arrival of nine members of the hit squad on 1 May and that the squad included Sivarasan, Shubha and Dhanu. But he firmly denied his presence at the time of their arrival. He said he hadn't received Sivarasan in person. He spoke freely and did not look under pressure when he reiterated that he had never met Sivarasan. Verma asked Ragothaman to get Koneswaran. He was sure he would negate Shanmugham's claims. Smuggler Shankar, caught earlier, was junior to Shanmugham and had testified that Shanmugham was close to both Sivarasan and Murugan.

But the smuggler changed his statement with a smile the moment Verma divulged Koneswaran's and Murugan's testimony on Shanmugham's relationship with Sivarasan. He admitted that Murugan had kept a bag with him, which contained material that could become clinching evidence in the case. Shanmugham said he would hand it over to the interrogators. He also said he would guide the SIT to the forests of Vedaranyam, where the LTTE had hidden arms and ammunition.

At the behest of the SIT, the Tamil Nadu Police set up a large team to raid Vedaranyam. Aware of Shanmugham's clout in the region, the police knew resistance could come from some locals who worked for him and owed their livelihood to him. Also, his arrest had ruffled many feathers. He could drag many other 'respectable' figures into custody with him. Shanmugham was a mine of information on the LTTE as he gave them logistical support in Tamil Nadu.

Shanmugham was taken to his house for the recovery of two letters written by Dhanu and Shubha. One was to Pottu Amman and the other to the LTTE's women's intelligence-wing head, Akila. Akila was another name that Athirai was known by. In their letters, both the human bombs reassured them that they would remain loyal to their mission.

The next person to give the SIT information was Mariappan, Shanmugham's neighbour in Kodiakkarai. He had seen Murugan and other LTTE cadres staying in Shanmugham's luxurious house. He had been given Murugan's box to bury in the forest for safekeeping, but for some reason, Shanmugham had taken it back from him the very same day. He had admitted that that had been done at the behest of a Tamil Nadu politician. The SIT continued Mariappan's interrogation to figure out the nexus between Shanmugham and the powers that be who had extended support to the LTTE through his services. Else, the SIT believed, Shanmugham would have been arrested much earlier.[5]

A large team consisting of the Tamil Nadu police, the CRPF, Verma and Ragothaman launched a combing operation in the Kodiakkarai forests from that evening until the next morning and recovered six VHF Japan-made wireless sets, arms, ammunitions, 121 cartons of high explosives, sixty-six drums of fuel, and Indian currency of over Rs 20 lakh buried in deep pits. Even in pitch dark, Shanmugham guided the SIT to the exact locations of the pits without a problem. To win his trust further, the sleuths granted him permission to meet his family and have food from home. But they took him back to the government circuit house in Vedaranyam in an attempt to maintain pressure on him. He had much more to disclose. The LTTE had hidden gold biscuits in the forest too, and Murugan's bag was hidden somewhere around.[6]

Incidentally, Shanmugham's maternal uncle, Seetharaman, also a smuggler and known for his closeness to the LTTE, was also in police custody. The SIT brought him face to face with

Shanmugham. In no time they were fighting with each other. The uncle abused his nephew in front of everyone for helping 'Rajiv Gandhi's assassins'. The SIT had thought interrogation of the two face to face would help them figure out where the gold was hidden, but instead, their fight almost turned violent, and the SIT had to handcuff Shanmugham and send him off to a nearby police station. It was about nine at night. Shanmugham wanted to have dinner at the circuit house before being sent to the police station. His handcuffs were removed.

Seetharaman was not in sight as Shanmugham quietly finished his dinner. He got up to wash his hands when, in a sudden surprise move, Shanmugham bolted the door from outside and disappeared in a flash. The two constables guarding him were caught unawares and couldn't catch him. Shanmugham must have scaled the walls of the circuit house as there was no sign of him inside the premises. The guards raised an alarm, and the constables who were posted on the front of the police station ran around looking for him. The first thing they found was his clothes, dropped on the ground—he had taken them off, probably to hide better at night and escape easily. The police immediately issued an alert and sought the people's help in tracing the smuggler. Police dogs were brought in, followed by raids on houses belonging to his kin. A joint search by the SIT and the local police continued through the night. But Shanmugham seemed to have vanished into thin air.

Around dawn, Shanmugham was found hanging from a tree in a public park about fifty metres from the circuit house. The SIT and the local police claimed it was a suicide. The news spread like wildfire and the press suspected foul play. Either the accused had died in custody from torture or was killed by those Shanmugham was going to expose. In either case, the blame had gone squarely to the SIT, since the accused was found dead while in 'custody'.

The alleged suicide by a key witness had turned the spotlight of investigation back on the investigators themselves. This was a huge setback for the SIT.[7]

The top brass in the CBI was upset with the development. If they admitted it was an outsider's job, they were accepting there had been a big security lapse on their part. And if they said it was a suicide, it showed negligence on their part. Death from torture would have a charge far more serious.

Shanmugham's lawyer, Ramalinga Raju, had rushed to the court and filed a petition seeking immediate suspension of the SIT unit that had been handling Shanmugham's case. As Anirudhya later mentioned in his story, he claimed that the 'mistakes are disturbing as they point to a death-in-custody, and a more deep-rooted conspiracy. No prompt action is taken to book the guilty is indicative of a cover-up by the SIT.'[8] An officer sent a telex to Malligai saying that Shanmugam appeared to have died of asphyxiation and could be a victim of foul play with the involvement of external players. More so because Shanmugham opening his mouth before the CBI exposed the smuggler-politician-terrorist nexus. Verma had dispatched a report to Kaarthikeyan by telex on the developments. Kaarthikeyan rushed Sri Kumar to Vedaranyam.

Anirudhya, much against the wishes of the SIT, exposed the loopholes in his next story, titled 'A Dubious Twist to Rajiv Gandhi Assassination Probe'. He wrote:

*Glaring Loopholes*

- There was no rope mark or bruise on the victim's neck.
- The tongue wasn't protruding, nor had the eyes popped out.
- How did he acquire the 14-feet-long rope away from any habitation in the middle of the night?

- How did he give the slip to one DIG, two SPs and 20 policemen?
- If an alert was sounded how did he manage to hang himself just 50 yards from where he was held?

> Police sources say that fearing more revelations, someone could have ordered his killing. Perhaps the LTTE, which had threatened last fortnight to 'rescue' its members from SIT custody.[9]

The SIT's version is that Shanmugam had his dinner brought in by his uncle Seetharaman around 9 p.m. on July 19 at the Traveller's Bungalow in Vedaranyam where he was being held. Then under the pretext of washing his hands, he went to the backyard accompanied by a lone guard.

And in the dark disappeared scaling the compound wall, leaving behind his khadi dhoti and white shirt. Next morning his body was found hanging from a tree in a nearby park. A blue lungi was found at the spot. The post-mortem was conducted the same day at Nagapattinam, 40 km from Vedaranyam.

The report, taking note of the saliva, emission of semen and stools, declared it a suicide. But the SIT story and post-mortem are riddled with loopholes that militate against forensic wisdom.[10]

The followers of Shanmugham had surrounded the SIT officials at the police station and demanded an explanation. Their action was justified.

The victims' supporters asserted that emission of saliva, stool and/or semen could also have come from his strangling. And if Shanmugham was tied up, how could he commit suicide? Neither were any skin cells found under his nails. Advocate Ramalinga Raju asked dramatically if it was humanly possible for Shanmugham to climb the tree first, then put the rope around his neck and then jump. All by himself. He refused to believe the victim would find a fourteen-foot-long rope in the middle of the night unless someone from the police station had abated his act. The advocate demanded a magisterial inquiry be set up immediately.

Again there were many questions asked while no answer was available. Why was Seetharaman allowed to visit Shanmugham, get his dinner from outside and chat with him for over an hour when a lawyer was not permitted to be present during the interrogation? It may be noted here that a lawyer is not allowed to sit during interrogation of an accused booked under TADA. None of the constables entrusted with Shanmugham's physical custody had any convincing answer to offer either. Stranger still was why the guards didn't carry any guns on their persons. They could have fired in the air to warn Shanmugham while he was fleeing. Even if an alarm was raised after his escape, the victim could not have reached the park, not more than fifty yards from the police station, and complete the act of suicide without anyone from the police station catching up with him.

That night, a local police officer who was present at the circuit house told the SIT that it was a case of death in custody. According to him, the victim's uncle, Seetharaman, was a local landlord, a money lender and a known LTTE sympathizer. He was already in police custody in connection with another case. The cops sent him to get Shanmugham's dinner. Incidentally, he had a professional rivalry with Shanmugham over the latter's financial rise and proximity to the LTTE, as anyone close to the Tigers enjoyed power in the region. After getting dinner for his nephew, Seetharaman reportedly blamed Shanmugham for settling scores with his competitors by getting them falsely implicated in the assassination case. It was half past ten already. Neither Seetharaman nor Shanmugham had touched their food, even as the argument continued. The DIG and the SSP had gone to sleep. Suddenly a constable started thrashing Shanmugham, and no one intervened. He collapsed on the floor. Yet no one raised an alarm. The victim's clothes were removed, the body was taken out under the cover of darkness and hanged. The lungi that was found, in fact, belonged to Shanmugham's uncle's driver, Das.[11]

Kaarthikeyan refused to take questions on the incident from the media. After much persuasion, he summed up the drama in just a line: 'It's a controversy we could have done without.'

Even as Kaarthikeyan was able to douse the resentment and anger of the locals using his relationship with the Tamil Nadu police, the matter had reached New Delhi by then as some of the DMK MPs had raised the issue in Parliament. The SIT got a bashing from all sides—from the press, from human rights organizations that took a soft view on the Tamil Tigers, and from political parties and NGOs. Union Home Minister S.B. Chavan assured the public that New Delhi was determined to get to the root of the incident even as a magisterial inquiry was instituted, besides an internal inquiry by the vigilance department of the CBI. The Shanmugham incident was a loss of momentum for the SIT.

# 10

Kaarthikeyan did two things after the death-in-custody episode. First, he tried to boost the morale of the team. He told the entire team that Sivarasan was feeling trapped—it was evident from his frequent SOS messages to Jaffna. One-Eyed Jack already knew that he could not keep the SIT off his tracks. It could also be that he was not feeling safe under the political group of the LTTE. Was he operating now on his own instead of depending on his handlers for movements? He understood that his fellow LTTE members were under the constant watch of the SIT and other security agencies. He didn't want to risk availing their protection any more. If ever there was a time, Kaarthikeyan told his team, to charge ahead full steam to catch Sivarasan, this was it.

Second, Kaarthikeyan requested the Tamil Nadu government to lodge all the accused in a regular prison. They were still being kept at Malligai. Although they were in handcuffs all the time and kept under the constant vigil of the CRPF and the CBI armed constables, he didn't want to take any chance after the Shanmugham incident.

The state government promptly agreed and allotted the Poonamallee sub-jail, twenty-five kilometres off Malligai, for keeping the accused. The entire route from Malligai to Poonamallee sub-jail was blocked to transfer the accused safely, which took almost a full day.

Three names had been appearing in the interrogation of Jayakumar, Robert Payas and Athirai—Vicky, Dixon and Suresh Master, all of whom worked under Trichy Santhan. It was established that the political group of the LTTE was in control of the post-assassination 'escape' operation, since the job of the INT group was over. The SIT was getting desperate to catch at least one of these three.

In response to the SIT's release of Dixon's photo in the press and a subsequent release of a photo of Sivarasan, too, in which he was not seen wearing his false eye, on 24 July, an informer from Coimbatore claimed to have seen 'Dixon' often making calls from a particular telephone booth opposite the Punjab National Bank in Jawahar Nagar. Kaarthikeyan immediately moved the tracking team to Coimbatore.

Around the same time in Coimbatore, local police detained two men for violating traffic rules and tripling on a bike in the Gounderpalayam area. All three were made to sit in 'murga' (sitting in a squat, with heads hanging down and hands holding the ears through the back of their legs) in one corner of a police post. The idea was to release them after a couple of hours, the usual drill for such offences. The trio kept seeking forgiveness in their repeated pleas for release. The SP of the area was on his daily round. He had casually dropped in at the police post for a glass of water. The trio, speaking Tamil with a strong Sinhala accent, did not go unnoticed. He took extra interest in them and found, to his horror, that they were members of the LTTE. They were immediately taken to the district police headquarters for interrogation.

One was named 'Vicky' and turned out to be an insider working closely with the Tigers' political group leader Trichy Santhan. Another was 'Raghu'. The third, 'Vijay', was a real estate broker who was taking them to show a new place available for rent.

Vicky, or Vigneshwaran, was a Sri Lankan national. The cloth store his father owned had been destroyed in an air raid by the Sri Lankan air force in 1985. He started ferrying contraband goods between Jaffna and Madras for a living. Two years later, his house was destroyed in a bomb blast. He was sent to a refugee camp in Batticaloa, where he met people who believed only Prabhakaran could get them 'freedom'. Finding no other means of livelihood in violence-stricken Jaffna, Vicky visited Madras again, along with a few wounded LTTE cadres seeking treatment in Tamil Nadu. Vicky's grooming in the rebel cause began. He started working as an assistant to LTTE cadres and gained their confidence. A trusted lieutenant of Pottu Amman, Trichy Santhan was overall in charge of looking after the LTTE's wounded cadres seeking treatment in India, their movements, settlement and safety. He was impressed with Vicky's dedication. He took him as his assistant in mid-1990 and paired him with Dixon. Vicky handled wounded LTTE cadres in hideouts in Trichy and Dixon sent coded messages from Trichy Santhan to Jaffna.[1]

Trichy Santhan shifted Vicky and Dixon to Coimbatore. Vicky was thoroughly briefed on how to assist Dixon in managing Sivarasan's movements in case Trichy Santhan wanted to send the mastermind to Coimbatore. Sivarasan was not alone. Shubha and Nero were with him. In his interrogation, the twenty-two-year-old admitted that working for 'Sivarasan anna' would have been a matter of pride for him.

There was a third associate—Guna—who specialized in obtaining explosives from Indian sources. Vicky confessed to the Coimbatore Police that he was witness to Dixon and Guna making plastic bombs, grenades and grenade shells, but Vicky never got involved in procuring explosives for bombs. However, Dixon sent hand grenades in large numbers concealed in cartons of medicine through Vicky to Jaffna via secret routes. Their activities ran smoothly until the assassination. Indian security agencies tightened their nets around LTTE activists and sympathizers after the assassination. The state police was on the lookout for Sri Lankans who did not possess passports and visas, and made it compulsory for landlords to report such matters to the police. They could not rent out their place to a Sri Lankan national without police verification.

But money did the talking. Vicky succeeded in renting houses where he could keep grenades and explosives from Dixon. He kept moving Guna and Dixon from one place to another. The LTTE was in desperate need of hand grenades and explosives. But with increasing security on the Palk Strait, Jaffna was reluctant to accept more consignments. As a result, the inventory in Coimbatore was swelling. Where to store them was Vicky's biggest concern. A local real estate broker, Vijay, agreed to take a house in his own name and help Vicky. Of course, for a hefty consideration. Both fell into the police dragnet.

Inter-city communication between security agencies is not their strongest suit. And that's precisely what happened in Coimbatore too. Neither did the tracking team of the SIT inform the Coimbatore Police about their arrival in the city to catch Dixon, and nor did the latter think it necessary to inform the SIT about Vicky, an associate of Dixon, in their custody. Enthused by its catch, the local police went overboard. Instead of handing Vicky over to the SIT, it took a heavily armed unit and raided the house where Dixon would supposedly be found. But with the sudden disappearance of Vicky and Raghu, Dixon and Guna knew something was wrong. Both took their cyanide pills when the armed police tried to break into their house in Muthusamy Servai Street.

Anticipating that the LTTE operatives might be carrying cyanide pills, the SP, Muththu Karuppan, had asked Dixon and Guna to surrender, saying no harm would come to them. Dixon, as intercepted by the police, tried to inform Pottu Amman about the situation. Pottu Amman instructed them to destroy whatever material there was in the house before biting the cyanide pills in a quick reply and had closed the communication. Dixon ensured that the police team was caught up in negotiation as Guna destroyed all incriminating documents pertaining to the LTTE's operations, photo albums, the VHF transmitter set and large sums of currency notes. He burnt them over a gas stove in the kitchen. Once done, Dixon and Guna took no chances. They blasted the interior with grenades to wipe out whatever evidence was still left. After that they shot each other and took their cyanide pills. Such was their dedication to the LTTE.

And all this was happening while the SIT's tracking team was looking for Dixon in the same city.

After the botched operation, realizing that it had overestimated its ability to deal with LTTE operatives, the Coimbatore Police handed over Vicky and Raghu to the SIT and sent the bodies of Dixon and Guna for post-mortem. But the SIT was obviously upset with the Coimbatore Police for not informing them about Vicky and not even bothering to tell them that he had revealed Dixon's hideout in Coimbatore. The tracking team had the Black Cat commandos, specially trained to disarm terrorists in close-combat warfare and always carried anti-cyanide kits. It was the first cyanide death after Rajiv Gandhi's assassination. Radhavinod

Raju, on their way back to Madras in an MI-8 chopper, said they should not be surprised if there were more such setbacks.

—∾—

The Ludlum-like plot continued to thicken. Former top cop of the state Kondath Mohandas went on to write a strong letter to Prime Minister P.V. Narasimha Rao, reiterating his earlier claim of 'intriguing circumstances in which Sriperumbudur was added to Rajiv Gandhi's itinerary' without having consulted the state Congress chief V.K. Ramamurthy. He also underlined the incident of the 'snag in the aircraft from Vizag', which was immediately rectified. These, he claimed, were 'proof of information that the plot had been leaked'. Even as the SIT cited Mohandas's action 'seeking attention', New Delhi could not ignore apprehensions raised by a police officer of his stature and experience. Even before any response could reach him, Mohandas held a press conference in Madras where he repeated his earlier statement to *India Today* about a 'foreign hand' in the assassination. He told the press, 'I strongly suspect some foreign hand behind the assassination. If the LTTE is involved, it is only as a tool.' He also urged the press to look into the warning that had come from Yasser Arafat to Rajiv Gandhi. 'I strongly suspect the LTTE was used as a front for some other organization. Ask Mr Arafat what he had told Rajiv Gandhi about the possibility of Mossad staging a coup in India.'[2]

Unfortunately for Mohandas, his press conference did not elicit the attention he wanted. That Mossad wanted to stage a coup to topple Rajiv Gandhi's government sounded far-fetched. Although there was little evidence of a 'foreign hand' other than the LTTE's, Union Home Minister S.B. Chavan's statement in Parliament about 'certain forces in superpower countries conspiring to kill Rajiv Gandhi' fuelled such speculations further. The US ambassador, in particular, took strong exception to such a claim. The minister later tried to play it down, claiming it was a slip of tongue. But the ambassador was not willing to give up so easily. He was heard later saying at an informal gathering that Chavan's tongue could not have been slipping for five minutes.

But criticism was mounting, with no news of Sivarasan. New Delhi questioned the progress of the SIT, as none of their raids had produced the desired results. The argument behind questioning the SIT was that Sivarasan had not even fled after assassinating Rajiv Gandhi but was also already readying to strike at three more VIPs. Intelligence reports revealed that Sivarasan had planted two assassins in the state guest house in the capital. But this was unsubstantiated since even sustained interrogation of the two LTTE cadres, Athirai and Kanagasabapathy, did not reveal anything to confirm this diabolical plan. They were in the capital as part of Plan B to kill Rajiv Gandhi.

Kaarthikeyan proudly backed his team. In a meeting at the PMO, he stressed that thanks to his team, major LTTE establishments in the state had been wiped out. There had been a rich haul of arms, explosives, high-powered communication gadgets and money. Also, more than thirty of their members were either dead or cooling their heels in prison. The fact that Sivarasan had become a liability for the LTTE was a big achievement for the SIT. It was established news by then that Jaffna hadn't sent a boat for Sivarasan despite the latter's repeated requests. And if reports of the IB and the R&AW were anything to go by, the LTTE bosses in Jaffna were not happy to see their carefully created empire in Tamil Nadu crashing like a house of cards. Yet, the spirit of a section of the political wing of the LTTE in Tamil Nadu was so high that keeping Sivarasan away from the SIT did not seem difficult. A major concern for the SIT at that point was that in the event of getting nabbed, Sivarasan would bite the cyanide pill that always hung around his neck.

Using computer-generated imagery (CGI), the SIT conjured up over a dozen faces of Sivarasan both with one eye and in disguises that showed him as a Sikh, a maulvi, a Hindu priest and a parish priest, and released them in newspapers. They printed thousands of flyers with photographs of Shubha and Nero, and distributed them to drivers of autorickshaws and taxis, and to the traffic police. The trio (Sivarasan, Shubha and Nero) was believed to be travelling in autorickshaws.

Around that time, an anonymous call from the Bangalore airport shook everyone in the SIT. The caller said he was travelling on the Cochin–Madras flight via Bangalore and was sure that Sivarasan was his co-passenger. It was a stop-over flight, and the caller had got off at Bangalore, but Sivarasan had continued to Madras. Raju informed the Madras Police. Airport security swung into action and surrounded the flight as soon as it landed. The man suspected to be Sivarasan was quietly picked up and brought to Malligai, but he turned out to be the branch manager of a nationalized bank. There were similar anonymous calls one after another. The SIT and the police couldn't ignore even a single one of them. As a result, the SIT ended up catching criminals who were not known to the local police—be it a smuggler, a drug dealer, a forger of passports or a dealer of illicit foreign exchange. Such was the enormity of the case and its investigation that it started to take a toll on the officers.[3]

Ragothaman had lost considerable weight; Verma and Kanth had dark circles around their eyes from lack of sleep; some had started smoking more frequently. There was hardly any communication with their families. One day over lunch, Kaarthikeyan shared with his team that he had laid down a few conditions with Vijay Karan before accepting the assignment of heading the SIT. One of those was that he would visit his family in Hyderabad once a week. He had done that only twice on his way back from Delhi.

The SIT had taken Vicky and Raghu from the custody of the Coimbatore Police to Madras. Both belonged to the LTTE's political group and worked under Trichy Santhan, who was entrusted with the safety of Sivarasan and his escape from India. Kaarthikeyan knew Vicky and Guna had to be cracked soon to get to Trichy Santhan. The news of his arrest must have put the political group on high alert. Trichy Santhan could be anywhere between Trichy, Salem and Coimbatore, where wounded LTTE men underwent treatment in designated 'safe houses'. Vicky had also anticipated Sivarasan taking some steps on his own to escape, if not totally convinced with Trichy's plans. With Vicky, Raghu, Guna and Dixon gone, Trichy would have to look for the right replacement. Till then, he might be visiting hideouts to check on the wounded. Vicky revealed the frequency of the station that was used to communicate from Trichy's UHF wireless set. But neither the intelligence agencies nor the SIT could intercept any messages. It could be that there was no one to operate it, Guna felt.

Ragothaman's moles in the LTTE endorsed Vicky's prediction of Sivarasan making his own arrangements for escaping. Some reports suggested that he had asked for more AK-47 rifles and ammunition. Obviously, those were unconfirmed reports. Kaarthikeyan knew the only way to One-Eyed Jack was through Trichy. The only lead Vicky could give them was a sketchy description of a hideout in Thippasandra in Bangalore. He had an idea about the area. Ragothaman thought the boy's memory would not be failing him since he had visited the said house with cash for Trichy two weeks before his arrest. Vicky gave two more pieces of information—that Trichy used a blue AC Premier Padmini car and the political groups had a green Maruti Gypsy.

—ɷ—

On 31 July, Kaarthikeyan sent out two teams—one to Trichy to check the Mutharasanallur hideout and another to Bangalore, where Trichy Santhan could be cooling his heels if Vicky's admission was correct. As suspected, there was no sign of the wanted in the hideout in Trichy. However, it was loaded with medicines, empty grenade shells, grenades, splinters used in hand grenades and bombs, ammunition, explosives and two UHF wireless sets, all concealed in wooden boxes purported to be a shipment of fruits. A homoeopathy doctor owned the place. On questioning him, he denied any knowledge of what his tenants did. However, such replies had become standard from landlords if and when their tenants were caught indulging in unlawful activities or linked with the Tamil Tigers. He was taken to the police station for interrogation.

Sri Kumar was leading the team to Bangalore. Within hours they had identified the hideout based on Vicky's rough description. It was located in Bangalore's posh residential area, Indira Nagar. Inquiries made with the neighbours confirmed the occasional presence of a green Maruti Gypsy and a blue Premier Padmini car outside the house, in a clear indication of the political group operating from there. Trichy had been using those cars. The house was immediately put under round-the-clock surveillance. Sri Kumar made sure the team worked with extra caution. Even the slightest mistake could alert the suspects and they would bite the cyanide pill. There was no sign of life from the house. All its doors and windows were shut and no movement was noticed. After an entire day passed, suddenly there was light from inside, negating the SIT's initial apprehensions that everyone had fled.[4]

Sri Kumar asked Malligai for the tracking team, along with a doctor and cyanide antidote kits. The local police were also alerted. The SIT had no jurisdictional authority to raid a place. Taking the help and permission of the local police was a must in India's federal structure. The tracking team arrived in an MI-8 chopper within hours. A meeting was held between the NSG's Ravindran and Sri Kumar's team at the VIP lounge of the Bangalore airport.[5]

The NSG Black Cats were trained in close-combat warfare. They were trained in storming hideouts of terrorists and capturing them alive, or rescuing victims held hostage by terrorists. The SIT knew Sivarasan was armed with an AK-47 assault rifle and a 9-mm pistol. Just like the INT group, the political group also had its stock of cyanide capsules, and arms and explosives, as was evident from the recent raids in Coimbatore, Salem and Trichy. In addition, Suthenthiraraja and Vijayan had disclosed earlier during interrogation that one of the three—Sivarasan, Neru or Shubha—would always be awake and armed to counter any attack on their hideout.[6]

In the meeting, Sri Kumar shared a piece of intelligence to help the tracking team understand how alert their target could be. After shutting down Sivarasan's wireless set, Pottu Amman was sending him messages through Trichy and others. An insider from the LTTE had brought to the SIT's attention that Pottu Amman had warned Sivarasan of Indian security agencies using gas to catch him alive. The gas would make him numb and prevent him from reaching for the cyanide pill. Pottu Amman had underlined his instructions that, come what may, Sivarasan should never be caught alive. Swearing on Prabhakaran, Sivarasan had assured his boss that he was aware of the SIT tailing him like a 'dog' but that he would never allow a stigma to be attached to the LTTE on his account. Sri Kumar concluded the meeting saying, 'It's already late at night. Any movement outside the house will catch the inmates' attention. The element of surprise will be compromised. Let's strike tomorrow morning.' The meeting was over.

On the morning of 2 August, the tracking team led by Sri Kumar reached the location. The plan was for two innocuous officers in disguise to knock on the door of the house, pretending to be lost in the area, even as the Black Cats would take their positions. The two officers rang the bell. A side window opened for a moment and was almost immediately shut. Sri Kumar understood that the inmates were alert—maybe they had been alert since yesterday and hence the lights were kept switched off until night. He signalled to Ravindran to move. The commandos broke open the front and back entry points of the house. The scene inside was frightening. One boy was biting a cyanide capsule while another was rushing into a bathroom. A commando broke into the bathroom and gave cyanide antidote shots to the boys hiding inside. They were handed over to the local police. The boys were rushed to the hospital. However, neither could be saved for want of time.[7]

The commissioner of Bangalore Police was shocked to learn about how the LTTE was operating in his city. It was undoubtedly an intelligence failure on the part of his force as well as of the central agencies responsible for collecting domestic intelligence. One more time, One-Eyed Jack had shown a clean pair of heels to the SIT. There was a mixed feeling among the members of the tracking team. If, on the one hand, there was the increasing worry about how to stop the fugitives from biting the cyanide pills, on the other, the trackers had seen a silver lining too—Sivarasan and gang must have been in the city. And with that came the million-dollar question on everybody's mind—how did Sivarasan reach Bangalore, slipping past so many barricades, police pickets and a distance of about 350 km between Madras and Bangalore. His confidence must have escalated with every slip he gave to the security agencies, who he knew were desperately looking for him.

# 11

Vicky was the only member of the LTTE's political group who was in the SIT's custody. Ragothaman sat up with him in Madras and started digging for a fresh lead for the tracking team in Bangalore. Vicky started singing. The house in Indira Nagar was taken on rent by a married couple and LTTE activist K. Jagannathan and Sivapackiam in the third week of March, when Irumborai, Suresh Master's assistant, was planning to shift an injured cadre, Jamuna, from Neyveli to Bangalore. But nobody ever moved any injured cadre from one hideout to another unless there was approval from the top. In the second week of June, Irumborai visited the girls in Neyveli to see if Jamuna had her amputated leg replaced by an artificial one. She was barely seventeen years old and had lost her right leg in an ambush in the Jaffna fort earlier. She seemed fine with a perfect artificial leg. He told her to be ready to leave for a new hideout soon, where she would have to undergo physiotherapy. Hopefully she could return to Jaffna soon.[1]

When Irumborai returned to Madras and met Suresh Master to debrief him about the progress in Neyveli, the latter gave him unpleasant news. The CBI had got his photograph from a raid and was looking for him. He cautioned him not to venture out of the house and to wait for his instructions. In about three or four days, Suresh Master got back with a Maruti van. Accompanying him was Rangan, who would drive the van to Bangalore and take Irumborai with him.

Rangan was a Sri Lankan national who had joined the LTTE movement in 1983 and was trained in military drills. He proved his mettle in the war with the Sri Lankan army in 1984 and earned accolades from Prabhakaran. However, he was seriously injured in the war and was 'grounded', or removed from field operations. Prabhakaran gave him logistics to handle, and he was soon inducted into the political group. He had met Sivarasan during the war. Soon, he was shifted to India with the responsibility of transporting LTTE guerrillas from one hideout to another. He ran an unlicensed travel agency in India for that.[2]

Two injured boys were already present in Rangan's house. Irumborai was the new entrant. And then came Trichy Santhan at the end of June. He asked Irumborai to relocate Jamuna from Neyveli. And then he talked about Sivarasan, who had to be either shifted out of India in a boat or brought into that city by road. The Indian navy and the Indian Coast Guard were patrolling the sea route to Jaffna, so taking Sivarasan in a boat would be very risky. The other option he had in mind was trying the Naxalites from Andhra Pradesh. But Irumborai could not find a via media to approach the Naxalites.

Two days later, Trichy Santhan returned to Bangalore. He could not trust telephone communication, which was under the vigil of the Indian police. So he came physically to give the news of transporting Sivarasan, Shubha and Nero to the Indira Nagar house in the next two days. Therefore, Irumborai should be ready to receive them and take care of their needs, and whatever else Sivarasan asked for. On 28 June, Sivarasan came with Shubha, Nero, Rangan, Dhanasekaran and Vicky.

As Vicky narrated this, Ragothaman jumped hearing Vicky take his own name—he, in his deposition after his arrest in Coimbatore, had categorically denied having anything to do with Sivarasan in person. Ragothaman, instead of giving Vicky a piece of his mind for withholding crucial information, asked, 'How did you manage to pass through so many checkpoints and reach Bangalore without getting caught?'[3]

'We took Sivarasan in an oil tanker,' said Vicky, with a slightly smug smile on his face.

'Oil tanker? Whose oil tanker?'

'Dhanasekaran's oil tanker.'

'Who is Dhanasekaran?'

'He is in the transport business—DK Transporters. He owns lorries, buses.',

'DK? Is he a member of the political party DK?'

'I don't know. But he is an admirer of Prabhakaran. And he helps the LTTE with transport.'

Ragothaman quickly briefed Kaarthikeyan on the developments and information on Dhanasekaran and got back to Vicky. Kaarthikeyan immediately alerted the concerned people to find out everything they could on Dhanasekaran. Anyone entrusted with the responsibility of keeping Sivarasan safe must have been close to Prabhakaran.

Vicky resumed his story. The huge oil tanker that Dhanasekaran usually rented out to government-owned oil companies had picked up Sivarasan, Shubha and Nero from Kodungaiyur in Madras after midnight. The registration number of the vehicle was changed. Vicky remembered only the fake one—TAM 8998.

Adequate care was taken to avoid any suspicion. The oil storage gauge had shown 'full'. The air pressure in the tyres gave the tanker a heavy look. The three cylindrical interiors of the tanker were equipped with a mattress and pillows, a reading lamp, coffee, water, towels, snacks and analgesic medicines. Sivarasan had kept the AK-47 with him and given the 9-mm pistol to Shubha. Nero was without a weapon. He carried three duffel bags in his chamber. Dhanasekaran, Amman and Vicky had travelled in the front cabin while driver Selvaraj drove the tanker from Madras to Bangalore.[4]

Vicky could not tell Ragothaman whose idea it was to escape in a tanker. Vicky was to tap the wall between the driver's cabin and the chambers twice if the tanker was stopped by the police. That would be the signal for Sivarasan and Shubha to take combat positions. And if the police insisted on checking inside the tanker, Vicky would tap four times and the fugitives would open fire. All this was due to the unavailability of a boat under increased surveillance by the Indian navy. Travelling in a boat was impossible, but the tanker was not stopped and checked at a single check post over the seven-hour-long journey. It was just one more oil tanker entering Bangalore. Sivarasan, Shubha and Nero were delivered to the house in Domalur, a developing Bangalore suburb near Indira Nagar. It was not an easy or comfortable journey for the fugitives. From there, Vicky took them in a white Premier Padmini Fiat car to the house in Indira Nagar. The house was filled with over a dozen injured cadres. Trichy Santhan and Irumborai were already there.[5]

Ragothaman and Verma left for Bangalore soon after Vicky's interrogation was over. The next day, Jagannathan, a real estate broker who had been in touch with Rangan when the latter was looking for houses, was picked up with the help of the Bangalore Police. The SIT had reached his doorstep through the owner of the house in Indira Nagar. The investigators' priority was to go after the fugitives. Verma had asked Jagannathan to disclose the locations of other hideouts. He broke down during the interrogation and revealed the hideout at Domalur, close to Indira Nagar. The house was immediately placed under surveillance.[6]

Around ten at night, the silhouette of a man was spotted approaching the Domalur house. The area of late had seen a spate of burglaries. A small vigilance team had been formed and local residents sprung into action, suspecting it was a thief. But it turned out to be Miresh, a sixteen-year-old LTTE guerrilla who had come to the city for medical treatment. He was waiting to be sent back to Jaffna. Cornered and fearing police arrest, Miresh unsuccessfully tried to grab his cyanide capsule. The tracking team was around, watching the drama. Neither Verma nor Ragothaman had anticipated the sudden intervention of the locals. At the Domalur hideout, the entire tracking team realized how close it had been to catching Sivarasan. According to locals, Sivarasan, Shubha and Nero had all been in the house until the day before. They were there at Domalur when the tracking team was raiding the Indira Nagar hideout to catch them—only two kilometres away.[7]

---

Miresh told Verma and Ragothaman that Suresh Master had moved out the injured cadres from the Domalur house when the raid was under way at the other house in Indira Nagar. As a result, he and some others were spending the night on pavements, in parks and bus stands. Ragothaman extracted the details of the others but got nothing about their whereabouts. All the cadres had been told to fend for themselves. The local police were alerted, but not a single character was found from the list.

Miresh had also talked about three female LTTE cadres in the Indira Nagar house while about six male cadres were being treated at a local nursing home. Acting on the sketchy description of the facility, the local police launched a series of raids. But everyone from the Indira Nagar house had vanished.

Kulathan and Arsalan were the only injured cadres who had come to Tamil Nadu for medical treatment. Why did they die by suicide? Miresh and senior activist Jagannathan, who were in custody, estimated that Trichy Santhan had given clear instructions to everyone to not get caught alive. They had to bite the cyanide capsule in the event of a police raid and that they should never forget the sacrifice Dhanu had made to make Prabhakaran's mission a success. They must follow suit. But the LTTE boys who were looking for a cover in the city could not have revealed much to the SIT even if they were captured alive, except that Sivarasan, Shubha and Nero were part of the LTTE and that they had been shifted to the nearby Domalur hideout from the Coimbatore hideout, where Dixon and Guna had died by suicide on 28 July. The LTTE's involvement in the assassination would have been established beyond any doubt, which is why Trichy Santhan's order to bite the cyanide pills.[8]

The tracking team was back to square one with no further leads. All it was left with was that the LTTE cadres were still around and getting medical treatment at various hideouts. The state police of Karnataka had sealed the borders with Tamil Nadu and a large number of police check posts were set up on the periphery of Bangalore. But One-Eyed Jack was getting more and more alert with every failed attempt by the SIT to catch him. The question, therefore, in the minds of every member of the tracking team was: Would Sivarasan continue to avail shelter provided by Trichy Santhan and his assistant Suresh Master? Most likely not. Nevertheless, Sri Kumar asked the Bangalore Police to discreetly check any new Tamil arrivals. He also shared the details of the two cars used by Santhan's group—the blue Premier Padmini Fiat and the green Maruti Gypsy that Sivarasan was using.[9]

Sri Kumar, Verma, Ragothaman and Ravindran got back to the drawing board and reviewed where they had gone wrong in the Indira Nagar operation. Everyone had felt that a 'swift operation' would be their best bet at capturing the LTTE operatives alive. They had a doctor in the team, along with an antidote for cyanide. Despite that, they had failed to catch the targets alive. Was it because of a flawed approach or the strong determination of the LTTE cadres to not be caught alive? Nobody had an answer to that. The LTTE was not in their control, and their dedication to the organization was above board. So if any course correction had to be done, it had to be in the SIT's approach.

Verma and Ragothaman resumed further interrogation of those in custody. Miresh, who had been caught two days ago, revealed that Suresh Master was in troubled waters. The LTTE had rented two houses in Bangalore to keep the injured cadres. One was at Indira Nagar and the other at Domalur (near Indira Nagar). Their attempts to acquire a third hideout through their Bangalore supporters had not been successful. Very few landlords were ready to rent out their houses to young Tamils without police verification, just like the situation in Tamil Nadu after the assassination. Sri Lankan Tamils were suspected in general in most parts of southern India. The news of the commando operation at Indira Nagar had made Suresh Master desperate to find new hideouts for Sivarasan.

Tamil sympathizer Ranganath, a small-time lathe machine operator in Bangalore, was also a desperate man, as his business had failed. He needed money. A local Tamil activist, who was negotiating with Ranganath to purchase his lathe machine workshop, had introduced him to Suresh Master. Ranganath lived in a friend's house in Puttenahalli. The two had worked out a deal.

Suresh Master would arrange finances and bail him out of his crisis. In turn, Ranganath would give shelter to some 'friends' in his house—friends who were 'injured'. Suresh Master would move them out as soon as he had found suitable accommodation. A few hours later, past midnight, Trichy Santhan's green Maruti Gypsy had arrived outside the house where Ranganath was staying. Sivarasan, along with Shubha, Nero, Suresh Master, Amman (Trichy Santhan's wireless operator) and Rangan (who was helping Trichy Santhan arrange transport for shifting injured cadres from hospital to hospital), got out of the Gypsy and sneaked into their new hideout.[10]

Ranganath's entry into the scene turned out to be an obstacle for the SIT. He was not a regular member of the LTTE and didn't figure in any record of either the intelligence bureau or the Bangalore Police. Tracking Suresh Master through him, therefore, was not possible. The trail the SIT was following had snapped, giving Sivarasan enough time to plan his next move. And Ranganath had no clue about the real identity of Suresh Master's 'injured friends'. He had only let his house be used in an attempt to wriggle out of his financial issues.[11]

Suresh Master had kept the carrot dangling in front of Ranganath by offering him more financial help against new accommodations. Suresh Master knew the situation was becoming hot for him and could not risk going around looking for a new house. Ranganath helped him for money. The Tamil activist secured another house in Anekal. Suresh Master found it crowded, so he suggested that Ranganath continue his search. He found two new places within two days—at Biroota and Muthati in Madya district. Ranganath understood that Suresh Master's 'injured friends' were LTTE cadres who had sustained injuries in Jaffna. Their interactions had made it easy for Ranganath. He also understood that the rest were none other than the assassins of Rajiv Gandhi. Identifying Sivarasan or

Shubha was no rocket science in those days. He knew he would face questions from the landlords about the identity of so many injured people. He had to make up a story. He told the landlords the houses required were for shooting a film. Those who would stay in the house were 'film extras', Ranganath added.[12]

But even though Ranganath tried to stay cool about giving shelter to Rajiv Gandhi's killers, his wife Mridula could not. She was terrified about the consequences but didn't know how to defy her husband when he was getting paid for it. Suresh Master would use the couple as much as he could, from shifting the injured from nursing homes to the rented houses and shifting them between the houses to shopping for Sivarasan's daily requirements. They were Bangaloreans, and hence no one suspected them and believed their film-shooting story. Their presence lent credibility to the fugitives and the injured cadres, some of whom were undergoing treatment at Kalappa Nursing Home.

---

Meanwhile, Vicky was questioned again. He spoke about a personal wireless set that Sivarasan owned, which he had not destroyed and carried along with his personal belongings. Trichy Santhan had taken it away after the fugitives were brought under his care by Amman. Trichy's personal wireless set was destroyed by Dixon just before he and Guna died by suicide in Coimbatore. All code sheets had been destroyed too, leaving Trichy with neither a code sheet nor an operator. He had one injured LTTE boy, though—Vardhan—who had some basic knowledge in operating a wireless set. Trichy had asked the boy to take the set to an empty, quiet place and try to contact Jaffna. He had categorically warned Vardhan against using it in the house, as it would affect TV transmission, which would alert the police. Vicky's revelation was shared with the Trichy Police immediately.[13]

Luckily for the Trichy Police, Vardhan didn't heed Trichy's note of caution and used the wireless set in the house. The police intercepted the transmission and raided the house. They caught Vardhan and a girl, Sumathi. Once there, it was easy to find Sivarasan's wireless set along with records of LTTE militants belonging to the political group who were under the control of Trichy. The records revealed their real names, cadre names, addresses and details of family members. The only Indian to figure on the list was Irumborai. The loss of the wireless set left Trichy helpless as he was cut off from Jaffna.

Sri Kumar believed the fugitives were still in Bangalore. But the possibility of their getting caught alive was increasingly doubtful. His experience from the last raid was that the cyanide antidote had prolonged the time, but eventually the two boys, Kulathan and Arsalan, from the Indira Nagar house had died before they could be treated. And it was horrific to watch them die—it was not a painless death, as is often thought. Their bodies had started to convulse and their mouths had filled with saliva mixed with blood and vomit. And then they had passed out. The antidote might have earned them maybe thirty minutes more of life, but that was it. They were declared brought dead at the hospital. A similar situation might arise with Sivarasan and gang too.

While the tracking team was struggling to catch Sivarasan, Manoharan of the Tamil Nadu Police was busy studying old cases of the LTTE at Malligai. He discovered some DK activists in Tamil Nadu who were very close to the LTTE's political group. He shortlisted them and approached one of them for a sting operation. The man's background showed his full involvement in helping the LTTE's political group. But there was nothing to indicate his link with the INT group in Tamil Nadu. His interrogation after the sting operation revealed his links with Trichy Santhan. He was shocked to see Manoharan on his doorstep. The DIG made his intentions clear—he told the DK activist that the SIT wanted to catch Sivarasan 'alive' and wanted to talk to Trichy about it. Would he be able to convince Trichy? But he was only an activist and not a well-trained cadre or terrorist. He could not take pressure from the investigators and the round-the-clock surveillance on him and his family. He gave in.

The DK was essentially a social movement aimed at promoting a casteless society for the Tamils. The DK had actively and openly supported the Sri Lankan Tamils in their violent struggle against the Sri Lankan army. Even though there were two groups in the DK—the main group led by K. Veeramani and a splinter group led by Ramakrishnan—both had accepted the LTTE as the only representative of the Sri Lankan Tamils.

—∾—

Feeling the heat, Suresh Master had got both the cars—the green Maruti Gypsy and the blue Premier Padmini Fiat—repainted in white. He knew the SIT must have come to know about the vehicles and therefore would be looking for those colours and models. The registration plates of the cars were frequently changed. Using Ranganath's connections, Suresh Master had another house rented in Bangalore's Konanakunte. A drama took place when Suresh Master wanted to shift Sivarasan, Shubha, Nero, Amman, Jamuna and others to the new house. Sivarasan insisted that Ranganath and his wife Mridula shift with them. He had acted in a similar fashion with Vijayan and Selvaluxmi in the Kodungaiyur hideout earlier in Madras, as he didn't trust anyone beyond a point. Ranganath didn't like Sivarasan's suspicious attitude. To reiterate his loyalty, Ranganath claimed that he could have got more than fifteen lakh rupees in reward by handing him over to the SIT, but he didn't, despite the severe financial crisis he was going through. Sivarasan had raised his gun on him and asked what the guarantee was that he wouldn't do so in future. An unruffled Ranganath had simply produced a cyanide capsule from his pocket and said that he always carried it with him and that his loyalty need not be questioned. Sivarasan was impressed.

Following the raid on the Indira Nagar house and the subsequent death of the two LTTE cadres from cyanide pills, people in Karnataka had become watchful. The residents of Muthati, where Ranganath had rented a house for 'film-shooting', had become suspicious of the injured boys in the house. They started doubting if they were film extras at all. Some of them called up the police. But repeating the same mistake that the Coimbatore Police had made in their overenthusiasm in trying to catch Dixon and Guna, the Bangalore Police, too, didn't inform the tracking team before going to raid the houses in Muthati and Biroota. There were nine boys in the Muthati house and eight in Biroota. Of them, twelve bit their cyanide capsules and died while the remaining were hospitalized. The Bangalore Police did not have cyanide antidotes or a doctor and had never dealt with a case of mass suicide. They were clueless. Most of the raiding policemen could not bear the ghastly sight of the young boys convulsing from acute pain and vomiting blood and had to rush out of the house, leaving the boys to their fate.[14]

—ꟿ—

Nobody in the SIT could understand what the hurry was in raiding the house without informing the tracking team. The tracking team arrived in Muthati and Biroota just as the boys were dying. No administration of an antidote helped. The team also did not find anything significant, but the police had traced the address of Ranganath's house. His antecedents were still unclear—the only thing they knew was that it was he who had taken the house on rent. Instead of going to that address and catching Ranganath, the police passed on the address to the office of the director general of police, Karnataka.

The next morning all newspapers had carried news of the raid and suicides on their front pages, and questions were again raised about the efficiency of the SIT. But of the three arrested from the raid, Dhanasekaran was a prized catch. Even though there was still no sign of Sivarasan, Dhanasekaran admitted that the mastermind had travelled to Bangalore in his oil tanker.

Ranganath had gone to buy milk for his guests in Konanakunte. The newspapers on display in the stall caught his attention. He bought copies and showed them to Sivarasan. Tension was writ large on all their faces; Sivarasan looked desperate. He said, 'The dogs of the CBI are everywhere. They will come here too.' Then he turned to look at Ranganath, as if expecting an answer from him. Mridula suddenly had an attack of asthma and fell to the floor, but she gathered herself and wanted to go out of the house for some fresh air. But Sivarasan blocked her way and threatened her. She didn't care. Everyone was shocked at her guts. Ranganath swung into action. He pleaded with Sivarasan not to get angry. He said he would take his wife to a doctor and come back with her soon.

It was clear to Ranganath that the police would be reaching his house in Putanahally soon. The first thing he checked with his wife was if she had been feigning the asthma attack in front of Sivarasan. He had to plan his next moves accordingly—whether to take her to a doctor or head home. Mridula wanted to go back home. The couple rushed home, picked up their essentials, hired a Matador van from a neighbour and went to Mridula's brother's house in the Shanthi Oliver Church campus, where he was the pastor.[15]

The situation was now a ticking time bomb. The DGP's office had passed on Ranganath's address to the commissioner of police in Bangalore. The city police had reached Ranganath's house in Putanahally. Apparently, his landlord, E. Anjanappa, had gone there to find out if what he had heard was true—that his tenant had sublet the house to Sri Lankans. But Ranganath had left minutes ago. Anjanappa heard about the Matador. Seeing the police at his doorstep, the landlord gave the police the details of the vehicle from his neighbour. The police stayed put for the Matador van to return.[16]

The driver was back in the afternoon. By evening the police had picked up Mridula from her brother's house and taken her to Jaya Nagar police station in Bangalore. When asked about her husband Ranganath, she said she would speak to the commissioner of police, Bangalore, and no one else. Shortly, the DCP Crime of Bangalore arrived, posing as the commissioner of police. To that Mridula reiterated that she had asked for the commissioner of police and no one else. Shortly, B.P. Ramalingam, the commissioner of police, arrived at the Jaya Nagar police station. By the late evening of 18 August, Mridula began describing her experiences of the past sixteen days with Rajiv Gandhi's killers to a stunned city police.[17]

# 12

Mridula used to teach English at a primary school. Having lost that job six months ago, she had been offering home tuitions. Both she and Ranganath struggled to make ends meet. On the night of 2 August, Ranganath returned with Suresh Master. The latter had been told to accommodate a few more persons in the house for four days. He would move them to a new place after that. It was only a stop-gap arrangement.

Suresh Master had posed the question directly to Mridula and she was still struggling to come up with an answer when Ranganath suddenly took Suresh Master outside. While leaving the room, he signalled to her about more money coming in if there were more guests to accommodate. Within minutes, both were back with four more people—Amman, Sivarasan, Rangan and Driver Anna. Around the same time, two persons entered the house through the back door. They were Shubha and Nero. However, Mridula clarified to the police that she had no clue about their identity at that point of time. She watched the development without a word. She felt Sivarasan had sensed that she was not happy about the arrival of the new guests. She said she and Ranganath could not sleep that night.[1]

Next morning, when she went out to collect milk from the regular vendor, she noticed a green Maruti Gypsy parked in front of her house, partially covered in tarpaulin. Ranganath, Suresh Master and Rangan left after having coffee. Rangan and Suresh Master returned in the afternoon with bags full of groceries. That night, when her husband returned, Mridula said she sensed something fishy about the guests. 'Why are these people so hesitant to go out?' she asked Ranganath. 'Just ignore these things. They are here just for three or four days. After that they will leave.'

After four days, Mridula received the biggest shock of her life. Photographs of Sivarasan and Shubha were broadcast on television news. And it happened while Shubha was sitting a yard away from Mridula. Shubha didn't react. She watched Mridula's reaction for a while and left the room. Mridula could not wait for her husband to return. She took it up with Ranganath the moment he came home. Ranganath advised her not to raise the subject again, with the assurance that they would leave soon. Mridula reminded him of Suresh Master asking them for four days only and that those four days would be over that night. Ranganath had no reply to offer. However, Shubha tried to make it easier for Mridula. She spoke to her about her life and how eager she was to return to Jaffna and meet her supreme leader Prabhakaran to express gratitude.[2]

Mridula was uncomfortable with the developments. But she was gathering confidence to be able to deal with the situation. One evening, Sivarasan was cleaning his false eye when Mridula asked him why they killed Rajiv Gandhi. Shubha immediately chipped in with the stock reply that all assassins gave—Rajiv Gandhi was responsible for sending the IPKF to Sri Lanka and therefore responsible for all the atrocities the force had heaped upon innocent people, including women and children. But Sivarasan replied to Mridula. He asked her if she was satisfied with Shubha's answer. Mridula was not, but she didn't dare say that to the world's most-wanted fugitive at that point. She tried to change the subject to the cyanide capsule that hung around Shubha's neck. Mridula asked her if the capsule really did carry cyanide. Shubha's reply came attached with a sense of pride. She said it indeed did and that she would be proud to take it if the need arose. Mridula was stunned. Perhaps Sivarasan wanted the conversation to end there. He told Mridula quietly not to mention any of this to anyone outside, or the consequences would be fatal for her and her husband.[3]

On 16 August, Ranganath told Mridula that he had fixed a new house in Konanakunte for the group and that they would be leaving. But Ranganath and Mridula had to first go and set up the new house with 'provisions, drinking water, a gas cylinder and stove and toiletries' and then perform a puja for their well-being. Mridula prayed at the puja for a quick end to their ordeal. That night, when the group was leaving for Konanakunte, Mridula saw Nero carrying the AK-47 rifle and Shubha a pistol. She couldn't help herself when she asked them why they still needed weapons when their mission of killing Rajiv Gandhi had already been achieved. None of the assassins were expecting such a question from her—she almost sounded like a cop. Nero lost his cool. He advised Mridula to keep her mouth shut, or she knew what the consequence would be—death. All of them left at 10.30 p.m. Ranganath, Mridula, Sivarasan, Suresh Master, Shubha, Nero, Driver Anna and Amman left in the Maruti Gypsy. Nine people fitting into one Gypsy was difficult and Mridula said she had put her foot down by refusing to go with them. But Suresh Master and

Nero forced her into the vehicle. Mridula said she was praying for an end to her situation all through the journey.[4]

On the morning of 18 August, Mridula came across sketches of KRS Dam and Vidhan Soudha, the state legislature building of Karnataka. Were they planning to bomb those places? She could not help asking them about it. Shubha tried to give her an answer but Mridula was not convinced. At that point, Shubha came down hard on her—either Mridula stopped asking questions, or she faced the consequences. But Mridula didn't stop there. She asked Shubha what she meant by 'consequences', as she had been hearing it from their mouths time and again. Shubha didn't react. She just smiled and left the room. Suddenly a newspaper lying around caught Mridula's attention. It carried the news of twelve LTTE cadres taking cyanide capsules in Muthati during a police raid. That day, Mridula and Ranganath had a series of arguments. She insisted that they leave the house as the situation was becoming dangerous. The police might be coming to their doorstep at any moment. But none of the fugitives liked the idea of Ranganath leaving. It was at that point that Mridula had an asthma attack. She did not fake it. But instead of going to the doctor, she decided to go back to her house in Putanahally.

A neighbour from Putanahally had helped them get a Matador van to carry their stuff. They had gone straight to Mridula's brother's house in the Shanthi Oliver Church campus. On the way, Ranganath had got off to make a phone call and told Mridula to continue on her journey—he would meet her later. Around 4.30 p.m. the next day, Mridula was taking a few saris to a nearby laundry shop when she was stopped by some men and told to accompany them to Jaya Nagar police station.

Until that morning of Mridula's confession, the Bangalore Police were not even sure if the most-wanted Sivarasan was hiding in their city. And here they were, hearing Sivarasan's story from someone who, till one day back, had shared a house with him and his gang of assassins. The commissioner of police asked Mridula if she could show them the house. Mridula said yes, provided the police gave her protection. The DCP Crime, an ACP and a female constable accompanied her in a private car to Konankunte.[5]

Again, the Bangalore Police had not yet informed the tracking team about Mridula being in their custody. The matter reached the SIT's ears through some friends in the IB. Sri Kumar and Verma rushed to the Jaya Nagar police station, where they were given second-hand information, since Mridula was not there. The SIT had lost Rangan's track in Trichy, but it had learnt from the police that according to Mridula, Rangan was in Bangalore and had been driving them around in a green Maruti Gypsy. The tracking team realized they would have to move on their own. Waiting for the local police to be proactive was wishful thinking. Verma and Ragothaman wanted to take up the matter of 'non-cooperation of the Bangalore Police' with the higher authorities but was placated by Sri Kumar. Rubbing a single officer in the Bangalore Police the wrong way could be catastrophic at this point in their investigation.

Accompanying the DCP Crime in a private car, Mridula explained that the front of the Konanakunte house faced the rear area of a neighbour's house, separated by a few yards. From one of the bathrooms of the neighbour's house, one could peep into the Konanakunte house and watch the movements of the assassin gang. The DCP, by then, had mounted a watch on the Konanakunte house from the neighbour's bathroom. He had also brought a few men and officers for assistance. Their vehicles were parked on the road, behind the neighbour's house, hidden from view by a row of houses. From inside the hideout, these vehicles could not be seen. But anyone coming to the hideout could clearly see the vehicles. And that's what happened. Driver Rangan had gone out and spotted the police vehicles on his return. He fled the scene immediately. At that time, the tracking team was still waiting at the Bangalore office of the CBI. Despite knowing Ranganath's factory address, they could not make any move, since it was a Sunday and the factory was closed. Sri Kumar, Verma and Ragothaman had no clue about the developments in Konanakunte following Mridula's disclosure before the city's police commissioner. The DCP had no instructions from the top about taking the tracking team along.

—w—

After listening to Ragothaman's interaction with Mridula at her parents' house, Sri Kumar's take was that Sivarasan would soon feel helpless and desperate. Neither Ranganath nor Mridula had returned to the Konankunte hideout. Rangan, too, had gone missing. It would have checked Sivarasan's movements—Rangan had the Gypsy with him, and the Premier Padmini Fiat had gone to the workshop. Sri Kumar asked Verma and Ragothaman to do a recce of the area and get back soon. But reaching Konankunte did not lift their spirits. They saw that the hideout was surrounded by police vehicles and uniformed men. It was clear that the element of surprise had again been lost to the tracking team.

Anirudhya had reached Bangalore on the morning of 19 August. Verma had told him to head for Konanakunte straight from the airport, although no exact directions to the hideout were available. Verma could not speak for more than ten seconds on the phone. The private taxi brought Anirudhya to Konanakunte. It was a southern suburb of Bangalore. After about two hours of driving, the taxi stopped at the JP Nagar bus terminus, and the driver, Gopal, sought directions to Konanakunte from a tea-stall owner. Anirudhya wanted a cup of tea but time was short. Gopal made it easy for him—he brought out a thermos from his car and filled it with tea so that his customer could have it on the way and not lose any time.

Back in the car, Gopal asked if something had happened in Konanakunte. Apparently, while buying tea, he had heard bystanders talk about fire engines and police vans rushing to Konanakunte. Anirudhya, too, had noticed a fire engine heading in the same direction as his taxi. They followed the speeding fire engine into a dusty, bumpy road and then to a poor locality with thatched-roof houses and many under-construction structures. The vast, barren spaces between the houses were punctuated with stray cattle, storage areas for paddy and heaps of cow dung. It didn't take long, though, for the scene to change dramatically the moment the taxi came close to the house under the scanner.

Policemen were everywhere—on rooftops and various strategic positions. Everyone's gaze was fixed on a light-yellow house stained with rainwater marks. Everyone present there, from cop to peanut seller to children playing in the streets, knew the mastermind of Rajiv Gandhi's assassination and his gang were holed up there.

Anirudhya quickly tore a blank page off his notepad, scribbled 'PRESS' on it and pasted it on the windscreen of the taxi. The cops did not stop his taxi, but when asked what was going on, didn't say anything wither, simply waving the car on. Anirudhya was wondering if his Bangalore bureau chief Saritha Rai would be there. She had filed her copies independently to Delhi even as the news desk of *India Today* kept updating its next big story. Nevertheless, for Anirudhya it was more important to find a contact or a source than a colleague.

Senior members of the SIT had started reaching Bangalore. It looked like the time for the grand finale had come. But the SIT's primary concern was the complete lack of cooperation from the local police. The question of catching Sivarasan alive had been discussed over and over again within the SIT. The chase was being led by the tracking team. However, they could not raid the hideouts or catch the assassins without the permission of the local police. The NSG's Black Cat commandos were an integral part of the tracking team. The situation at Konanakunte was ideal for their skill sets and expertise. The incident during the Indira Nagar operation, when the LTTE cadres had bitten their cyanide capsules, was enough to suggest that Sivarasan and gang would do the same.

In fact, Captain Ravindran of the NSG had asked Vijay Karan whether he had the authority to act the moment they tracked down the fugitives. The idea was to figure out a way to bypass the local police. Tracking teams can usually take calls on their own and do not need the approval of the top bosses, but in the case of the Rajiv Gandhi assassination, there had been several lapses and failures in catching the fugitives, which had resulted in a lot of criticism in the media and in Parliament. Naturally, it had been demoralizing to the team. Karan's reply was that if the choice was between 'One-Eyed Jack killed' and 'One-Eyed Jack escaping', he would opt for the latter as it would give them another chance to catch Sivarasan alive. The top cop's response brought the officers no satisfaction.

The tracking team had only a section of the Black Cats available in Konanakunte. But within a couple of hours, the rest of the NSG team had assembled in Bangalore and was on operational alert. The commissioner of police, DCP Crime, Sri Kumar, Verma, Ravindran and Ragothaman sat together and went through all the options available to them. They admitted that the element of surprise had been lost. Nevertheless, whatever little chance they had of catching at least some of them alive and seizing at least some documents or records intact lay in a quick operation.

The Black Cats, in a separate conversation, told Ravindran to keep the police away, so they could enter through the windows with the cyanide antidote kits, and if Sivarasan did bite his cyanide capsule, treat him without losing more than ten to thirty seconds, depending on how far Sivarasan was from the window. They felt that Sivarasan would never reach for his cyanide capsule until he had seen the commandos barge into the house. The last thing a mastermind like him would want was to die by suicide. The commandos looked really charged, and that, in turn, raised the SIT officers' hope of catching Sivarasan alive.[6]

Kaarthikeyan was in Hyderabad. Around midnight Sri Kumar telephoned him and briefed him on the situation in Bangalore. Kaarthikeyan felt there was no point in wasting any more time—they should strike immediately. He, however, added with a note of caution that the CBI director should be consulted before the strike. Vijay Karan was in Delhi at that time. Verma called him at 1 a.m. He clearly stated that the tracking team had to wait till his arrival in Bangalore. He did not think there was any chance of catching Sivarasan alive, even if the raid was conducted right away. Verma, who used to report to Karan in the CBI, tried to convince him about the urgency of the situation, but to no avail.[7]

There was no way the fugitives could be driven out of the house. Their hideouts were always well stocked with food and water that could see them through weeks. They had kept all the doors and windows closed. If Rangan had returned to their hideout in the evening, there was a small chance that they might have made an attempt to escape. But by then, the city police had surrounded the house. While it looked like the tracking team was about the strike, the order was to wait. The commissioner of police, Ramalingam, did not agree with the instant raid. He felt it would lead to massive casualties among his men, thanks to the AK-47 rifles and 9-mm pistols the fugitives were carrying. Also, he would not move without a green signal from Delhi. Earlier he had said that the tracking team had no jurisdictional authority and had to cooperate with the Bangalore Police for the strike. Now he said he needed orders from the higher-ups in Delhi. The tracking team felt helpless. No one was even allowing them to try and catch Sivarasan alive.[8]

The plan chalked out by the Black Cats appeared promising, but they, too, could not do anything without their seniors' nod. And there were too many seniors calling the shots—including Vijay Karan from Delhi and Kaarthikeyan from Hyderabad. Kaarthikeyan was home at that critical phase of the chase. Then there was the commissioner of the Bangalore Police and Radhavinod Raju from Malligai.

The night-long vigil continued till the next day. The presence of policemen and their vehicles surrounding the house drew the attention of the locals. People started crowding the area. Managing them required a full-fledged police team. But no one was willing to miss the drama. Word went around that Rajiv Gandhi's killers had been traced. Despite requests, the DCP Traffic refused to cordon off the area and keep traffic at bay. The tracking team could not understand how an operation of that magnitude was possible with such immense public presence. In the meantime, Kaarthikeyan arrived from Hyderabad around 10 a.m. and went into a closed-door meeting with the commissioner of police, Bangalore.[9]

Ranganath came to know about Mridula's police detention from his brother-in-law. He did not know where she was. Also, he suspected police presence around where she was being kept. Going there would not be safe. He had spent the night at a local lodge. In the morning he had gone back to Konanakunte. Even as he was getting off the autorickshaw, the milk-delivery woman had recognized him as the man who had taken the house on rent.

Ranganath had tried to run away. The crowd that had gathered to watch the drama caught him and handed him over to the police. Verma and Ragothaman were frustrated and angry at this bungling by the local police. It had to be a quiet operation, but the hideout was swarming with police in uniform, thereby alerting Sivarasan about the operation. But they held in their anger, knowing that any outburst at that stage would only add fuel to the fire.

Vijay Karan finally arrived, along with a cyanide expert, Dr Ramachari, around 4 p.m. The doctor immediately suggested that the SIT collect another set of cyanide antidote kits from Gwalior as the existing ones had reached their expiry date. Arrangements were made to do so, even though it would delay the raid by many more hours. Ravindran refused to agree with the doctor. He asserted that the antidotes remained effective until about fourteen days after the official date of expiry. Any further delay would take away from them even the iota of chance they had to catch Sivarasan alive. He got into an argument with the doctor but was stopped by Karan, who made it clear that the NSG had to wait until the fresh stocks arrived. Ravindran could not understand the need for these fresh stocks if the CBI director was so convinced that they would not catch Sivarasan alive. Verma joined in and asked Karan if the NSG could try their 'thirty-second' storming plan. But the bosses remained staunch on their decision. Strangely, Kaarthikeyan was not around while his junior kept pleading for permission to catch Sivarasan alive.[10]

Meanwhile, the tracking team and the Bangalore Police were engaged in examining options other than storming the house, which would invariably provoke Sivarasan and gang to bite the cyanide capsules. Sending a milk vendor or Mridula as a decoy was considered and immediately rejected—the fugitives were already on alert after Ranganath, Mridula and Rangan's disappearance. Another option was adding sedatives to the water supply.

But maybe they would have water stored in the refrigerator and not drink from the water supply. So this idea was dropped too. The only feasible option was to storm the house. The Black Cats were asking for fifteen to thirty seconds, within which they said they would capture Sivarasan and administer the antidote shots to him. The fugitive could then be transferred in their MI-8 helicopter to the nearest hospital. The plan was presented before the commissioner of police. He said there was no permission to allow helicopters to fly in the area—it would be a violation of the state's Low Flying Annoyance Act. Ravindran tried to intervene. 'Sir, we never had to take permission for a rescue act by a helicopter in an emergency situation,' he said. But the commissioner just gave him a polite smile in reply.

Sri Kumar suggested that the local police could alert the nearby hospitals to get ready for treating 'cyanide-poisoning patients' and also keep the road to the hospitals cleared of traffic. But nothing was done. Most of the police officers felt that Sivarasan would take the lives of many in their force before choosing to die by suicide. To that, Ravindran made a promise—his team alone would handle the operation and the Bangalore Police personnel need not come close to the hideout. The Black Cats were dying to give the plan a shot. Commissioner of Police Ramalingam intervened again and asked Ravindran to wait till further orders, and left the room. The DCP Crime, on a personal note, apologized to Ravindran—he could not overrule the 'bosses', he said.

The entire day passed without any action. But suddenly a log-laden lorry broke down on a muddy patch about fifty metres from Sivarasan's hideout. The truck driver and an assistant got down to fix the problem. But Sivarasan mistook that as part of the police operation and opened fire. The neighbour's bathroom, from where policemen were watching, was sprayed with AK-47 bullets. The police and the NSG commandos returned fire.

In exchange, a commando and a police officer sustained grievous bullet injuries. They were rushed to the hospital. The firing stopped after thirty minutes.

The truck incident had sparked a shootout even as whatever semblance of order was left crumbled. And with the news of the firing spreading from the wireless sets in the Jaya Nagar police station, there was panic at the top. Kaarthikeyan was heard screaming on the wireless, 'Where is Captain Ravi? Where is he?' The site of action turned even more chaotic. Floodlights were switched on, paramedics arrived at the door of the house, fire engines switched on their ignitions and the public address system told the entire Bangalore police force to be on standby. A team from Doordarshan was also recording the action live. A loud gunshot was heard. The NSG thought that the fugitive had again started firing from his AK-47—but it was the sound of Sivarasan shooting himself in the head. Kaarthikeyan came out with a statement for the press even before Sivarasan's body could be officially inspected. He said, 'The SIT was criticized for being too rash during the Indira Nagar raids. So we decided to wait and do our best to catch Sivarasan alive.' The best, unfortunately, was far from good enough.[11]

The fresh cyanide antidotes arrived the next morning around 5 a.m. No one understood what took fourteen hours for the kits to travel from Gwalior to Bangalore, despite having special planes and helicopters to do the job. At 6 a.m., the NSG finally raided the house. All seven fugitives—Sivarasan, Shubha, Driver Anna, Jamuna, Nero, Amman and Suresh Master—were found dead inside.

Sivarasan had a bullet wound on his temple. The rest had bitten cyanide capsules on a day that happened to be Rajiv Gandhi's birthday. It was a botched-up operation. Too many cooks had spoilt the broth, yet so many security officials were jostling for media attention, trying to take credit for the operation. But for those officers who genuinely tried to catch Sivarasan alive, it was salt rubbed on their wounds, for they could not see any victory in the spectacle that was created due to the complete lack of coordination between the various agencies.[12]

Naturally there were excuses galore that had come from the officers. While Vijay Karan avoided the press, Kaarthikeyan was at his diplomatic best. For him, 'it was next to impossible to catch Sivarasan and Shubha alive', although he was in agreement with the officers who wanted to storm the hideout at Konanakunte on 18 August, when Mridula had informed the police about Sivarasan's presence in the house. Saritha Rai from *India Today*'s Bangalore bureau and Anirudhya went on to write that the 'SIT, the Bangalore police and the think tanks of the operation representing various agencies had slipped on a banana peel while at a shouting distance of Rajiv Gandhi's assassin'. When Anirudhya asked Ramalingam why his force could not conduct the operation without drawing the attention of the public, and particularly the fugitives, he had no answer except 'we did our best'. But Anirudhya had heard that Ramalingam wanted to raid the hideout soon after he got wind of Sivarasan's whereabouts on the afternoon of 18 August. But he had got cold feet after hearing from Mridula that Sivarasan carried an assault rifle. He had feared a violent retaliation from the fugitive. So the commissioner had played safe. He had left it to the CBI to decide when to raid the house. Anirudhya chased the commissioner for the next hour, trying to get a comment. He finally came up with one: 'All members of the tracking team knew catching Sivarasan alive would be impossible. The fugitives would have taken the cyanide in any case. Therefore, we acted as per the demand of the situation.'[13]

What was even more intriguing was that neither the CBI nor the Bangalore Police gave the NSG Black Cats a chance to execute their plan of storming the house and catching Sivarasan alive. All in thirty seconds maximum. In any case, neither the local police nor any member of the SIT or the CBI was to physically raid the hideout. It was for the NSG to break into. But the Black Cats were never given the green signal even though they waited for thirty-six long hours. After the bodies had been taken out, the SIT looked for whatever evidence was left behind. One was a sheet of paper from Sivarasan—it was a poem in Tamil in the mastermind's own handwriting, where he had glorified Prabhakaran and the flag of liberation (Eelam) while urging the Tamils of the world to wake up and strengthen the leader's fight to win freedom. None of the investigators ever had any doubt about Sivarasan's loyalty and dedication to the cause of the Tamil movement. And he had fought until his last breath for it.[14]

For Anirudhya, an end like that was a setback. Not that he had expected to get an opportunity to interview Sivarasan in person after his arrest, but, as a reporter who had been with the sleuths all through the investigation, such a concluding chapter was a bit of an anticlimax. Later at night, over a drink, Verma had tried to cheer him up. 'This is just the beginning of unfolding the larger conspiracy. The big players of the drama will now be unmasked.' In fact, for some of the officers, the deaths were not a setback. They never believed catching Sivarasan alive was possible.

# ACKNOWLEDGEMENTS

THE SPECIAL INVESTIGATION TEAM OF THE CBI WITH D.R. Kaarthikeyan at its helm, followed by Radhavinod Raju, Amod Kanth, Amit Verma and K. Ragothaman. None of my stories or this could have happened without their unconditional support.

The *India Today* magazine that sent me to Madras to investigate the case and always encouraged me to chase the big story. Endless support came from Aroon Purie, Inderjit Badhwar, Dilip Bobb, Shekhar Gupta, Ajit Ninan, Harpal Singh and Arun Suri.

S. Sripal, then DGP, Tamil Nadu Police.

Kondath Mohandas, former DGP (Intelligence), Tamil Nadu Police.

Dr P. Chandrasekharan of the Forensics Lab, Tamil Nadu.

K. Ravindran of the National Security Guard.

Officials from the IB, R&AW and Q Branch of Tamil Nadu Police.

Dr K. Chokalingam of Devki Hospital, who took me around places, introduced me to people who could throw light on the case during my investigation.

And Sameer Nair, who changed the face of Indian television with *KBC*, for encouraging me to write the book.

# NOTES

## PROLOGUE

1. Excerpts from Supreme Court judgment by Justice K.T.Thomas dated 11 May 1999, upholding the death sentence of the seven key accused.

## PREFACE

1. Charu Lata Joshi, 'Jain panel report suggests deliberate attempt to tamper with Rajiv assassination evidence', *India Today*, 28 February 1997; https://www.indiatoday.in/magazine/nation/story/19970228-jain-panel-report-suggests-deliberate-attempt-to-tamper-with-rajiv-assassination-evidence-830192-1997-02-28
2. Sonia Gandhi and Narsimha Rao had strained relations, *Economic Times,* 16 February 2014 https://economictimes.indiatimes.com/news/politics-and-nation/sonia-gandhi-and-narasimha-

rao-had-strained-relations-k-v-thomas/articleshow/30503304.cms?from=mdr;

## A BRIEF NOTE ON THE INDIAN PEACE KEEPING FORCE (IPKF)

1. Frances Harrison, 'Twenty years on – riots that led to war', BBC News, 23 July 2003, http://news.bbc.co.uk/2/hi/south_asia/3090111.stm; Rajan Hoole, 'Sri Lanka's Black July', *Colombo Telegraph*, 24 July 2013, https://www.colombotelegraph.com/index.php/sri-lankas-black-july-borella-24th-evening/
2. K.T. Rajasingham, 'Sri Lanka: The Untold Story, Chapter 35', *Asian Times*, 2002, https://sangam.org/sri-lanka-the-untold-story-chapter-35/
3. Dilip Bobb, 'After 16 days of bloody battle, IPKF finally captures LTTE stronghold Jaffna', *India Today*, 15 November 1987, https://www.indiatoday.in/magazine/cover-story/story/19871115-after-16-days-of-bloody-battle-ipkf-finally-captures-ltte-stronghold-jaffna-799481-1987-11-15; A.G. Noorani, 'Shocking disclosures – Indian Peace Keeping Forces (IPKF) played double game in Sri Lanka', Tamil Sydney, https://web.archive.org/web/20110929150947/http://www.tamilsydney.com/content/view/865/37/
4. S.H. Venkatramani, 'Situation takes a dangerous turn with IPKF now in Sri Lanka engaged in battle against LTTE', *India Today*, 31 October 1987, https://www.indiatoday.in/magazine/special-report/story/19871031-situation-takes-a-dangerous-turn-with-ipkf-in-sri-lanka-now-engaged-in-battle-against-ltte-799473-1987-10-31; K.T. Rajasingham, 'Sri Lanka: The Untold Story, Chapter 35', *Asian Times*, 2002, https://sangam.org/sri-lanka-the-untold-story-chapter-35/ (archived from the original on 1 October 2002; retrieved on 26 November 2014).

## A BRIEF NOTE ON THE LIBERATION TIGERS OF TAMIL EELAM (LTTE)

1. Joanne Richards, 'An Institutional History of the Liberation Tigers of Tamil Eelam (LTTE)', The Centre on Conflict, Development and Peacebuilding Working Paper, 2014, https://repository.graduateinstitute.ch/record/292651/files/CCDP-Working-Paper-10-LTTE-1.pdf
2. Ibid.
3. 'Liberation Tigers of Tamil Eelam', CISAC, Stanford, https://cisac.fsi.stanford.edu/mappingmilitants/profiles/liberation-tigers-tamil-elam
4. Amy Gunia, '"The Birthplace of the Suicide Belt." Sri Lanka's Deadly History of Suicide Bombings', Time, 25 April 2019, https://time.com/5575956/sri-lanka-history-suicide-bombings-birthplace-invented/
5. A.G. Noorani, 'Shocking disclosures – Indian Peace Keeping Forces (IPKF) played double game in Sri Lanka', Tamil Sydney, https://web.archive.org/web/20110929150947/http://www.tamilsydney.com/content/view/865/37/

## CAST OF CHARACTERS

1. Excerpts from the Supreme Court judgment of Justice K.T. Thomas dated 11 May 1991.
2. Ibid.

## CHAPTER 1

1. Jain Inquiry Commission Report by Justice M.C. Jain in October 1997, looking into the larger conspiracy of Rajiv Gandhi's assassination; Prabhu Chawla, 'Jain report not only scripted history but defined the future too', *India Today*, 26 December 2005, https://www.indiatoday.in/magazine/cover-

story/story/20051226-jain-report-not-only-scripted-history-but-defined-the-future-too-786408-2005-12-26

2. Ibid.

## CHAPTER 2

1. Anirudhya Mitra, 'Rajiv Gandhi assassination: How plot was hatched and executed by LTTE', *India Today*, 15 July 1991, https://www.indiatoday.in/magazine/investigation/story/19910715-rajiv-gandhi-assassination-ltte-supremo-pirabhakaran-ordered-the-killing-in-jaffna-in-october-1990-814580-1991-07-15
2. AnandViswanathan, 'DMK accused of inaction over LTTE in Tamil Nadu', *India Today*, 31 December 1990, https://www.indiatoday.in/magazine/indiascope/story/19901231-dmk-accused-of-inaction-over-ltte-in-tamil-nadu-813463-1990-12-31
3. Anirudhya Mitra, 'Rajiv Assassination: How the plot was hatched and executed by LTTE', *India Today*, 15 July 1991, https://www.indiatoday.in/magazine/investigation/story/19910715-rajiv-gandhi-assassination-ltte-supremo-pirabhakaran-ordered-the-killing-in-jaffna-in-october-1990-814580-1991-07-15

## CHAPTER 3

1. CBI charge sheet dated 20 May 1991; Supreme Court judgment dated 11 May 1999.
2. My interview with the Director General of Police (DGP), Tamil Nadu, S. Sripal, in *India Today* magazine, 15 June 1991; Anirudhya Mitra, 'Rajiv Gandhi assassination: How plot was hatched and executed by LTTE', *India Today*, 15 July 1991, https://www.indiatoday.in/magazine/investigation/story/19910715-rajiv-gandhi-assassination-ltte-supremo-pirabhakaran-ordered-the-killing-in-jaffna-in-october-1990-814580-1991-07-15

3. *The Hindu*, 10 June 1991.

## CHAPTER 4

1. Anirudhya Mitra, 'Rajiv Gandhi assassination: How plot was hatched and executed by LTTE', *India Today*, 15 July 1991, https://www.indiatoday.in/magazine/investigation/story/19910715-rajiv-gandhi-assassination-ltte-supremo-pirabhakaran-ordered-the-killing-in-jaffna-in-october-1990-814580-1991-07-15
2. Excerpts paraphrased from the CBI charge sheet dated 20 May 1992, submitted to the TADA Court, Chennai.
3. Ibid.
4. Anirudhya Mitra, 'Rajiv Gandhi assassination: How plot was hatched and executed by LTTE', *India Today*, 15 July 1991, https://www.indiatoday.in/magazine/investigation/story/19910715-rajiv-gandhi-assassination-ltte-supremo-pirabhakaran-ordered-the-killing-in-jaffna-in-october-1990-814580-1991-07-15
5. Excerpts paraphrased from the CBI charge sheet dated 20 May 1992, submitted to the TADA Court, Chennai; excerpts paraphrased from the Supreme Court judgment dated 11 May 1991.
6. Excerpts from the Madras TADA court judgment dated 28 January 1998 sentencing all the twenty-three accused to death; excerpts from the Supreme Court judgment by Justice K.T. Thomas on 11 May 1999.
7. Excerpts from the CBI charge sheet dated 20 May 1992; excerpts from the Supreme Court judgment dated 11 May 1999.
8. Anirudhya Mitra, 'Rajiv Gandhi assassination: How plot was hatched and executed by LTTE', *India Today*, 15 July 1991, https://www.indiatoday.in/magazine/investigation/story/19910715-rajiv-gandhi-assassination-ltte-supremo-pirabhakaran-ordered-the-killing-in-jaffna-in-october-1990-814580-1991-07-15
9. Ibid.

10. Excerpts from the Supreme Court judgment by Justice K.T. Thomas dated 11 May 1999.
11. Excerpts from the TADA court judgment dated January 1998; excerpts from the Supreme Court judgment by Justice K.T. Thomas, dated 11 May 1999.
12. CBI charge sheet filed before the TADA court in Madras dated 20 May 1992; excerpts from the Supreme Court judgment by Justice K.T. Thomas, dated 11 May 1999.
13. Anirudhya Mitra, 'Rajiv Gandhi assassination: How plot was hatched and executed by LTTE', *India Today*, 15 July 1991, https://www.indiatoday.in/magazine/investigation/story/19910715-rajiv-gandhi-assassination-ltte-supremo-pirabhakaran-ordered-the-killing-in-jaffna-in-october-1990-814580-1991-07-15
14. Supreme Court judgment by Justice K.T. Thomas, dated 11 May 1999, upholding the death sentences of the seven accused.
15. D.R. Kaarthikeyan and Radhavinod Raju, *Triumph of Truth: The Rajiv Gandhi Assassination*, New Dawn Press, 2004.

## CHAPTER 5

1. T.S. Subramanian, 'Anatomy of an investigation', *Frontline*, 7 February, 1998, https://frontline.thehindu.com/cover-story/article30160829.ece
2. Supreme Court judgment by Justice K.T. Thomas, dated 11 May 1999 upholding the death sentences of the seven accused.
3. CBI charge sheet filed before the TADA court in Madras dated 20 May 1992.
4. Anirudhya Mitra, 'Rajiv Gandhi assassination: How plot was hatched and executed by LTTE', *India Today*, 15 July 1991, https://www.indiatoday.in/magazine/investigation/story/19910715-
5. Anirudhya Mitra, 'Rajiv Gandhi assassination: How plot was hatched and executed by LTTE', *India Today*, 15 July 1991, https://www.indiatoday.in/magazine/investigation/story/19910715-

rajiv-gandhi-assassination-ltte-supremo-pirabhakaran-ordered-the-killing-in-jaffna-in-october-1990-814580-1991-07-15; excerpts from the CBI charge sheet in the TADA court dated 20 May 1992; excerpts from the Supreme Court judgment by Justice K.T. Thomas, dated 11 May 1999.

6. Anirudhya Mitra, 'Rajiv Gandhi assassination probe casts its net wider', *India Today*, 31 August 1991, https://www.indiatoday.in/magazine/special-report/story/19910831-sit-investigations-focus-on-conspiracy-international-ramifications-and-sivarasan-visits-to-several-countries-814776-1991-08-31
7. Anirudhya Mitra, 'Rajiv Gandhi assassination: How plot was hatched and executed by LTTE', *India Today*, 15 July 1991, https://www.indiatoday.in/magazine/investigation/story/19910715-rajiv-gandhi-assassination-ltte-supremo-pirabhakaran-ordered-the-killing-in-jaffna-in-october-1990-814580-1991-07-15
8. Ibid.
9. Ibid.
10. Supreme Court judgment by Justice K.T. Thomas, dated 11 May 1999.
11. Anirudhya Mitra, 'Rajiv Gandhi assassination probe casts its net wider', *India Today*, 31 July 1991, https://www.indiatoday.in/magazine/special-report/story/19910831-sit-investigations-focus-on-conspiracy-international-ramifications-and-sivarasan-visits-to-several-countries-814776-1991-08-31
12. CBI charge sheet filed before the Madras TADA court on 20 May 1992.
13. Ibid.
14. Ibid.
15. This story is now online as 'Rajiv Gandhi assassination: How plot was hatched and executed by LTTE'.
16. Ibid.

## CHAPTER 6

1. Excerpts from the Supreme Court judgment by Justice K.T. Thomas dated 11 May 1999.
2. Prabhu Chawla, 'Rajiv Gandhi killing: Jain Commission report indicts DMK for colluding with LTTE', *India Today*, 17 November 1997, https://www.indiatoday.in/magazine/cover-story/story/19971117-rajiv-gandhi-killing-jain-commission-report-indicts-dmk-for-colluding-with-ltte-832134-1997-11-17
3. Ibid.
4. Charu Lata Joshi, 'Gaps in the probe', *India Today*, 31 May 1996, https://www.indiatoday.in/magazine/investigation/story/19960531-gaps-in-the-probe-753114-1996-05-31
5. Ibid.
6. Anirudhya Mitra, 'Rajiv Gandhi's assassination only first layer of LTTE conspiracy', *India Today*, 15 December 1991, https://www.indiatoday.in/magazine/investigation/story/19911215-rajiv-gandhi-assassination-only-first-layer-of-ltte-conspiracy-815187-1991-12-15
7. Ibid.
8. Anirudhya Mitra, 'Rajiv Gandhi assassination: How plot was hatched and executed by LTTE', *India Today*, 15 July 1991, https://www.indiatoday.in/magazine/investigation/story/19910715-rajiv-gandhi-assassination-ltte-supremo-pirabhakaran-ordered-the-killing-in-jaffna-in-october-1990-814580-1991-07-15
9. D.R. Kaarthikeyan and Radhavinod Raju, *Triumph of Truth: The Rajiv Gandhi Assassination*, New Dawn Press, 2004.
10. Anirudhya Mitra, 'Rajiv Gandhi's assassination only first layer of LTTE conspiracy', *India Today,* 15 December 1991, https://www.indiatoday.in/magazine/investigation/story/19911215-rajiv-gandhi-assassination-only-first-layer-of-ltte-conspiracy-815187-1991-12-15

11. D.B.S. Jeyaraj, '"One-eyed Sivarasan" the mastermind behind the Rajiv Gandhi assassination', *Daily Mirror Online*, 29 May 1992, https://www.dailymirror.lk/dbs-jeyaraj-column/One-eyed-Sivarasan-the-mastermind-behind-the-Rajiv-Gandhi-assassination/192-109816; Anirudhya Mitra, 'Rajiv Gandhi assassination probe casts its net wider', *India Today*, 31 August 1991, https://www.indiatoday.in/magazine/special-report/story/19910831-sit-investigations-focus-on-conspiracy-international-ramifications-and-sivarasan-visits-to-several-countries-814776-1991-08-31
12. Ibid.
13. Anirudhya Mitra, 'CBI's net closes on operational mastermind behind Rajiv's killing', *India Today* magazine, 31 July 1991, https://www.indiatoday.in/magazine/special-report/story/19910731-cbi-net-closes-on-operational-mastermind-behind-rajiv-killing-814615-1991-07-31
14. Ibid.
15. Anirudhya Mitra, 'Rajiv Gandhi assassination probe casts its net wider', *India Today*, 31 August 1991, https://www.indiatoday.in/magazine/special-report/story/19910831-sit-investigations-focus-on-conspiracy-international-ramifications-and-sivarasan-visits-to-several-countries-814776-1991-08-31

## CHAPTER 7

1. Excerpts from the Supreme Court judgment by Justice K.T. Thomas dated 11 May 1999; excerpts from the CBI charge sheet filed before the Madras TADA court dated 20 May 1992.
2. Ibid.
3. Ibid.
4. Ibid.
5. Anirudhya Mitra, 'CBI's net closes on operational mastermind behind Rajiv's killing', *India Today* magazine, 31 July 1991, https://

www.indiatoday.in/magazine/special-report/story/19910731-cbi-net-closes-on-operational-mastermind-behind-rajiv-killing-814615-1991-07-31

6. Prabhu Chawla, 'Cyanide capsule delayed Prabhakaran's meeting with Rajiv Gandhi', *India Today*, 23 May 2009; https://www.indiatoday.in/headlines-today-top-stories/story/how-a-cyanide-capsule-delayed-prabhakarans-meeting-with-rajiv-gandhi-48358-2009-05-23
7. Shekhar Gupta, Kavitha Shetty and Anand Viswanathan, 'LTTE key suspect in Rajiv Gandhi assassination probe', *India Today*, 30 June 1991, https://www.indiatoday.in/magazine/cover-story/story/19910630-ltte-key-suspect-in-rajiv-gandhi-assassination-probe-815528-1991-06-30
8. 'Obituary: Velupillai Prabhakaran', BBC News, 18 May 2009, http://news.bbc.co.uk/2/hi/7885473.stm

## CHAPTER 8

1. Excerpts from the Supreme Court judgment by Justice K.T. Thomas dated 11 May 1999.
2. Anirudhya Mitra, 'Rajiv Gandhi assassination probe casts its net wider', *India Today*, 31 August, 1991., https://www.indiatoday.in/magazine/special-report/story/19910831-sit-investigations-focus-on-conspiracy-international-ramifications-and-sivarasan-visits-to-several-countries-814776-1991-08-31
3. Excerpts from the Supreme Court judgment by Justice K.T. Thomas dated 11 May 1999.
4. Ibid.
5. Ibid.
6. Ibid.
7. Ibid.
8. Ibid.
9. Ibid.

10. Ibid.
11. Ibid.
12. CBI charge sheet filed before the Madras TADA court dated 20 May 1992; Supreme Court judgment by Justice K.T.Thomas dated 11 May 1999.
13. Ibid.
14. Ibid.
15. CBI charge sheet filed before the Madras TADA Court dated 20 May 1992.
16. Anirudhya Mitra, 'CBI's net closes on operational mastermind behind Rajiv's killing', *India Today,* 31 July 1991, https://www.indiatoday.in/magazine/special-report/story/19910731-cbi-net-closes-on-operational-mastermind-behind-rajiv-killing-814615-1991-07-31
17. Anirudhya Mitra, 'Rajiv Gandhi assassination probe casts its net wider', *India Today*, 31 August 1991, https://www.indiatoday.in/magazine/special-report/story/19910831-sit-investigations-focus-on-conspiracy-international-ramifications-and-sivarasan-visits-to-several-countries-814776-1991-08-31
18. Ibid.

## CHAPTER 9

1. Excerpts from Supreme Court judgment by Justice K.T.Thomas dated 11 May 1999.
2. Ibid.
3. Sandeep Unnithan, 'Rajiv Gandhi assassination: Explosive revelations from mastermind Sivarasan's notes of the plot to kill former prime minister', *India Today*, 30 November 1999, https://www.indiatoday.in/magazine/cover-story/story/20140310-rajiv-gandhi-assassin-diary-sivarasan-exclusive-revelations-about-sivarasan-plot-to-kill-rajiv-gandhi-800337-1999-11-30

4. Excerpts from Supreme Court judgment by Justice K.T.Thomas dated 11 May 1999.
5. Excerpts from CBI charge sheet filed before the Madras TADA court in May 1992.
6. Ibid.
7. Anirudhya Mitra, 'A dubious twist to Rajiv Gandhi assassination probe', India Today, 15 August 1991, https://www.indiatoday.in/magazine/special-report/story/19910815-key-suspect-sudden-death-under-suspicious-circumstances-casts-shadow-over-rajiv-assassination-probe-814658-1991-08-15
8. Ibid.
9. Ibid.
10. Ibid.

## CHAPTER 10

1. Excerpts from CBI charge sheet filed before the Madras TADA court in May 1992.
2. Anirudhya Mitra, 'Rajiv Gandhi assassination probe casts its net wider', *India Today*, 31 August 1991, https://www.indiatoday.in/magazine/special-report/story/19910831-sit-investigations-focus-on-conspiracy-international-ramifications-and-sivarasan-visits-to-several-countries-814776-1991-08-31
3. Anirudhya Mitra, 'CBI net closes on operational mastermind behind Rajiv's killing', *India Today*, 31 July 1991, https://www.indiatoday.in/magazine/special-report/story/19910731-cbi-net-closes-on-operational-mastermind-behind-rajiv-killing-814615-1991-07-31
4. Anirudhya Mitra, 'CBI's net closes on operational mastermind behind Rajiv's killing', *India Today*, 31 July 1991, https://www.indiatoday.in/magazine/special-report/story/19910731-cbi-net-closes-on-operational-mastermind-behind-rajiv-killing-814615-1991-07-31
5. Ibid.

6. Ibid.
7. Ibid.

## CHAPTER 11

1. Excerpts from the CBI charge sheet filed before the Madras TADA court dated 20 May 1991; excerpts from the Supreme Court judgment by Justice K.T. Thomas dated 11 May 1999.
2. Ibid.
3. Ibid.
4. Ibid.
5. Ibid.
6. Ibid.
7. Ibid.
8. Excerpts from the CBI charge sheet filed before the Madras TADA Court dated 20 May 1992; Supreme Court judgment by Justice K.T. Thomas dated 11 May 1999; excerpts from the Madras TADA court judgment dated 28 January 1998.
9. Ibid.
10. Ibid.
11. Ibid.
12. Ibid.
13. Ibid.
14. Excerpts from the CBI charge sheet filed before the Madras TADA Court dated 20 May 1992; excerpts from the Madras TADA Court judgment dated 28 January, 1998.
15. Ibid.
16. Ibid.
17. Ibid.

## CHAPTER 12

1. Excerpts from the CBI charge sheet filed before the Madras TADA court dated 20 May 1992.

2. Ibid.
3. Ibid.
4. Ibid.
5. Ibid.
6. Saritha Rai and Anirudhya Mitra, 'Rajiv Gandhi assassination probe: By dithering, policemen lose opportunity to capture Sivarasan alive', *India Today*, 15 September 1991, https://www.indiatoday.in/magazine/special-report/story/19910915-rajiv-gandhi-assassination-probe-by-dithering-policemen-lose-opportunity-to-capture-sivarasan-alive-814788-1991-09-15
7. Ibid.
8. Ibid.
9. Ibid.
10. Ibid.
11. Ibid.
12. Ibid.
13. Ibid.
14. Ibid.

# ABOUT THE AUTHOR

**Anirudhya Mitra** is a journalist-turned-filmmaker. During his successful stint of news reporting at the *Times of India* and the *India Today* magazine (1982–93), Mitra broke several stories, including the Rajiv Gandhi assassination; the Bofors gun deal; the drug wars in India, Pakistan and Afghanistan; the money laundering operation by the BCCI bank that led to its worldwide closure; corruption in the judiciary; the life and times of Indian model-turned-spy Pamella Bordes; and Godman Chandraswami, among others. He moved to writing and creating television series with UTV in Mumbai in 1994. Notable among his works are *Sea Hawks* on Doordarshan Metro and Star TV and Govinda-starrer *Jeeto Chappar Phaad Ke* on Sony TV. He also wrote and produced movies in South East Asia, of which *Under the Protection of Ka'bah* competed at the Oscars in 2012. The biopic on Indonesian President B.J. Habibie, *Habibie & Ainun*, also became a blockbuster. The Hindi film *Tahaan*, of which Mitra was a co-writer, won major awards at festivals, including the London Independent Film Festival and the International Istanbul Film Festival.